BANKING ALLIANCES

BANKING ALLIANCES

Hazel J. Johnson

Distinguished University Scholar
University of Louisville
Louisville, Kentucky, USA

World Scientific
Singapore • New Jersey • London • Hong Kong

Published by

World Scientific Publishing Co. Pte. Ltd.
P O Box 128, Farrer Road, Singapore 912805
USA office: Suite 1B, 1060 Main Street, River Edge, NJ 07661
UK office: 57 Shelton Street, Covent Garden, London WC2H 9HE

British Library Cataloguing-in-Publication Data
A catalogue record for this book is available from the British Library.

BANKING ALLIANCES

ISBN 981-02-4272-7

Printed in Singapore.

In loving memory of

Ida Wilma Kelly

who taught me the meaning of compassion

Preface

A banking *keiretsu* is the Japanese version of a combination of industrial firms that may be linked through cross-holdings of common stock, through supplier relationships, and through government ties. Although they may have different structures in different countries, all banking *keiretsu* have one thing in common--they all receive strategic direction and long-term financial support from a bank.

In Japan, the bank and trading company share these responsibilities. The relationships within *keiretsu* are long-standing and far-reaching. The Mitsubishi *keiretsu*, for example, is composed of 160 formal members that generate annual sales of $145 billion. The *keiretsu* bank is the primary source of financing for all the industrial members of the group, extending loans and making equity investments. The world's largest bank, Dai-Ichi Kangyo, is the bank for the *keiretsu* of the same name. Mitsubishi, Sakura, Sumitomo, Fuji, and Sanwa banks all lead *keiretsu* that are composed of Japan's leading firms in automobiles, electronics, and heavy industries. As a result of these liaisons, Japanese financial institutions have also reached world-class status and fill the ranks of the world's five largest banks.

In Germany, the *keiretsu* is led by the universal "house bank" which owns stock in the members of the industrial group. The three largest German banks--Deutsche Bank, Dresdner Bank and Commerzbank--are virtually financial department stores in which a full range of banking services have been made available to group members. These universal banks, with their nationwide branch networks, have provided not only financial support but also technical expertise in specific industries. Today, the Deutsche Bank holds stock in and occupies seats on the boards of Germany's largest and most powerful firms.

In China, at the top of the banking *keiretsu* is the People's Bank of China which works closely with the Chinese government to establish economic priorities for the country. In turn, the People's Bank coordinates the activities of the Industrial and Commercial Bank of China for the purpose of domestic loans for working capital and equipment. The Industrial and Commercial Bank has a nationwide branch network of over 20,000 locations. The Bank of China follows the direction of the People's Bank in conducting international business with branches in Hong Kong, London, Singapore, Luxembourg, New York, and Tokyo. The Bank of China extends credit to enterprises engaged in foreign trade, participates in joint ventures abroad, and issues foreign-currency financial instruments (including bonds). The Hong Kong branch of the Bank of China oversees the operations of 13 sister Chinese banks and manages Chinese government investments in real estate companies, airlines, hotels, stores, warehouses, and factories of all kinds.

The Korean equivalent of a banking *keiretsu* is a *chaebol*. In Korea, economic decision making power is shared by the government, the banks, and the industrial firms. The *chaebol* banks include Hanil, Cho Heung, Korea First, Bank of Seoul and Commercial Bank. The major industrial firms hold stakes in all these leading Korean banks instead of one (as is the usual case in Japan). With strong financial backing from the banks, Korea has become a major producer in steelmaking, shipbuilding, textiles, and electronics.

In the United Kingdom, the banking *keiretsu* are lead by the clearing (commercial) banks of Barclays, Lloyds, Midland, and National Westminster. These institutions have merchant bank and investment bank subsidiaries that enable them to offer the same universal banking services offered by their German counterparts. Recent modernization of the U.K. banking system, combined with privatization of major industries, has facilitated an increase in the market value of British firms of several hundred billion dollars.

In the United States, banking *keiretsu* thrived prior to enactment of the 1933 Glass-Steagall Act, which outlawed commercial bank involvement in the leadership of industrial corporations and in the underwriting of securities for nonfinancial firms. The House of Morgan was a prime example of an American banking *keiretsu*, with J.P. Morgan overseeing the direction of over 100 U.S. companies in the areas of banking, transportation, and public utilities. The Mellon empire encompassed banking, steel, oil, and aluminum. Had the American banking *keiretsu* not been disbanded, it is likely that the United States could have preserved much of the international competitiveness that has been lost in recent decades. As history shows, the banking *keiretsu* is a viable economic concept--in whatever its form--that can facilitate growth and industrial development.

Contents

Preface vii

1. Origins of Banking Alliances 1
    - Introduction 1
    - A Contemporary Overview 2
    - The Earliest Days of Banking 5
    - The 18th Century 8
        - The Birth of the Baring Brothers 8
        - The Rothschilds 9
    - The 19th Century 12
        - English Bankers--Financiers to the World 13
        - The Emergence of Strong German Banking 18
        - Chinese Bankers and the Western World 24
        - Japanese Banking--A Rapid Transformation 28
        - The Ascendancy of U.S. Banking 34
    - Conclusion 51
    - Selected References 52

2. International Leadership in the United Kingdom 55
    - Introduction 55
        - Clearing vs. Merchant Banks 56
    - An Archaic System in a World Class City 58
    - The Reform Movement 59
        - Privatizing Major Industries 60
        - Scrutinizing the Financial Sector 61
    - The Eurodollar Markets 63
        - The Monetary Goals of the European Union 63
        - The United Kingdom and Monetary Union 66
        - The Off-Shore Market in U.S. Dollars 66
    - Deregulation and the Big Bang 70

Early Liberalization 70
The Big Bang 72
Important Lessons 74
Merging Different Cultures 74
Managing Branch Networks 75
Capital vs. Skill 75
Adequate Supervision: The Case of Barings 76
The New Financial Services Authority and Future Directions 78
Future Indications 79
Selected References 81

3. Dedicated Capital in Germany 83
Introduction 83
Setting the Stage for Economic Development 83
A Post War Economic Miracle 87
Reforming the System After the War 87
Insights into the German Company 89
Two Forms of Development 91
The Growth of Universal Banking in the German Economy 96
Conclusion 99
Selected References 100

4. Formal and Informal Ties in Japan 103
Introduction 103
Early Modernization 104
Breaking Up the *Zaibatsu* 106
Reestablishing Powerful Alliances 108
The High Growth Years 109
The Income Doubling Plan 110
The New Keiretsu 111
Coordination of Government, Industry, and Banking 113
International Expansion 114
Japan: The Control Center 116
Expanding Into the United States 117
Penetrating the *Keiretsu* 121
Reforming the Financial System of Japan? 124
Conclusion 126
Selected References 127

5. Forging Banking Alliances in China, Hong Kong, and Korea 129
Introduction 129
China: Breaking Economic Ties with the Past 130
Transition to the People's Republic of China 130
The Socialist Banking System 131
Economic Reform 133
Support from the Banking Sector 135
Hong Kong Industry and Banking 137
Hong Kong as an Industrial Center 138
The Hong Kong Trading Companies 139
Greater China 142
South Korea: Adapting the Japanese Model 143
The Economic Plan 143
The Chaebols 146
Conclusion 149
Selected References 150

6. Steps Toward Financial Modernization in the United States 153
Introduction 153
Misconceptions About the U.S. Banking Industry 155
The True Cause of Early U.S. Money Panics 155
The Great Depression: Facts and Myths 163
The Glass-Steagall Act 165
The Provisions of the Act 165
The Effects of Glass-Steagall 167
The Investment Shortfall 168
Aggregate Investment 168
Lack of Dedicated Capital 169
The American Banking *Keiretsu* 172
Selected References 176

1. Origins of Banking Alliances

Introduction

History shows--in England, Germany, China, Japan, and the United States--that a close working relationship between banking and industry has benefitted both sectors. When banking, business, and government share risk, the net result is dynamic economic growth. Beginning with the underwriting of trade bills of exchange in Europe, the Barings went on virtually to help underwrite the development of the United States, from the Louisiana Purchase to state bond issues to construction of U.S. railroads. The Rothschilds, initially risking physical safety, accommodated the financial needs of government and business throughout Europe. The Deutsche Bank, which epitomizes the German joint-stock banking system, began with the primary goal of promoting German business and assumed ownership positions in the firms to help accomplish this goal. The traditional bankers of China created a buffer between Chinese merchants and the Western world--a buffer that allowed the Chinese to develop their economic system while not sacrificing their own culture. A coalition between the former *samurai* and the merchant class propelled Japan from a feudal state to a country in which banking, industry, and government provided support for the common goal of economic development.

In the United States, J.P. Morgan espoused the philosophy of relationship banking--in which spirit he rescued any number of troubled industrial firms and even rescued the U.S. government from financial collapse. With a $10,000 loan, the Mellons backed a fledgling company that was to become the foundation of the U.S. aluminum industry. The Mellon union of banking and industry also furthered the development of many other industries, including steel, oil, and coal. Citibank began a credit union for its merchant-owners. It later developed into a veritable financial department store that was instrumental in bringing to market the securities of a wide range of companies *and* in delivering those securities to the households of America.

Clearly, U.S. banking was on pace to compete with any other banking system in the industrialized world. But the Glass-Steagall Act of 1933 would change all this. It appeared that the close relationship between U.S. banking and industry constituted a conflict of interest that was undesirable and could no longer be tolerated. Commercial banking and investment banking could no longer be conducted by the same firm. At this point, the upward momentum of U.S. commercial banking in the world marketplace ground to a halt. Because of legal restrictions such as the prohibition against investment banking, U.S. banks no longer rank among the world's largest. Instead, the largest banks are now primarily Japanese as are some of the most powerful industrial firms. Instead of being a closed issue in the United States, the close relationship between banking and industry in other countries must be examined and the wisdom of past U.S. restrictions revisited.

A Contemporary Overview

The Japanese *keiretsu* is a business combination involving interlocking ownership of financial and industrial firms, with a bank acting as one of the dominant firms in the group. A *keiretsu* bank not only provides loans to the members of the group, but holds ownership shares in them as well. Consider the Mitsubishi group as a case in point (Table 1.1).

TABLE 1.1		
THE MITSUBISHI KEIRETSU		
		Percentage of Firm Owned by Keiretsu Members
1.	Mitsubishi Corporation	32%
2.	Mitsubishi Bank	26
3.	Mitsubishi Heavy Industries	20
4.	Mitsubishi Trust and Banking	28
5.	Tokio Marine & Fire Insurance	24
6.	Meiji Mutual Life Insurance	0
7.	Mitsubishi Motors	55
8.	Nikon Corporation	27
9.	Kirin Brewery	19
10.	Mitsubishi Oil	41
11.	Mitsubishi Electric	17
12.	Mitsubishi Plastics Industries	57
13.	Mitsubishi Petrochemical	37
14.	Mitsubishi Gas Chemical	24
15.	Mitsubishi Metal	21
16.	Mitsubishi Aluminum	100
17.	Mitsubishi Steel Manufacturing	38
18.	Asahi Glass	28
19.	Mitsubishi Construction	100
20.	Mitsubishi Cable Industries	48
21.	Mitsubishi Paper Mills	32
22.	Mitsubishi Rayon	26
23.	Mitsubishi Mining & Cement	37
24.	Mitsubishi Estate	25
25.	Mitsubishi Kasei	23
26.	Mitsubishi Warehouse and Transportation	40
27.	Mitsubishi Kakoki	37
28.	Nippon Yusen	25

The three dominant firms are Mitsubishi Corporation (a trading company), Mitsubishi Bank, and Mitsubishi Heavy Industries. Other financial affiliates include two insurance companies and a trust company. The industrial members are in diverse industries including motor vehicles, construction, metal, and textiles. In almost all cases, at least 20 percent of the stock of these 28 companies is owned by members of the group. Every member firm benefits from this close working relationship because, if it should find itself in financial difficulty, the other members are there to support it, notably the bank. Such relationships are illegal in the United States and have been branded as an "unfair competitive practice."

Yet the truth of the matter is that the *keiretsu* typifies a long-standing arrangement between banking and industry that is not restricted to Japan. The banking system of the United States was patterned after that of the United Kingdom. Nevertheless, deregulation during the 1980s has enabled banks in the U.K. system to offer a full range of services to industry, as industry itself has been privatized on a large scale. Financial services and industry have been liberalized at the same time so that each can complement the other in the Single European Market. Still closer ties may be observed in Germany, where bank representatives routinely sit on the boards of their industrial clients and give advice to management with respect to day-to-day operations. Even in the Communist-run People's Republic of China, free enterprise areas such as Quangdong Province thrive partially because of the strong banking presence in Hong Kong. As a case in point, the Hong Kong/Quangdong export mechanism is so efficient that the U.S. textile industry has crumbled largely because of exports from that region.

In contrast, U.S. banks are not permitted to own shares in industrial firms, are not uniformly allowed to underwrite industrial issues of stocks and bonds, and may not underwrite most insurance policies. While these prohibitions are intended to encourage "safety and soundness" within the industry, they also limit bank earnings and stifle economic development. Small- and medium-size firms have far less access to capital markets than larger firms. Yet each of these smaller firms has at least one banking relationship--a relationship that is constrained by laws and regulations that restrict the scope of permissible bank activity.

This book compares the banking systems in the United Kingdom, Germany, Japan, and China to that of the United States. While it necessarily describes differential banking system structures, its focus is on the *relationships* of banking. The primary focus is the relationship of banking with industry and, because government can certainly influence the industry/banking relationship, it also focuses on government relationships.

A description of current financial systems can be best understood, however, when placed in historical perspective. In observing the development of banking, several points will become abundantly clear:

- Banking has never been a risk-free industry.
- Successful bankers have historically adapted to adverse circumstances with innovative financing for industry.
- Without close collaboration of industry and banking, much of the economic development of the past would not have occurred.
- The Glass-Steagall Act of 1933 created an unnatural separation of banking and industry in the United States, reversing the trend of powerful banks in this country.

The Earliest Days of Banking

While precious metal coins were exchanged in Mesopotamia (ancient Iraq) as early as 2000 B.C., the merchants of Italy are credited as the world's first true modern bankers. Italian merchants in the 13th century financed local government, businesses, and international trade. In one of the earliest examples of monetizing a government's debt, claims on the government of Venice that arose from financing its international disputes changed hands in the city in a kind of payments mechanism. Money changers facilitated these exchanges and other exchanges that involved "full-bodied" money or coins of precious metal. On a *bancherius* or bench, from which the term *bank* is derived, merchants took deposits and gave credit to local businesses.

While loans to local business were important in the promotion of commercial activities, it is the response of the Genoese bankers (in northern Italy) to the needs of international trade that lends special significance to the early merchant bankers. Trade fairs began in Champagne, France where the vast majority of textile merchandising took place. Eventually six different fairs were held throughout the year. The Genoese merchant bankers went from one to the other, settling accounts at the end of each, or carrying the balance forward to the next fair. Soon they were joined by money-changers from Cologne, Barcelona, Rome, and Toulouse (France).

As the Genoese merchant bankers became more involved in the financial end of international trade, they started banking firms and traded their "benches" for more permanent facilities, sending agents to the trade fairs to settle accounts and gather information. The agencies evolved into bank branches. In the 14th century, the House of Bardi, for example, operated over 30 branches in Italy and locations abroad, including London, Bruges (Belgium), and Moorish Africa.

Besides fostering economic development by making on-the-spot international trade possible, the Italian bankers also developed an important financial instrument, the bill of exchange. For example, a local merchant (A) in Genoa—who wished to pay for goods purchased from a merchant (B) in Toulouse (southern France)—could make payment through banks in the two cities. Upon the request of merchant A, the bank in Genoa would write an order to the bank in Toulouse to pay merchant B. Delays in delivery of the paid draft back to the Genoese bank meant that these bills represented short-term loans to business. This form of finance remains an important element of international trade today in the form of the bankers' acceptance.

The Medici of Florence combined the art of mastering information with the convenience of the bill of exchange. The Medici maintained up to ten branches and a network of agents and correspondents throughout Europe. Through these contacts, the Medici could continuously feel the pulse of business at home and abroad. Each branch, agent, and correspondent had an open account with the others through which bills of exchange and other loans could be efficiently settled. From this very early example of banking it can be seen that while the business of banking contained risks, the risks were controlled through strong networks and solid information management. Interestingly, it was not the trade finance element of the Medici house that led to its ultimate failure. Instead, it was loans to government, that is, defaults by King Edward IV. It is ironic, or perhaps prophetic, that sovereign lending, not business-related ventures, should bring down a banking house that was so advanced.

During the 15th and 16th centuries, banking activity greatly expanded and not always under the most favorable conditions. Population growth and the growth of trade along Middle East and Far East trade routes increased the demand for precious metal coins and bullion. Even with the hundreds of tons of gold and silver that were brought in from the Americas (Spain alone obtained over 100 tons of silver a year from the Americas), the demand for credit remained unsatisfied. Banks responded by making the bill of exchange and other forms of "bank" currency available to support business and trade. In the early part of the 16th century the fairs at Lyons (France) were especially important in the international settlement of trades involving silk and spices from along the new trade routes--so important that 169 banks operated in the city year-round, of which 143 were Italian. At this point, banks had begun to have a significant impact on the money supply. Without bills of exchange and bank notes, the expansion of trade could not have taken place, at least not to the extent that it did.

The dominance of Italian banking faded, however, when more organized commodity exchanges developed in Holland and England as industries from these countries overtook the textile industry. In the late 16th and early 17th centuries, Amsterdam put in place institutional mechanisms to support trade and became the leading international market for shipping, commodities, and capital. The Chamber of Assurance (insurance), the United East India Company (trading company), a stock exchange, and a grain exchange facilitated the physical exchange of all manner of goods. The Wisselbank or Exchange Bank (1609) completed the foundation of support for business by providing financial services, including accepting deposits. All bills of exchange in excess of 600 florins were stipulated for payment through the Wisselbank, effectively forcing all major concerns to open an account there. The bank was also responsible for domestic coinage and foreign exchange and acted as the "state" bank in that a large proportion of its assets consisted of loans to the City of Amsterdam. The success of the Amsterdam economy was at least partially attributable to the powerful Wisselbank.

The model of the Wisselbank as a state bank was adapted throughout Europe, including the Bank of Sweden (1668) and the Bank of England (1694). The Bank of Sweden's primary customer was the government of Sweden, instead of the more customary business community. This distinction has caused this 17th century bank to be designated as the first central bank. On the other hand, the Bank of England was constituted as a private company, as it remained until the 20th century, with all the attendant duties and responsibilities. The Bank opened accounts for private citizens, accepted and paid bills of exchange, and issued bank notes--a new form of money. Nevertheless, its primary function was to manage the debt of the government and to make payments as ordered by the Exchequer. The first management team of the Bank of England was composed of merchants of the highest reputation and skills. Success from the earliest days of the Bank of England, with its dual responsibilities to industry and government, may be directly attributed to the thorough and intimate understanding of business enterprise by those in top management.

The 18th Century

As state banks were being established, the seeds of powerful, modern banking houses were being sown. The Baring Brothers and the Rothschilds followed the tradition of merchant banking, with remarkably humble beginnings.

The Birth of the Baring Brothers

Twenty-three years after the Bank of England was established, a young merchant by the name of John Baring arrived in Exeter, England. Born of German parents, John was raised by his grandparents when his own father died shortly before his birth. The family was involved in the textile industry, as was much of northern Germany. Large amounts of wool were imported from England while linen was exported in return. With £500, his share of his father's estate, the young Baring set out to England to learn that side of the business and to make useful contacts, planning to stay no more than two years. His first duties were to sell the family's linen inventory on consignment, earning a commission on the sales. He became more involved in wool trading and decided to stay in Exeter, marrying Elizabeth Vowler and starting his own family. By the time he died, leaving an estate of £40,000, he had become one of the richest merchants in that area with considerable land holdings. His sons John, Thomas, Francis, and Charles Baring assisted their mother in running the business. When Thomas died at an early age, the three remaining Baring brothers became the foundation upon which one of the world's powerful banking houses would be built.

Francis Baring was the most talented of the three Barings. He served an apprenticeship for seven years in Manchester, England, then became a partner in a firm in London when the family's London agent retired and suggested that Francis take over the business. The Barings now had two operations in England--the John and Charles Baring Company in Exeter and the John and Francis Baring Company in London. The London operation, run by Francis, was to buy the raw materials needed by the Exeter operation and to spot new markets for their products. By this time, London was a very active trading post and the financial center of England. The scope of the London business soon expanded to other commodities including copper and diamonds. The financial services that Francis also performed--collecting money due them and honoring the bills drawn on the Barings--were to evolve into the central function of this merchant family in later years.

Elizabeth Baring was not always comfortable with the financial affairs of her son Francis and warned him to not overexpose himself in the acceptance business, that is, the business of accepting bills of exchange. This advice was perhaps not overly cautious since in the fourteen years that Francis Baring was a member of the Exeter partnership, he lost money in eight of them. He lamented that it had cost him the better part of £10,000 to acquire merely the "knowledge of trade and commerce."

To add to his problems, he and his brother Charles were frequently at odds over Charles' poor investment decisions. After a particularly bitter dispute, Francis formed his own London-based firm in 1776, Francis Baring and Company, while remaining a partner of John and Francis Baring and Company. In the first year of operation, the new company doubled acceptance fees over the previous year and began to facilitate trade finance with the rich and influential Dutch firm, Hope and Company. The two firms accepted and exchanged trade bills that arouse from English/Dutch trade. In 1776, Baring began to invest for his own account in the East India Company, which held a monopoly on English imports and exports from and to India, and in 1783 he was made a director of the company. These affiliations also led to Baring's introduction to government officials. In the early 1780s, the British government needed funds to finance its war with America. The John and Francis Baring Company was selected as the sole underwriter of this public finance. It was a profitable undertaking and the Baring Brothers, with their close ties to business and government, were well on their way to becoming one of the most powerful financial houses in England, indeed, the world. It should be remembered, however, that without those initial days of risk-taking in the London acceptance market, the House of Barings would have never attained the prominence that would later be theirs.

The Rothschilds

While London was a relatively stable environment for trade finance and bill exchange, Germany of the 18th century was not nearly so advanced. This was primarily attributable to the many political subdivisions in the country. As late as 1790, Germany had 300 different rulers, a fact that led to the use of something other than a single domestic currency. At one time, 70 types of foreign coins circulated and gold was hoarded.

While the Barings were in the midst of the turmoil connected with the Exeter and London partnerships, Meyer Amshel Rothschild returned to Frankfurt, the city of his birth, in 1764. Earlier, he had been orphaned at a young age and taken in by relatives in Hanover, Germany. His benefactors found work for him in the merchant and banking house of Oppenheim, where he worked for eight years. His younger brothers Moses and Kalmann were apprenticed to a dealer in second-hand goods in Frankfurt after some meager schooling. When Meyer returned to Frankfurt, he had vague notions of setting up the equivalent of the House of Oppenheim--a house involved in wholesale import and export, where business was conducted directly with the merchants, and no merchandise actually changed hands. But as a fairly low-level employee in only the rare coin division of Oppenheim, Meyer had acquired little real knowledge of the business and no capital. Meyer would not have the benefit of an inheritance to finance his on-the-job training, as was possible for Francis Baring. His brothers offered little more in the way of skills or financing. The first enterprise of young Meyer Amshel Rothschild and his brothers in the Jewish ghetto of Frankfurt built on their combined knowledge—the trading of rare coins, old jewelry, curio items, and antiques.

While Moses and Kalmann operated the shop, Meyer was more often traveling between Frankfurt and nearby towns to respond to inquiries prompted by their catalog. In these travels he noted the chaos of the German money supply and became very much involved in money changing, both during the Frankfurt trade fairs and in the shop itself. Meyer began to train his brothers in the business of currency exchange and the discounting of bills of exchange. His ambitions were, however, to win the "account" of one of the dozen monarchs within 50 miles of Frankfurt. To win the patronage of one of the ruling class would make him a highly respected member of his neighborhood and allow him to travel and trade without the restrictions which were common for Jews at the time.

Meyer's dream began to be realized in 1769 when he was granted a modest title of nobility from the monarch of Hanau, the nearest sovereign capital to Frankfurt. With this enhanced respectability, Meyer gained the approval to wed the seventeen-year-old object of his affections--Guetele. Shortly thereafter, Moses also married. Upon his marriage, Moses left the family business. When Kalmann died in 1782, the business was left to Meyer, Guetele, and their five sons--Amschel, Salomon, Nathan, James, and Carl. Unfortunately, with both of his brothers gone, the business in the shop stagnated. Meyer was not particularly aggressive in his dealings with the curios and antiques. In fact, these items were eventually replaced by wine and coffee, tea and chocolate, cloth and ready-made garments. His real passions were the rare coins and the history that surrounded them. Sadly, it appeared that his dream of wealth and prestige would not be completely fulfilled after all.

But his eldest son Amschel more than compensated for Meyer's lack of commercial drive, first helping in the shop and then buying and selling (usually cotton cloth) on his own. But he lacked capital, which forced him to act primarily as a middleman earning commissions. He conceived a plan to relieve this capital shortage.

A young prince Landgrave William of Hesse-Cassel was the son of the monarch who had granted Meyer his nobility twenty years earlier. William had invested considerable amounts in obligations of the English government, among other investments. When the interest fell due on the English investments, he received English drafts (orders payable by the British government). He gave these to merchants with instructions not to discount them (cash them) until the Frankfurt fairs so as not to depress their market value in the interim. Thus, the merchants were given interest free loans. At the same time, cloth dealers in Manchester, England required payment in drafts on London. If the dealers could be paid with the Landgrave's drafts, a source of capital was assured! He urged his father to approach the Landgrave.

Not a particularly easy man to work with or to please, the Landgrave nevertheless gave Meyer a modest allotment of drafts, £1,000 per year which increased over time. Using these drafts, the Rothschild firm received first choice of the cotton fabric and the business prospered. By now the French Revolution had erupted, but a sufficient number of English textile dealers continued to make the trek to Manchester.

Then the worst possible scenario threatened--loss of their supply of textiles. While accompanying his father as he looked at the samples of a Manchester dealer, the spirited Nathan infuriated the British salesman who then refused to sell to them. The 21-year-old Nathan, who barely spoke English, assured his father that he would obtain all the cloth they needed and promptly left for Manchester. Once there, he provided a regular supply of cotton cloth for Frankfurt with the capital that he brought with him. But, he reasoned in his never-ending letters on the subject, if he had more capital, he could go to London and really expand the family's enterprises. The Landgrave was the answer. This was an opportunity of a lifetime!

The Landgrave much preferred to conduct his larger financial affairs through bankers that had a more noble pedigree than the Rothschilds, such as the Bethmann Brothers and Rueppell & Harnier. Understanding this and the fact that the Landgrave was not exactly the most favorite client of such high-brow bankers, Nathan convinced the bankers to allow the Rothschilds to work directly with the

Landgrave for a broker's commission. This enabled the bankers to keep the account without having to actually work with him. In this capacity, the Rothschilds sold Danish bonds originated by the bankers to the Landgrave, converted interest coupons, and repaid principal amounts. The arrangement was working to everyone's satisfaction.

Suddenly, in 1804, the Rothschilds stopped servicing the account. No explanation was given and the bankers were too proud to ask for one. The Rothschilds had learned the secrets of high finance and were ready to enter the world of bond trading. Nathan departed for London in the same year. The patience and risk-taking had paid off. The Rothschilds were ready to take a more central role in securities dealing in the financial capital of the world.

The 19th Century

The 19th century would witness the development of major banking institutions that supported economic development in their home countries and abroad. The Barings became heavily involved in financing in the Americas and almost stumbled into financial collapse along the way. The Rothschilds concentrated primarily on the European continent. Both houses contributed significantly to the industrialization of the countries in which they invested. Yet private bankers of this sort would yield some of their power to a new form of banking in Europe--the joint-stock or limited liability company. The new breed would also include American firms as the center of gravity of the financial world moved from London to New York. The names of Morgan and Mellon would take on the same connotation that those of Baring and Rothschild had for so many years. The expansion of economic activity would dramatically affect China as it adapted to sometimes-forced foreign influence on its soil. The Chinese culture would not be lost, however, as Chinese traditional banks acted as a buffer between the old world and the new, all the while maintaining the close ties between Chinese merchants and bankers. Japan would watch the activity in China with alarm. Internal change and external forces would precipitate one of history's most rapid transformations from agriculture to industry. Essentially, during the 19th century seeds of collaboration between banking and industry were sown, the fruits of which can still be seen.

English Bankers--Financiers to the World

In London, John Baring retired and officially ended the partnership of John and Francis Baring and Company. Francis Baring and Company was reconstituted with Francis, his elder son Thomas, and his son-in-law Charles Wall. Of course, there were other offspring of Francis that were involved with the firm including Alexander, Henry, William, and George, although not all were of equal qualification. Alexander, who had worked in Amsterdam with Hope and Company, was sent to the United States to develop business there after the French invasion of Holland disrupted the operations of the Hopes. Henry became an important operative in London. William and George were sent to the Far East to work in the East India Company. But William, a promising banker by all accounts, was prone to illness and died in 1820. George, on the other hand, was more plagued by personal problems. After marrying against the family's wishes, speculating and losing money in the opium market (which was to have significant impact on the trade patterns in China), George left the East India Company and became more religious. The religious conversion did little to curb his extravagant tastes, however, and he soon went bankrupt. While the other brothers did bail him out, George never again had a significant role in the House of Baring.

When Francis retired in 1803, he left the firm in the capable hands of Thomas, Alexander, Henry, and son-in-law Charles Wall. The company's focus was decidedly international. Trade in the United States accounted for a large share of the Barings' acceptance business. In the four years ended 1797, acceptance liabilities (those bills for which the Barings were obligated) went from £89,458 to £454,807, much of it attributable to "American and colonial" trade.

The alliance with Hope and Company brought the Barings into the realm of government finance, as well. The Portuguese government needed financing in 1801 to repay war debts. The Hopes took responsibility for the bulk of the offering, but the Barings assumed 5 million of the 13 million guilder issue. It was not well received; only 1.5 million guilders had been sold in London by 1802.

It was the Barings' role in London government finance, however, that brought the house the reputation of power. Alexander took personal charge of these issues and they were almost always profitable, that is, unless the market had reason to doubt either the government or the Barings. When Francis Baring died in 1810 and certain members of Parliament urged a reduction in paper money (in favor of payments in gold), the market collapsed on the £22.3 million British government issue for which Barings was primarily responsible, forcing the issue to sell 8 percent below face value. For the most part, however, the Baring name ensured the success of a government issue.

In their U.S. dealings, the Barings were oriented to trade and to government finance. North America was one of the best markets for British cloth, but without North American exports, there was no way to pay for the cloth. The Barings facilitated trade in both directions. When the American William Bingham approached the Barings about buying 3 million acres in Maine, Francis Baring sent Alexander to investigate. After the deal was completed, Alexander looked for other investment opportunities. With great enthusiasm for the former colonies, he prompted the house to become involved in other long term investments. In 1803, fully half of the $32 million of foreign investment in U.S. stocks was held by the British, and the Barings were squarely in the center of these dealings. In fact, they were responsible, along with the London merchants C.T. Cazenove and Batard, for distributing all U.S. stock dividends to British investors.

There was also a close alliance with the U.S. government. As early as 1795, the Barings provided the government with $800,000 to facilitate negotiations about shipping rights in the Mediterranean. To cover an emergency need only a month later, another $200,000 was forthcoming. The Barings even provided £45,000, 10,000 muskets, and 330 cannons when it appeared that the U.S. would become involved in a war with France. The house was essentially an agent of the U.S. government without officially receiving the designation.

In 1803 the United States had the opportunity to purchase the French colony of Louisiana, doubling its own land mass and avoiding the presence of the French on its southern border. The negotiated price was $11.25 million and the lead manager in the bond issue was Alexander Baring, assuming responsibility for 60 percent of the total. In exchange for 6 percent bonds in this amount, the Barings delivered 52 million francs to the French in 3 installments.

In 1828, Alexander promoted an issue of State of Massachusetts bonds to be sold in London. Ohio, Pennsylvania, and Maryland were also believed to be quite creditworthy because so many residents were from New England. All states were not so favored. For example, the Barings avoided Indiana and Mississippi as not yet worthy of serious investment. But London had unfailing confidence in the Barings' ability to discern the difference.

Then the dam broke in the 1840s. It became apparent that Florida, Mississippi, Indiana, Illinois, Arkansas, Michigan, and even Maryland and Pennsylvania would default on their bonds. Practically overnight, the Americans became as despised in England as they were during the war between the two countries. Americans were attacked on the street and barred from public establishments. What is now seen as a safe haven for the world's money was at that time considered no better than a capital-starved, debt-ridden, underdeveloped country.

Despite these defaults, the Barings worked with those states with which they had particularly close affiliations--Pennsylvania, Louisiana, and Maryland--urging them to resume payments so as to have access to capital in the future. Nevertheless, it would be a number of years before London regarded the United States with anything other than disdain.

After the Civil War, the House of Baring became involved in the industrial revitalization of the United States. Amid strong optimism, the rush of California gold, and major capital investment, the house participated in 22 new issues of stock in the 1870s and 1880s. Of these new issues, 14 were rail stocks. In fact, the Barings were responsible for almost 30 percent of the U.S. railroad stocks issued through London merchant banks. Some of these issues ran into trouble, but the Barings supported the market and the country as a direct result. Gradually, the financial sophistication of home-grown U.S. financial firms increased such that the Barings held a less prominent role in the United States. But it is safe to say that the development of the United States in no small way can be attributed to the House of Barings.

If the Barings present a convincing case for the establishment of a strong relationship between industry and banking, their Latin American dealings also illustrate the problems that can result from a less-than-well-informed approach to banking. The firm first became involved in Latin America in 1858 when Chile retained the house as agent for a £1.5 million government loan issued in London. The issue sold poorly and the firm was forced to buy back £200,000 to support the price after only a few days. An even less auspicious transaction in Venezuela was undertaken in 1867 when the Barings floated a £1 million issue for Venezuela secured by customs receipts. Within two years, the Venezuelan government took over all the customs duties and refused to service the bonds. The Barings appealed to the British foreign ministers, but to no avail.

Argentina was another matter, however, or so it seemed. A young member of the family, Ned Baring toured the Latin America in 1859 to try to work out payments for several delinquent issues of debt. He found very little to comfort him in Mexico, sensing a basic dislike for foreigners that he translated into little willingness to service foreign debt. Argentina was different; it was completely controlled by a dictator. But the dictator appeared to want to resolve the outstanding issues. Ned worked with the leader, Juan Rosas, over the course of several months and finally reached what seemed to be a reasonable repayment plan. However, within two years, Rosas was deposed and the repayment of the debt once again appeared questionable. Surprisingly, new terms were worked out fairly quickly and payments resumed.

The Barings had been fortunate, it seemed, to work out the terms of this troubled bond issue. To become more involved may have seemed foolhardy. But Argentina was rich in natural resources and at 18 percent interest rates, the prospect of new money into the country must have appeared enticing. What was not factored into this equation was the need for adequate intelligence gathering. While risk is an inevitable part of successful merchant banking, *information* is indispensable. At a time when Londoners knew almost nothing about South America, sometimes not even where specific countries were located, the Barings badly underestimated this simple truth.

In 1866, the Argentine government issued a small loan for £1.25 million, followed in 1868 by a £1.95 million issue. Both were slow to clear the market, leading Nicholas Bouwer, an employee of Barings for over 13 years to recommend a retrenchment from the government issues while looking for more favorable industrial projects. The first was the Buenos Aires Drainage and Waterworks, a massive water works project, as suggested by the local trading house of S.B. Hale and Company. Hale and Barings began to work together, identifying other projects in Argentina that showed promise. In the aggregate, the British investment in Argentina went from £25 million in 1880 to £45 million in 1885 to £150 million in 1890, representing 50 percent of all British overseas investment, with the House of Baring participating in roughly 10 percent of the new issues.

But there had been too much reliance on Hale and Company. When John Baring visited Argentina in 1889 he found a disaster in the making. Business was at a standstill, largely because of Buenos Aires Drainage and Waterworks. Streets had been torn apart, yet work was not progressing because of material shortages and misallocations of labor. The Waterworks refused to accept devaluating pesos, insisting instead on payment in gold-backed dollars, forcing residents into inability to repay and resulting in unpaid accounts of $1.65 million. The Argentine bubble was about to burst and catch the House of Barings holding a large proportion of its asset portfolio in inflated securities based on the fragile economy.

Back in London, the word soon spread that the house was in trouble. Depositors and investors essentially started a "run" on the House of Barings, requesting immediate repayment of deposits and other instruments of debt. A rescue effort was led by William Lidderdale, the Governor of the Bank of England, to raise the £8 million that would be necessary. It was all too clear to him that if the House of Baring fell, so would many other banking houses in the City. The Bank of England established a Guarantee Fund by borrowing £3 million in gold from Paris and another £1.5 million from St. Petersburg. Private money was contributed by many rivals of the firm including the Morgans and the Rothschilds. The crisis was averted, but the old partnership was disbanded, Barings' personal fortunes lost, and the reorganized operation downsized considerably.

The lessons to be learned from the Barings are mixed. A strong bank can be the key to growth and development. Indeed, if the firm had not been as large and powerful as it was, it would not have had the same beneficial impact. Until recently, it was virtually impossible for banks to have this kind of impact domestically because of geographic restrictions. On the other hand, without a close and informed operational relationship between banks and their clients, the safety of the bank itself can be threatened

While the Barings operated internationally as a partnership, other smaller institutions were forced to adopt the partnership form of business organization because the Bank of England had received the exclusive right to operate as a limited-liability, joint-stock bank (similar to a corporation as it is known today) and issue bank notes (money). However, as the Baring collapse illustrated, without the confidence of the banking public in an institution, a bank could quickly succumb to immediate demands for deposit withdrawals. Such demands fell exclusively to the partners and ultimately to their own assets if the partnerships assets were tied up in illiquid loans. This precarious situation erupted in 1825 when 73 of England's 770 banks failed. Especially hard-hit were the banks outside London.

The 1826 Banking Copartnerships Act attempted to remedy this situation. Under provisions of the Act, a bank could be constituted as a joint-stock company, with an unlimited number of shareholders, and have the right to issue their own notes. So as not to dilute the power of the Bank of England, which had been quite efficient in helping the government manage its debt, banks within 65 miles of London were precluded from taking advantage of these provisions. This law opened up the floodgates of the practice of banking in England. Many old partnerships converted and altogether new companies were formed, with the number of bank offices growing from 1,700 in 1850 to 3,300 in 1875 to over 6,600 by the end of the century.

These "country" banks made banking services now available to rural towns and villages and to industrial cities outside of London. It soon became apparent that there was strength in numbers. Instead of paying several correspondents for banking services, such as bill discounting, in other parts of the country, why not merge with those banks? Some of the nationwide networks that formed in England during the 19th century remain today as the country's most powerful banks, among them Lloyd's Bank (1884), Midland Bank (1891), and Barclays (1896). Savings in the countryside were mobilized to finance industry since virtually every village in England had at least two banks. Industry specialization also developed because the bankers in each region became quite knowledgeable of that area's primary commercial and industrial ventures. At the same time, the banking network was not entirely dependent on any one area or industry, improving the diversification of bank operations.

The early joint stock banks in England clearly illustrate a natural development of the banking system when not hampered by artificial barriers. It was as natural for a nationwide network of joint-stock banks to develop as it was for the Barings to develop an international presence in banking. To restrict nationwide operation, as was the case in the United States until recently, benefits neither the banks nor the clients that they serve.

The Emergence of Strong German Banking

In 1804, one year after Francis Baring turned over the reigns of the House of Baring to his sons and the Barings financed the Louisiana Purchase in the United States, an unknown merchant banker by the name of Nathan M. Rothschild arrived in London. His abrupt departure from Manchester marked a milestone toward the family's goal of eventually becoming the primary bankers to the German prince, Landgrave William of Hesse-Cassel.

While Nathan had been availing himself of the credit made possible by using the Landgrave's notes from London, brother Salomon had been laying the diplomatic groundwork for a nothing less than a financial coup d'état. He befriended Karl Friedrich Buderus, the man whom the Landgrave had entrusted with managing his investments. Buderus, a reserved but friendly individual, confided to Salomon that the Landgrave's practice of parceling out the financial services that he required--the Van Nottens in Amsterdam, the Russians in St. Petersburg and so on--was inefficient. The oversight of this vast fortune should be handled by one banker. Although not betraying the intensity of their desire to be that one banker, Salomon Rothschild knew that Buderus was the best ally that they could have in their quest for the Landgrave account.

As chief bankers for the Landgrave, their income would be derived from a number of sources. First, the terms of the investment were negotiating, generating fee income for the banker. Then the funds must be delivered--another fee. When interest coupons were due, these too had to be converted into cash, sometimes involving a foreign currency exchange. Lastly, when the principal amount was due, delivery of the final payment and any necessary currency conversions generated still more commissions and fees. With the prospect of tapping into this free-flowing stream of revenues, Salomon patiently cultivated his relationship with Buderus. But Buderus was not receptive to Salomon's subtle hints of the customary financial favors that were bestowed on the staff of the Landgrave. What would it take to gain an opening? After many seemingly casual conversations, Salomon realized that Buderus sought financial independence, that is, he wanted a share of the potential fees. Salomon proposed such an arrangement and it was accepted!

The first investment was a Danish loan currently being negotiated with the Bethmanns at an unusually high 8 percent interest rate. Buderus approached the Danish representative, Johann Daniel Lawaetz, with the proposition of investing in the entire bond issue and accepting a much more reasonable 4.5 percent interest, with the provision that the Rothschilds handle the transaction without disclosing the ultimate lender. Lawaetz was delighted and the Landgrave was willing because he had a surplus to invest and no great desire to have the full extent of his fortune publicly disclosed. It was 1804, the year of Nathan's departure from Manchester, his arrival in London, and the abrupt conclusion of the Rothschild's brokerage relationship with the Bertmanns and Rueppell & Harnier with respect to the business of the Landgrave. The plan worked perfectly and was replicated four times over the period of the next two years. Of course, the noble banking houses that lost the business were confused and dismayed at the turn of events.

Finally, the houses of Bertmann and Rueppell & Harnier learned the truth when yet another Danish bond issue was being negotiated. The Rothschilds were being considered to handle the offering. This was indeed laughable! These small, undercapitalized, inexperienced bunch could not possibly take responsibility for such a major undertaking. Little did they know that the Rothschilds had done exactly that for the last two years, by selling the bonds largely through the London-based firm of Nathan M. Rothschild. But it appeared that they would not rest until the absurdity of such an arrangement was clearly understood and the

Rothschilds eliminated from consideration. It looked as though the Rothschilds' good fortune had just about ended.

Or had it? The October 1806 invasion by Napoleon considerably changed the German financial landscape, disrupting the operations of the established German bankers and forcing Landgrave William to flee to Denmark in the middle of the night. Buderus, by now a silent partner of the Rothschilds, was left in Germany to manage the Landgrave's affairs. Napoleon issued a proclamation ordering confiscation of all the nobleman's property and the payment of all state revenue to his treasury. Buderus and others also left to safeguard the Landgrave's belongings hurriedly hid as much treasure as possible behind walls and under stairways at other castles, transferred it to warehouses in Frankfurt, and even deposited some in the basement of the Frankfurt home of Meyer Amschel Rothschild.

Having secured much of the Landgrave's valuables, Buderus then directed all payments to be made to the Rothschilds, with the English payments being made directly to Nathan in London. While this provided even more capital to work with in London and Frankfurt, Napoleon had imposed a blockade on all goods from England, forcing prices to black-market levels. But with Rothschilds on both sides of the Channel, new opportunities for profitable trade opened to the family. Meyer opened a receiving depot in northern Germany and smuggling became a major operation for the Rothschild clan. The goods were reexported throughout Germany, Holland, Scandinavian countries, and even France itself.

The family furthered ingratiated itself with the Landgrave by transporting his hidden Treasure to their own Hamburg warehouses until they could be moved to safer locations, by making sure that all the former soldiers of the Landgrave continued to receive their pay, by enforcing collection from those to whom the Landgrave had made loans (in spite of Napoleon's degree that all such payments be made to him), and by helping him to move his bases of exile from Denmark to Prague. Though the Landgrave's general disposition was not at all improved by his exile, this "royal treatment" did inspire even more confidence in the Rothschilds.

However, the French police began to crack down on the smuggling activity from England. Fortunately, when they raided the Frankfurt shops and warehouses in October 1810, relatively little was found in the Rothschild's quarters. Part of this good fortune was attributable to the dual set of books that Meyer maintained--one for the French authorities and one true set of records. While they escaped any severe consequences, the episode did serve to convince the family that it was time to stop the merchandising of goods. From that time forth, their sole enterprise would be buying and selling *money*—exchanging currencies and making investments. In December 1810, Nathan convinced the Landgrave to let him invest £550,000 in British bonds. His brother Carl acted as a secret courier by transporting the securities, though delivery was not as speedy as the nobleman would have preferred. Smuggling securities was a risky business, the patriarch of the family would remind the Landgrave when he complained of receiving only £189,500 in certificates well into 1811. It is true enough that transporting the securities could only be handled most delicately, but it is also true that Nathan used the money to profitably speculate in the gold bullion market in London.

Ostensibly, the money that flowed through Nathan M. Rothschild was being invested by the principal, Nathan himself. Since no one was aware that it was primarily the Landgrave's funds, the general consensus was that the young Rothschild was quite well-to-do. This, in turn, enabled Nathan to build his own credibility in the City.

As Nathan continued his investment activities, he had also become aware of other dynamics in Europe. English forces in Spain, under the command of the Duke of Wellington, were attempting to marshall forces to fight Napoleon, but were having difficulty with supplies and provisions. It appeared that the ships from England to the peninsula were being intercepted by the French and the English notes were depreciating because of the difficulty of redeeming them for gold.

Nathan Rothschild had realized that his family's experience of moving goods through Germany and serving the needs of the Landgrave would serve them well to also move money through the dangerous regions of Germany, France, and Spain. Carl was dispatched to the Pyrenees, that is, the border between France and Spain. James was stationed on the English Channel, and Salomon positioned himself between them in Paris. After Carl had exchanged a satchel full of British notes (at a discount) for gold, he headed toward Paris, where he met Salomon outside the city under the cloak of darkness and passed along the British paper. The last leg of the land journey was from the outskirts of Paris to the Channel coast where Salomon passed the notes to James at the appointed spot. Then either Nathan traveled south by water to retrieve the notes from James or James crossed the Channel to deliver the notes to Nathan. The culmination of this dangerous enterprise was that Nathan then redeemed the notes in London at par, fetching a handsome profit for the family.

However, a shortage of gold to redeem these notes became a serious problem. When a ship of the East India Company landed in London in 1811 with £800,000 in gold bars for sale, Nathan appeared to have solved the liquidity problem. He arrived at the site of auction early and placed a bid that was certain to ensure that the gold bars would be his. But they would not be his without the interest of the British government. Charles Herries, Commissary General of the British government, sent Nathan Rothschild a letter requesting his presence at a conference. When Nathan arrived and was shown in, Herries was surprised at his humble attire. When he opened his mouth and spoke in his less-than-pedigreed dialect, Herries was astonished. Could this be the man who had snatched almost £1 million of gold right from under the nose of the British government? Upon inquiry, it seemed that indeed this was the man.

Herries explained the need for the government to purchase the gold, for a reasonable price, of course. When Nathan asked about the intent of the government for the gold, knowing full well the intent before he asked, Herries explained that the gold was needed for transport to Spain. Then Nathan Rothschild explained the land-based network that his family had established. Herries was so impressed that he requested that the Rothschild's put themselves in the service of the British government.

With the financial assistance of the Rothschilds, Napoleon was eventually defeated and the stature of the Rothschild family was never again challenged. The "Five Arrows" of the Rothschild crest became the permanent heads of the European-based financial dynasty. When fully developed, the network consisted of Nathan in London, James in Paris, Carl in Naples, Amschel in Frankfurt, and Salomon in Vienna.

Having established their place in government finance, the Rothschilds turned once again to financing commerce and industry, including the Liverpool-Manchester Railway in 1830, the railroad from Bochnia (Poland) to Vienna in 1835, and the Paris-Saint-Germain Railway in 1837. As the markets for public and private finance became more advanced, the dominance of the Rothschilds subsided. But family members went on to participate directly in government and to become philanthropists, patrons of the arts, writers, and physicians. By understanding the markets in which they operated, being willing to take risks when warranted, and seizing opportunities that presented themselves, the Rothschilds evolved from a family of meager means to a financial powerhouse strong enough to affect the course of world events and to have major impact on the economic development of Europe.

While the Rothschild dynasty was being established, German banking was evolving into a coherent system of strong regional banks. The unification of the currency was accomplished in 1871 when the gold mark, divided into 100 phennigs, replaced the Prussian thaler, the silver mark of Cologne, the Dutch gulden, and other coins circulating at the time. This consolidation roughly coincided with the 1871 establishment of the Deutsche Bank, a joint-stock bank in Berlin. From the outset its charge was to facilitate trade. Section 2 outlines its purpose:

"The purpose of the company is to carry on banking transactions of every description, in particular to further and facilitate the trading relations between Germany, the other European countries and the overseas markets."

The Deutsche Bank sought to challenge the dominance of English banking in international trade. It was a difficult tradition to outdo, however, because by the time the German currency was unified, the British pound had been used in international trade for a century or more. The alternative approach was to foster growth of German companies themselves. By the late 1870s and early 1880s, the Deutsche Bank was underwriting stock issues of firms such as Krupp, the chemical company, and Siemens & Halske, the forerunner of the electronics giant.

Other major German banks began operation during the same period--the Dresdner Bank and the Commerzbank. These banks "promoted" the companies that they supported by first making the initial investment in the companies and then soliciting the public to follow suit. While the major banks, Deutsche Bank, Dresdner, and Commerzbank supported companies which would grow to have worldwide prominence, smaller, regional banks developed expertise in those industries important to their particular economies. This tradition has not changed since the inception of joint-stock banking in Germany. The arrangement has lead to an efficient regional system of banks with industry specialization, complemented by a strong system of the three major banks with close alliances to those German companies with international presence.

During the nineteenth century, Germany evolved from a financially chaotic country (with not even a currency of its own) to one with a private and joint-stock banking system completely focused on the country's economic development. The relationship that developed between banking and industry during this century would form the foundation of a manufacturing giant that, despite its relatively small size, would seriously challenge the United States in its ability to export goods throughout the world.

Chinese Bankers and the Western World

In the early 19th century, while the Rothschilds were moving from government to industry finance and the Barings were already financing the Louisiana Purchase, the traditional commercial bankers in China, called the *ch'ien chuang*, were operating as private bankers for the merchant trade. As early as 1796, the Shanghai guild of *ch'ien chuang*, the equivalent of a modern bankers' association, had 60 members. As was true with London, Shanghai became an important banking center because it was first an important trading center. The difference is that China's economy had not yet been touched by the British-led Industrial Revolution, a condition that would change violently later in the century.

Shanghai was the trading post for goods from the north and the south to be exchanged, including beans, wheat, oil, charcoal, and cloth, much of which was transported via junks, flat-bottomed ships of Chinese origin. The first function of the *ch'ien chuang* was currency exchange since the currencies of the north always differed from those of the south. In fact, provinces (states) and even smaller localities used individualized currencies, composed of various forms and combinations of gold, silver, or copper. The traditional Chinese bankers also provided important short-term financing in the form of *chung-p'iao*, a kind of promissory note, that came to be used in China very much in the same way that the bill of exchange was used in Europe.

Throughout their history, these Far Eastern bankers either directly financed or indirectly facilitated the entire merchant trade of China. The founder of the first *ch'ien chuang* is said to have owned a coal business and lent his surplus funds to neighboring shops and junk operators. Later, in the 1820s Fang Chieh-t'ang of Shanghai took profits from a grain business to open sugar and silk enterprises. Just as the Rothschilds moved from coins and second-hand merchandise into banking, the Fang family began operating a ch'ien chuang in the 1830s.

In another case, Li Yeh-t'ing arrived in Shanghai in 1822 at the tender age of 15, served an apprenticeship in a wineshop, where his duties included delivery to sampans, the smaller shipping vessels commonly used in 19th century China. With a small investment, Li started his own sampan company, which grew to a fleet of 10 boats. The Li *ch'ien chuang* was financed by the profits from this sampan enterprise.

The traditional bankers such as Fang and Li provided services including accepting deposits, making loans, issuing bank notes, and transmitting funds in addition to their currency exchange activities. Like the Rothschilds and the

Barings, the *ch'ien chuang* business passed from father to son. Perhaps even more than the case of their German and British counterparts, the conduct of banking business in China relied very much on the social contacts of the people involved--both family and geographic ties. Many of the *ch'ien chuang* were tied together in a friendly, noncompetitive relationship that enhanced their ability to provide a common front to their government and later to foreign commercial interests. Ironically, this kind of Confucian spirit would also later be a driving motivation for one of America's most dynamic financiers--J.P. Morgan.

However, this managed arrangement between banking and industry in China would not be left to develop on its own momentum. The expansionary trade of the English was to have significant impact on Chinese banking activities. China had historically maintained an isolationist posture with respect to the West, having fought for centuries to establish and maintain internal peace. The West would not be denied, however, and in 1834, Canton in the southern Chinese province of Quangdong was opened to limited overseas trade. American, British, French, and Dutch merchants ran operations in the trade of tea and silk. However, the British found the arrangement too restrictive.

The British East India Company (the same company upon whose board the Barings sat) was chartered in 1600 and given the exclusive right to conduct Britain's trade with Asia. The firm wielded significant power until the government of Britain took control of India in 1857. After the defeat of Napoleon in 1815, the British East India Company became even more assertive in the Far East, purchasing the island of Singapore in 1819.

Then there was trade with China beginning in 1834. This activity rapidly accelerated despite the fact that the reigning Manchu dynasty (1644-1912) in Beijing considered all foreigners to be barbarians. Canton was the China's interface with the rest of the world, because foreigners were permitted in no other part of the country. Within Canton, Manchu regulations prohibited foreigners from learning the Chinese language, bringing their wives to Canton, entering the walled portion of the city, riding in sedan chairs (carried on poles by two men), dealing with any Chinese merchant other than those 13 or so who had been officially appointed, or even pleasure boating without permission.

The foreigners sold woolens, cottons, furs, and a few manufactured goods. They purchased silk, tea, rhubarb, and works of art. The British essentially considered China to be an extension of their Indian operations and the defeat of France's Napoleon gave them confidence that the backward Chinese, led by the distant Manchus, poised no threat to their ambitions. East India Company abandoned its monopoly of Chinese trade and soon there were 30 British companies trading in Canton.

There was so much trading activity that the British had difficulty obtaining enough merchandise to exchange for Chinese goods because the Chinese were so self-sufficient. Then the British began to bring in Indian opium to exchange for the goods that they sought. Although the substance was banned in China, so much of it was brought in that in 1839 Lin Ze-xu, a high-ranking representative of the Manchu dynasty arrived in Canton with specific orders to eradicate the opium trade. Lin acted with authority, banning all opium imports and demanding the surrender of over 20,000 chests of opium held in inventory.

When the opium was destroyed, British merchants were infuriated and withdrew to emergency quarters on their ships. Lin issued an ordered forbidding any Chinese to provide the self-exiled British merchants any food or water. The British retaliated by having the Royal Navy fire upon three Chinese ships. Thus, began the Opium Wars (1839-1842). Not surprisingly, at the conclusion of the conflicts, the British emerged victorious. The price for the Chinese was a much greater foreign presence than ever before. In the Treaty of Nanking, the island of Hong Kong was ceded to the British. The ports of Canton, Amoy (Fujian province), Foochow (Fujian), Ninpo (Zhejiang), and Shanghai were designated "treaty ports" and opened to Western trade. The Brits were given the right of extra-territoriality, which meant that they were not subject to Chinese law, and the status of "Most Favored Nation," which meant that any future right given to any other foreign power in China would also automatically accrue to the British.

With the provisions of the Treaty of Nanking, British and other foreign merchants looked forward with great anticipation to enjoying their new freedom. But barriers between the British and the Chinese would remain. When merchants attempted to buy tea directly in Foochow, they found that they could not easily get the money into the interior. In fact, whenever they tried to negotiate with the source of the goods, they were frustrated. Eventually they retreated to the treaty ports, conceding control of the interior China to the Chinese.

The Treaty of Nanking changed the number of locations in which Western merchants could operate but it did not change Chinese culture. The culture clash was between a traditional, personality-dependent system on one hand and an impersonal, contractually oriented system on the other. If the Westerners were to operate successfully within the interior, they would first have to understand the Chinese system--difficult, if not impossible, under the circumstances.

This is not to suggest that the presence of the foreigners did not have an affect on the Chinese economy. In fact, the opening of foreign trade acted as a stimulus to the indigenous economy over which the foreigners had no control. This was especially true for the large merchant and banking families that acted as a buffer between traditional Chinese and Western sectors.

The British merchant now had the freedom to deal with any Chinese merchant he chose but ran into two problems: (1) With whom should he deal? (2) How could he determine, then obtain, the correct type and amount of currency especially given the language barrier? The solution to this problem was the *comprador*, a Chinese merchant who was also an employee of a Western company. As a Chinese merchant, he used his personal connections to do business in the traditional system. With his knowledge and connections in conducting business for a Western firm, the *comprador* would also advise the Western firm, guaranteeing the solvency of Chinese merchants with which the Western firm had business transactions, and sometimes even posting a bond. Because of this critical role in the East/West interface, the *comprador* enjoyed an enhanced status within the traditional system. Without this intermediary activity, trade between the two sectors would have been far more difficult.

The traditional bankers acted as kind of financial compradors. Through *ch'ien chuang*, foreign capital was loaned to Chinese merchants. Within China, there were few modern banks with advanced accounting systems during the 19th century. In fact, most accounts in these traditional banks were settled only once a year, during the Chinese New Year. Any foreign capital loaned to the *ch'ien chuang* was loaned to Chinese merchants, especially to those involved with Western trade in goods such as opium, tea, and silk. (The traditional bankers that were more involved with the domestic market financed trade in such goods as rice and cotton.) The promissory notes or chuang-p'iao which documented the indebtedness of the traditional bankers and their clients also circulated as money, in much the same way that Bank of England notes circulated in Europe. The viability of the system depended on the holder of *chuang-p'iao* being able to redeem the notes as promised and redemption depended completely on the traditional Chinese bankers.

Of course, this informal system was vulnerable in the sense that an imbalance in the market could have far-reaching impact, as the Shanghai financial crisis of 1882 illustrates. During that year the silk trade was particularly sluggish, leaving the traditional bankers with temporarily surplus funds. The surplus funds of no less than 20 traditional bankers had been loaned to a major silk company and, when it failed, this sent the bankers scrambling to collect from other borrowers to cover the losses. The time of the New Year's settlement was fast approaching, accelerating the panic within the financial sector because there was by then a shortage of hard currency. Some merchants hid their money, declared false bankruptcy, and fled Shanghai, making the shortage even worse. The ranks of traditional bankers shrank to half their original number.

The prominence of the traditional Chinese bankers would never be regained. When the Manchu dynasty was overthrown in 1911 and replaced by a republican form of government led by Sun Yat-sen, the banking climate changed as well. The government wanted more regulatory control over the traditional banks. Oversight and regulation were contrary to the basic premise of the *ch'ien chuang* but completely compatible with more contractually oriented modern banks.

The new government also sought more formal collaboration with respect to the financial affairs of the country. The Bank of China and the Bank of Communications filled this need by underwriting government's domestic borrowing, just as the Bank of England had assisted the British government since the late 1600s. The indigenous banking system of China was indeed coming of age. Modern banks became a much more acceptable part of China's culture and financial landscape. But the legacy of the *ch'ien chuang* would remain. The close ties between business and banking had supported the early development of Western trade under sometimes adverse circumstances. Playing the role of middlemen, the early Chinese bankers helped provide a conducive environment for the development of domestic commercial interests in that country, while maintaining their traditional values and culture.

Japanese Banking--A Rapid Transformation

It is difficult to appreciate the power of modern-day Japan without first understanding its origins. In terms of development 18th-century Japan was more like 16th-century Tudor England, primarily agricultural with a variety of domestic handicraft industries, but without the foundations of overseas trade or a Royal Navy. This is not to say that there had never been an outward focus in Japan. In the early 1600s, expeditions to Korea pointed the way to mercantilism and even colonialism. However, the ascendancy of the military regime of Tokugawa Ieyasu brought these activities to an abrupt end. After 1640, no foreigners or foreign traders were permitted in Japan with the exception of the Dutch and Chinese who had limited trading privileges in Nagasaki. Furthermore, no Japanese was permitted to leave the country and subsequently return. Any Japanese who did so was promptly put to death.

The feudalism of the Tokugawa era also established a rigid hierarchy of class. The Shogunate (military ruler) controlled the country, while the Emperor and his court were primarily official figureheads. Each social class was designated as either inferior or superior to the others and was subject to strict regulations with respect to every aspect of life, including dress and behavior. To violate the regulations was to face punishment for the transgression.

At the top of the hierarchy was the Tokugawa family (the Shogunate) with control of roughly one quarter of the land in Japan including the major trading centers of Edo (Tokyo, the seat of government), Sakai (Osaka), Kyoto, and Nagasaki. Their revenues were derived by extracting one quarter of the rice yield on the land they controlled.

The remaining three quarters of the Japanese territory was divided among the *daimyo* or feudal lords, some of which had opposed Tokugawa before his rise to power. To keep potential enemies under control, all feudal lords were required to reside part of the time in Edo and part of the time on their own land, leaving their wives and children in Edo while they returned to their own fiefdoms. Communication and travel between the fiefdoms were discouraged. Intermarriage among the families of the feudal lords was subject to ratification by the Shogunal government. Even building construction and repair within the fiefdom had to be cleared in this way. The Shogun exacted taxes on the feudal lords that kept their coffers empty for the most part.

Below the feudal lords were the *samurai*, ostensibly the protectors of the fiefdoms, being paid rice stipends by the lords. Before Tokugawa, the *samurai* had alternatively fought for their *daimyo* during times of war and cultivated the fields in times of peace. After Tokugawa, a distinction was drawn between the *samurai* and the farmer or peasant. With the military strength of the Shogunate and the long period of peace under his rule, the functional importance of the *samurai* dwindled along with their status, a substantial blow to their collective egos. When their feudal lords could no longer afford to provide their rice stipends some *samurai* dropped out of the system and went to cities where they studied Western ideas, becoming increasingly hostile to the Tokugawa regime.

At the bottom of feudal Japan's social system was the *chonin* or merchant. Merchants were considered no better than parasites because it was felt they would stoop to any level to make money. Their style of clothing and footwear was restricted. They were not permitted to use a name that sounded like that of a feudal lord, and they could not live in *samurai* districts. In fact, *samurai* had the legal right to kill merchants on the spot if they behaved "unbecomingly."

Despite the disdain with which merchants were regarded initially, they became a more important part of the feudal Japanese society. Before cities developed, a feudal lord's revenue in rice, not ownership of the land, determined his power. Thus, rice performed the function of money as a medium of exchange. As productivity in agriculture and manufacturing grew, trading centers and cities developed where hard currency, that is, money made of precious metal, replaced rice as a medium of exchange. As they became more urbanized, feudal lords found it necessary to convert their rice to hard currency. At the same time, many *samurai* were displaced from their fiefs, losing their rice stipend, and gravitated toward cities where they lived in abject poverty. As the rice economy was replaced by the money economy, many merchants in the cities realized substantial profits and lost much of the stigma that had been associated with them. Displaced *samurai* were quite receptive to being adopted by a prosperous merchant family, all the while becoming less enthusiastic about the feudal system and more intrigued by Western values including mercantilism.

Along with these developments in the Japanese economy, other circumstances threatened the Tokugawa Shogunate. The peasants left to till the land were often forced to turn to usurers to obtain money to buy fertilizer and tools. If the loans were not repaid, the peasant relinquished his rights to the land (his tenure) to the usurer who then forced the peasant to produce even more than before to pay a tribute to the new usurer-tenant as well as to the feudal lord. The natural disasters of earthquakes, flood, famine, and fire put particular stress on the rice economy. Shortages of rice and the accompanying starvation became so severe that in 1837, bodies were left unburied in city streets. "Rice riots" erupted--often led by *samurai*--and a real threat to Tokugawa's power emerged. No appeals to Confucian principles would discourage the peasants and disaffected *samurai* from insisting on conducting more trade with the West and gaining the skills of more efficient Western economies.

At the same time the Shogunal government was blundering badly in terms of its ability to manage the question of Western invasion. Geography had permitted Japan to remain isolated for many centuries, but that would soon change. The Russians threatened from the North and the West. The British had progressed from India to Singapore to Canton to Shanghai and then engaged the Dutch in preliminary skirmishes in Nagasaki. Their preoccupation with China after the 1842 Treaty of Nanking, however, kept the British at bay at least temporarily. Still, it appeared to be just a matter of time. So, in 1842, the

Shogunal government permitted foreign ships to refuel in specific Japanese ports. But many in the country saw this as a form of capitulation. The correct response, they reasoned, was *not* to give the foreigners what they wanted but to use Western know-how to beat them at their own game, that is, not to become another China.

The Meiji Restoration of 1868 was a response to both internal and external forces in Japan. Much needed to be accomplished in a short period of time. Democratic principles were less important than results. The *samurai*, backed financially by the merchant class, overthrew the Shogun and restored Emperor Meiji to power. The former *samurai* became the managers, administrators, and departmental officials of the Meiji government. The successful military operations of the Emperor had been largely financed by the House of Mitsui. Having inherited the bankrupt conditions of the former ruler, the Emperor again relied on Mitsui and other merchants for loans and outright contributions to restructure the government.

To ensure the cooperation of the feudal lords, Emperor Meiji agreed to pay them one half of their normal revenue, a generous offer in light of the unpredictability of rice harvests, the expense of maintaining the fiefdom, and the burden of supporting the *samurai*--all risks and responsibilities now assumed by the government. Former fiefs were converted to prefectures (states). The designated pensions were paid over a period of 15 years so as not to permanently overburden the new government. This measure both eliminated the need for feudal lords and minimized the probability of opposition. The cost of this program amounted to approximately ¥211 million.

The Emperor also guaranteed the repayment of loans made by merchants and usurers to the *daimyo* before the Restoration. Government bonds were issued to pay off these debts, adding another ¥41 million to the government debt. A side effect of the bond issue was the stimulation of modern commercial banking. Under the laws for establishment of national banks (patterned after the U.S. prototype), lenders used these bonds (assets) to back bank notes (liabilities) used as money in the economy. By 1880, shares of bank stock worth ¥42 million had been issued, with former feudal lords (44 percent), *samurai* (31 percent), and merchants (15 percent) as the primary shareholders. This provides an early example of the interlocking operations of the Japanese government, banking interests, and landowners--a pattern which would be repeated as the country's industrial foundation was laid.

Having settled with the more privileged members of the Tokugawa Shogunal government, Emperor Meiji was faced with the urgent need to prevent

Japan's being overrun by Western nations. This meant that Japan had to "catch up" with the West almost overnight. This could not be left to chance. What small amount of capital accumulation there was had to be directed by the government. Pre-Restoration merchants became post-Restoration directors of banks and industry. Trade, banking, and credit were the most familiar lines of business and most preferred by the new monied-class. Industrial development, however, required more risk-taking--risk that was assumed by the government. By obtaining *goyokin* (loans) from the major merchant houses, the Emperor directed the establishment of heavy industrial enterprises. Of course, additional government bond holdings made it possible for banks to back even more bank notes, creating an even larger concentration of capital within the banking sector.

These concentrations of capital formed the core of the *zaibatsu*, combinations of large, interrelated firms with a bank at the center. The Emperor's court considered this approach to business formation necessary in order to compete with large, joint-stock companies of the West, such as the British East India Company. Trusts or cartels were formed throughout Japan's industrial revolution, especially in the area of textiles during the 1880s. Large firms absorbed smaller ones when economic storms threatened so as to keep as many companies afloat as possible. The *zaibatsu* of Mitsui, Mitsubishi, Sumitomo, and Yasuda--familiar names even today--emerged during this period. These companies and companies like them controlled credit allocation, manufacturing activity, and distribution within capital intensive industries. Smaller firms pursued historically "Japanese" industries such as porcelain, silk, lacquer, straw, *sake*, and soy sauce.

The process of growth was managed by government in a system of shared risk. For a start-up industry, the government obtained loans from the *zaibatsu*, developed the industry, and then sold it back to the zaibatsu at a modest price. The first industries developed in this way were those related to national defense, "strategic" industries, that is, machinery which would prevent Japan from being defeated as China was in the Opium Wars. Early on, the government took over the existing arsenals at Tokyo (the former Edo) and Osaka, the shipyards at Nagasaki, and mines in ten different locations.

New transportation and communications systems were aggressively developed by the government. In one of the few examples of the use of foreign capital, the Meiji leaders floated a £913,000 loan in London. By the end of the century, however, private capital exceeded the government's investment in the railway system. Because of their strategic importance, telegraph and telephone systems remained government-owned operations.

The order of construction of these industries was reversed from the normal sequence. For example, textiles were the focus of Europe's early industrial development, beginning with the trade in 12th century. Later, heavy industry developed with the inventions associated with the English Industrial Revolution beginning in the 18th century. In Japan the first significant industrialization focused on arsenals, foundries, shipbuilding, and railroads. It was not until 1870 that the first modern equipment was installed at a silk factory, with the installation requiring foreign technical assistance from Italians and French. This sequence of development left a gap between "strategic" industries and traditionally "Japanese" industries--one which the government was not able to close through its own resources.

The 1880 legislation, Regulations or Law on the Transfer of Factories, outlined the goal of the government to abandon ownership of certain factories, especially those not connected with the military establishment. A few examples help illustrate the diversity of factories involved in this Meiji privatization. In 1882, the modern English cotton-spinning mills of Hiroshima were sold to that prefecture (state). Four years later, similar facilities in Aichi were sold to the Shinoda Company. In 1885 The Shinagawa Glass Factory was relinquished to the Ishimura Company. Mitsui received the Fukuoka and Shimmachi spinning facilities in 1883 and 1887, respectively. The Fukgawa Cement Factory was leased, then sold outright to the Asano Company in 1883.

A portion of the shares in the Nippon Railway Company were sold to the public in 1880, but the company continued to receive government loans and subsidies during the most active periods of construction. An even more graphic example of government support for industries through subsidies and other considerations is sea transportation and the Mitsubishi Company. Even before the 1880 privatization law, the government gave (*gratis*) Iwasaki Yataro, the founder of Mitsubishi, 13 ships that had been used in military transport. Not long thereafter, Mitsubishi was allowed to buy a quasi-government fleet, Yubin Jokisen Kaisha, for ¥320,000. The government's intention was to encourage a strong merchant marine, paying Mitsubishi an additional ¥250,000 per year for 15 years. Then the government tried to stimulate more competition in the industry by starting another line in 1883, the Kyodo Un'yu Kaisha. A bitter fight between the two companies ensued, but the final outcome was a merger between the two firms in 1885 to form Nippon Yusen Kaisha. Thereafter, the government supported the new shipping company even more enthusiastically with an annual subsidy of ¥880,000.

The Meiji government also turned over some of the enterprises that had been considered a part of "strategic" industries. Mitsubishi was permitted to buy the Nagasaki shipyards, the Ikuno silver mine, and the Sado gold mine. Mitsui Company bought portions of the Miike coal mine. The Furukawa Company was permitted to purchase the Ani and the Innai gold mines.

There is perhaps no more useful example than the Japanese Meiji Restoration to illustrate the critical need for cooperation between banking and industry in the face of urgent economic and social circumstances. With the help of bank-centered *zaibatsu*, the Emperor and his staff of former *samurai* transformed Japan from a nation of cottage industries to one whose industrial might would later be admired (and feared) throughout the world.

The Ascendancy of U.S. Banking

The 19th century witnessed the development of large banking institutions in the United States, both private bankers and joint-stock companies. The system would develop along similar lines as the European institutions, with an emphasis on government finance and large industry, especially with respect to the Morgan and Mellon families. Citibank would exhibit the ability to mobilize the resources of large groups of individuals for the purpose of distributing new securities and cultivating lasting banking relationships.

J.P. Morgan and Company

In 1835, at the height of the crisis of confidence in bonds issued in the United States, Baltimore merchant George Peabody sailed for London to become an ambassador for the country in general and the financial sector in particular. He faced an uphill battle because by this time Americans were considered to be swindlers having defaulted on a number of important bond issues. Once in London, Peabody organized a luxurious dinner for the London bankers during which he urged them to understand that without "new money" for the state of Maryland, the old money would be lost. He was not, he argued, pleading this case for his own personal gain--he would even waive his own fee, normally $60,000. It worked! He was able to raise another $8 million before returning to Baltimore.

Two years later, Peabody moved to London permanently, becoming the first American to set up a merchant banking operation there. He joined a group of other merchants who traded in dry goods and financed trade, specializing in high finance--governments, large companies, and rich individuals. His specialty was American bonds and the first few years were turbulent. During the severe depression of the 1840s, when Pennsylvania, Mississippi, Indiana, Arkansas, Michigan, and Florida defaulted on their bonds, the value of American bonds fell to $.50 on the dollar. Then Maryland defaulted! All was not lost, however. Upon urging by the Barings and Peabody, the states resumed payment. From his bond holdings and trade finance for everything from the silk trade with China to iron rail exports to America, Peabody's fortune grew to $20 million in the 1850s.

As Peabody approached retirement, he turned to the matter of an heir for his business. Since he was a bachelor, it was not possible to pass it on to a son. A trusted associate in Boston suggested his junior partner, Junius Morgan. In 1853, Junius visited London, bringing with him his son John Pierpont. Peabody offered Junius a ten-year arrangement: At the end of ten years, Peabody would retire, allow Junius to continue to use the Peabody name, contribute capital, and leave Junius in control. After looking over the books, Junius agreed. Junius Morgan, now partner in the firm George Peabody and Company, moved his family to London in 1854.

The partnership was profitable enough, encountering the normal ups and downs of the financial market place. In 1857, when Junius sent his son John Pierpont to New York to apprentice with the company's New York agent, Duncan, Sherman, and Company, he advised his son to maintain a *slow and sure* course in his business affairs. Junius had already developed a disdain for what he considered destructive price-competition among bankers, a principle that Pierpont would later extend to other arenas of the business world.

Pierpont did not always follow his father's advice about going slow and sure. On a visit to New Orleans in 1859, he gambled the company's capital on a shipload of coffee that had arrived from Brazil without a buyer. He resold the shipment for a quick profit, one of the first indications of his decisive, risk-taking approach to business. Yet the episode alarmed the more subdued principals of Duncan, Sherman and Company. Because of this and other similar incidents, Pierpont was not made a partner. In 1861, with his cousin James Goodwin, Pierpont started his own firm--J.P. Morgan and Company--and became the New York agent for George Peabody and Company.

In 1864, that is, at the end of the ten-year partnership, Peabody failed to live up to his promises to the elder Junius Morgan. He did not permit Junius to continue to use his name or his capital. In contrast to the miserly habits that he had exhibited during his career, Peabody left his fortune to a variety of charitable causes. It appeared that Peabody had become more concerned with having his name associated with philanthropy rather than finance. Nevertheless, Junius had inherited the chief American banking house in London and his share of the £444,000 of capital.

J.S. Morgan and Company was formed in 1864 in London. In the same year, Junius invested part of his capital in the New York partnership of Dabney, Morgan and Company, with Pierpont as the junior partner and Charles H. Dabney (30 years Pierpont's senior) the senior partner, with the latter selected to impose some restraint on the younger Morgan. The senior Morgan retained the right of final decision with respect to loans and other credits. Dabney, Morgan would act as the New York agent for J.S. Morgan.

In 1869, Pierpont became involved in a fight that would establish his reputation as a strong and powerful figure in New York finance. The Albany and Susquehanna Railroad (A&S) was a small 143-mile line with 17 locomotives and 214 cars that ran through the Catskill Mountains between Albany and Binghamton, New York. Jay Gould, owner of Erie Railroad, wanted to buy the A&S because it would give Erie the opportunity to sell Pennsylvania coal to New England and to compete with New York Central for freight business. The largest A&S shareholder, Joseph Ramsey, however, would not consider Gould's overtures. Gould launched a battle for control that included recruiting a dissident wing of the A&S board. Tensions accelerated until the two factions boarded trains on opposite ends of the line--Gould's heading east from Binghamton and Ramsey's heading west from Albany--and crashed head-on. Headlights of the locomotives were smashed, one of the locomotives partially derailed, and eight or ten people shot before the Gould contingent fled. Ramsey went to J.P. Morgan for help.

During the annual board meeting in September 1869, unusually tense under the circumstances, Pierpont bought 600 shares of stock for the account of Dabney, Morgan. But neither side won because of competing legal injunctions against each other. Later, Pierpont helped Ramsey find a friendly judge that ousted Gould's slate of directors and Ramsey's camp was back in control. In 1870, Morgan orchestrated a friendly merger between A&S and the Delaware and Hudson line. John Pierpont Morgan did not seek compensation for his assistance just in fees, but also in power. He became a director of the company, the first of many such seats that he would hold. His concept of banking was not an arm's length, detached approach. He believed in "relationship banking" whereby a company becomes committed to a particular bank and the bank acts as financier, adviser, and confidant. It is interesting to note that in the same year that J.P.

Morgan joined the board, the German Deutsche Bank was founded--a bank that was to become the quintessential example of relationship banking.

A year later in 1871, Charles Dabney retired, necessitating the identification of another partner for the New York firm. Anthony J. Drexel, a Philadelphia banker second only to Jay Cooke (also of Philadelphia) in the area of government finance, approached Junius about a possible partnership. The result was the firm of Drexel, Morgan and Company that was to specialize in railroad and government finance.

The U.S. Treasury Department decided to refinance at lower interest rates $300 million in bonds remaining from the Civil War in 1873. The firm of Drexel, Morgan challenged what had been up to that time a virtual monopoly on government finance by Jay Cooke. Drexel, Morgan led a syndicate of firms that included J.S. Morgan and the Barings. Unfortunately, in August of that year the French Credit Mobilier, that had built the Union Pacific Railroad, was revealed to be rife with scandal and fraud, involving many U.S. congressmen. Once again, Europeans developed an extreme distaste for American bonds and the market collapsed. Only four years earlier, Jay Cooke had financed the Northern Pacific Railroad for $100 million, but still held many of these bonds in his own portfolio. When the bond market collapsed it started a financial panic that took Jay Cooke, 57 Stock Exchange firms, and 5,000 commercial firms with it. The sudden departure of Jay Cooke thus placed Drexel, Morgan at the head of government finance.

After the death of Anthony Drexel in 1893 and the retirement of his son two years later, Drexel, Morgan was reorganized as J.P. Morgan and Company. J.P. Morgan had refined his theory of relationship banking into the concept of "voting trusts." In rescuing troubled companies, as had been the case with A&S Railroad, such an arrangement meant that Morgan and several of his associates controlled the company usually for a five-year period, overseeing the reorganization of operations as well as financing. He hired talented people who knew their business. The list of railroads that he controlled in this manner include the Erie, Chesapeake and Ohio, Philadelphia and Reading, Santa Fe, Northern Pacific, Great Northern, New York Central, Lehigh Valley, Jersey Central, and the Southern Railway--representing 33,000 miles of railroad or one-sixth of the country's trackage.

His philosophy against "destructive competition" would also later be evidenced in the combination of his own Federal Steel and National Tube with Andrew Carnegie's crude steel operation, Carnegie Steel. When Morgan learned of Carnegie's intentions to develop the business of finished steel products, he lamented that the same excessive competitiveness that had wrecked havoc in the railway industry would now do the same in the steel industry. When Carnegie expressed an interest in forming a vertically organized steel trust (or cartel), Morgan was receptive. The ultimate vision was a business combination that would handle all phases from mining ore to marketing steel. In the interim, however, the immediate result was a merger of the Carnegie and Morgan steel operations--including Carnegie Steel, Federal Steel, American Tin Plate, American Steel Hoop, American Sheet Steel, American Bridge, American Steel and Wire, National Tube, National Steel, Shelby Steel Tube, and Lake Superior Consolidated Mines--into one company, U.S. Steel.

In the same year that his firm was reorganized into J.P. Morgan and Company, Morgan would once again illustrate his ability to manage finance on a grand scale. A severe industrial recession began in 1892 when a steel workers' strike was crushed by the government. Before the recession ended, over 15,000 commercial firms and 600 banks failed. Europeans began to redeem their U.S. dollars for gold in large quantities.

Money was in short supply and the agrarian sector of the economy, still the largest sector, again faced finished goods prices that rose faster than the price of the agricultural products that they sold. It seemed to be a conspiracy between the industrial and banking sectors. The agrarians had long pushed for cheaper money--silver certificates, greenbacks (not backed by any precious metal)--anything to ease the money crunch. A legislative act in 1890 had compelled the Treasury to buy 4.5 million ounces of silver per year and issue certificates then redeemable in gold or silver. Now, in the face of the 1893 recession, agrarian populists called for silver coins, a position supported by silver-producing states. The recessionary conditions and this proposition, both being regarded as forces that devalue the U.S. currency, prompted Europeans to accelerate gold redemptions.

In 1894, the U.S. gold reserves dropped below the $100-million floor. By January 1895, it was possible to stand in New York harbors and watch the gold continuously being loaded on ships bound for Europe. Democratic President Grover Cleveland was a friend of the Republican House of Morgan and an advocate of the gold standard. J.P. Morgan had cast his only Democratic vote for Cleveland because of his position with respect to the monetary standard. However, the President faced a hostile Republican Congress that pushed for silver coinage and would not allow bond issues to purchase more gold. Neither, given the populist sentiment against bankers, could Cleveland reasonably turn to J.P. Morgan for help.

By January 1895, the gold reserves had dropped to $68 million and gold coin was especially scarce. On February 4, the gold coin in the government vaults on Wall Street amounted to only $9 million. J.P. Morgan traveled to Washington, informed the President that he was aware of a $10-million draft that was about to be presented, and that before 3:00 p.m. "it will all be over." Cleveland turned to Morgan for an alternative to this pending default.

Morgan recalled an 1862 statute that permitted President Abraham Lincoln to buy gold during a state of emergency. Morgan proposed the issuance of $65 million of 30-year gold bonds and assured the President that the gold would not leave the country. With no other alternative, the President agreed. The Morgan and Rothschild houses gathered 3.5 million ounces of gold and exchanged them for the bonds. The issue sold out in London in two hours and in 22 minutes in New York.

The crisis was averted, but not without cost. Populist sentiment was that the big money interests had done it once again. The interest rate of 3.5 percent was considered too high. The syndicate had bought the bonds at $104.50 per $100 of face value, immediately resold them for $112.25, then watched the price go to $119.00. In the 22-minute New York initial offering, the bankers had made profits of $6 or $7 million--proof, maintained the populists, that the syndicate cheated the government. There were even anti-Semitic criticisms of the inclusion of the Rothschilds in the syndicate.

Despite the fact that J.P. Morgan had saved the gold standard and averted the inevitable financial chaos that would have followed, populist frustrations ran high. There was not yet a real central bank in the United States. J.P. Morgan had only stepped forward to act as one in its absence. The system was not of his creation, but much of the blame was directed at him. He would also later be faulted for the great concentrations of wealth that he amassed in the private sector, much of that also accrued during rescue missions. In many ways, John Pierpont Morgan later became a lightning rod for public opinion against so-called money trusts and cartels. But the fact remains that his combined knowledge of finance, industry, and government supported and promoted this country during some of its most challenging times.

The Mellons

In 1839, just two years after George Peabody set up his dry goods operation in London that would eventually evolve into J.P. Morgan and Company, Thomas Mellon, Esquire, started his law practice in Pittsburgh. Thomas had worked in the county clerk's office during law school and invested small amounts in judgments, mechanic's liens, and other securities that holders were willing to sell at a discount prior to maturity. The accumulation of his proceeds from these activities, $700, was invested in his new office, mostly in his law library.

Between cases or clients, Thomas inspected properties in which he might invest or investigated the background of a potential borrower. He lent money only under the condition that the promissory note be secured by real or personal property and accompanied by a judgment bond, which entitled him to foreclose immediately. Within five years of opening his practice, Thomas had saved $12,000 from the combination of his lending activities and his frugal lifestyle.

After 20 years, in 1859, Thomas Mellon became a common pleas judge in county court. By this time, he was married with five children (three other children died before reaching maturity)--Thomas Alexander, James Ross (the two oldest), Andrew William, Richard Beatty, and George Negley (the three youngest). The boys were as industrious and enterprising as their father. While their father sat on the bench, they pursued the business activities in which Thomas could not engage because of potential conflicts of interest. In 1868, Judge Mellon purchased an orchard near the railroad where Thomas and James opened a lumber yard. At the end of the first year of operation, the company showed profits of $100,000. They branched into real estate, buying foreclosed real estate throughout Pittsburgh and creating residential subdivisions. An acre, costing $400 to $800, could be divided into 12 lots, each sold at $600 to $800. Thus, a $25,000 investment was turned into sales of $150,000.

When his term expired in 1869, Thomas Mellon left the bench to join his sons in such lucrative business ventures. In 1870, the private banking firm of T. Mellon & Sons opened for business in a rented store front building, with a long counter dividing the space and a stove positioned prominently in the center. In this humble office space began one of America's industrial and banking dynasties. T. Mellon and Sons conducted a general banking business and issued letters of credit for use in Pittsburgh, Canada, Mexico, the West Indies, and Central and South America. The bank benefitted from Judge Mellon's good name and an ample money supply at the time. Deposits flowed in and the bank was off to a promising start. Soon the offices were moved to a two-story, iron front structure built especially for the bank.

During the 1873 panic after the failure of Jay Cooke, the Judge and his sons approached every borrower for payment, if due, and sometimes payment even if not yet due. There was $60,000 in cash versus $600,000 in deposits. They needed cash badly because new deposits were slowing. One month after the Cooke failure, T. Mellon & Sons stopped payments to depositors--there was now only $12,000 in cash against deposits of $200,000. But the bank did not close, even though dozens of others had. The Judge was confident of the intrinsic value of the bank's gilt-edged bonds and mortgages.

After the worse of the money panic subsided a few months later, the Mellons began to foreclose on properties owned throughout the area. The sheriff was constantly occupied with serving notices on behalf of the Mellons, as unemployment and defaults continued to climb. By 1877, the suffering had become so intolerable that unemployed workers rioted, the Philadelphia troops were called in, and 20 unemployed people were killed. By 1880, the Mellon enterprises were still operating and had survived a severe economic test, with the result that their financial capabilities were unquestioned.

One of the Mellons' first involvements in heavy industry came as a result of the recession. The shareholders of the Ligonier Valley Railroad approached T. Mellon & Sons offering four-fifths of the stock and a mortgage to cover the cost of completing and equipping the rail line plus a $10,000 bonus. Thomas and Richard Mellon assumed supervision of the construction. The Mellons offered $1 per day for workers ($.10 more than the Pennsylvania Railroad was offering) and aggressively kept construction on schedule. Within 60 days the first train rolled into Ligonier (approximately 50 miles from Pittsburgh). Without the close coordination of efforts between the bankers and the company, it is unlikely that this project would have been completed in such an expeditious manner.

During the same period, Henry Clay Frick, not yet 21 years of age introduced himself to Judge Mellon and asked for a $10,000 loan. This was the beginning of a life-time alliance between the Mellons and the ambitious young Frick. Frick owned bee-hive ovens which converted coal into coke, an essential component in the production of iron and steel. Although somewhat cautious about this new line of business, the Judge authorized the $10,000 loan for six months at 10 percent. In a couple of months, Frick was back, not to repay the original loan but to request another $10,000! He needed another 50 ovens because he could not keep up with the demand. By then, Pittsburgh was a world leader in heavy industry producing an assortment of iron and steel products, including rails for the railroad systems that proliferated. The new loan was forthcoming and others followed later as needed.

After the panic that followed the failure of Philadelphia banker Jay Cooke in 1873, Judge Mellon could extend no further loans, but did help Frick negotiate the sale of a short railroad line connecting the coke fields for $50,000. A year later, the Mellons managed to advance another $15,000 and agree to discount $25,000 in Frick's commercial paper. With the help of the Mellons, the company survived the crisis. Later, when the price of coke soared from $.90 to $5.00 a ton, profits mounted quickly. By 1879, Henry Clay Frick was a millionaire.

When, in 1880, Thomas Mellon granted his third son Andrew William a general power of attorney over all his affairs, the young Mellon wasted no time in expanding the Mellon empire. A.W. Mellon and H.C. Frick purchased the Pittsburgh National Bank of Commerce and became directors of that institution. In 1883, the two purchased the Union Insurance Company and Andrew assumed the presidency. In this way, Mellon real estate ventures could also be insured by Mellons.

The private bank of T. Mellon & Sons prospered, making loans to iron and steel works, glass factories, and coal mines. The National Bank catered more to smaller businesses and individuals, while also taking advantage of banking laws that permitted national banks to issue their own bank notes. As the Pittsburgh suburbs developed, City Deposit Bank was opened to accommodate the new residents.

Then in 1889 another critical alliance was formed when Alfred E. Hunt and George H. Clapp visited A.W. Mellon. Both were former metallurgists for steel companies who had formed their own company, Pittsburgh Testing Laboratories. A young inventor of theirs, Charles M. Hall, had developed a process for smelting aluminum that they believed held promise. But it cost more to market aluminum than to produce it and they needed a loan.

Andrew was enthusiastic about the new featherweight metal. After doing his homework, he too believed that aluminum had some promising applications. He had also done his banking homework, learning that New York bankers no longer just made loans at a fixed rate of interest, but received a share of the borrowing company and control over the firm's financial affairs. Yes, he would provide financing for the aluminum project if he also received control of the company. They agreed, exchanging control in the new Pittsburgh Reduction Company for $250,000 in financing through T. Mellon & Sons. This venture would later evolve into the country's leading producer of the lightweight metal, the Aluminum Company of America (ALCOA).

Approximately 10 years later, a poor Yugoslav immigrant who had changed his name from Anthony Luchich to Anthony Lucas abandoned gold prospecting after realizing several small fortunes, only to loose them again. He placed a deposit on the $33,500 price that was being asked by the Gladys City Oil, Gas, and Manufacturing Company for land near Beaumont, Texas. For his money, he received a shack or two and a weather-beaten rig. He drilled for oil throughout the winter, finding none, and having to sell the furniture little by little to raise cash. Although he was encouraged by the content of the sand at the 575-foot level, he needed more pipe to drill deeper.

The Texas geological survey director, Dr. William Phillips, suggested that he contact Guffey & Galey in Pittsburgh. By this time, Guffey & Galey had become much more involved in the business aspects of oil than in the more exciting prospecting aspects. Upon receiving Lucas' correspondence, one of the principals of the firm, John H. Galey, was intrigued by the possibility of getting directly involved in the quest for oil once again. In exchange for majority interest, Galey agreed to back the needed drilling investment.

On January 9, 1901, the earth rumbled and shook so violently beneath Lucas' feet that he ran for his life. With a deafening roar, 700 feet of 4-inch pipe erupted from the ground, followed by a forceful rush of oil and mud that reached 200 feet above the ground, having been propelled by the millions of cubic feet of natural gas that were now unleashed. Before the gusher could be capped, thousands of barrels of oil accumulated in huge pool and were accidentally ignited. Oil valued in the six figures went up in smoke. Finally, the fire was extinguished and a heavy iron cylinder rolled over the head of the well. It held! The first well—in the field that would become known as Spindletop—had been capped!

Galey wired to his partner Guffey in Pittsburgh for more money. He obliged but the resources of the partnership were exhausted. It would require hundreds of thousands of dollars, perhaps millions, to bring this oil to market. Guffey then visited the offices of the Mellons. The family had invested in oil on occasion, having backed professional speculators like Galey & Guffey. In fact, William Larimer Mellon, son of James Ross, had a particular affinity for oil ventures. But the family had never undertaken an enterprise on this scale. Much needed to be considered. Who would need this much oil? Within three years, the yield from Spindletop alone could equal that of all the wells in Pennsylvania combined. New markets would have to be developed. Pipe lines to the coast would have to be built, along with storage tanks and refineries.

After careful consideration, the Mellons backed the new J.M. Guffey Petroleum Company, buying out Lucas' interest for $400,000 and receiving 40 percent of the stock. Guffey became president, receiving $1,000,000 in cash and $500,000 to be taken as future dividends. William Larimer Mellon was designated vice president in charge of the Pittsburgh office. The remaining 60 percent of the stock was subscribed by other financiers in the Pittsburgh area to spread the risk. Initially, $4.5 million was invested in the company, with $3 million immediately devoted to development. Later, a $4 million bond issue was also offered.

By 1901, the Mellons had expanded their investments in the Texas oil industry to include leases on a million acres of land in Texas and Louisiana, four wells in production, four more wells being drilled, and a six-inch pipeline to Port Arthur under construction. In 1904, the Mellon family began refining and distributing the oil from Spindletop and other fields. The S.S. *J.M. Guffey* and other tankers in the Mellon steamship line carried refined oil to Staten Island and to Europe. In 1906 these oil enterprises were consolidated into a holding company that would own and operate all of them--the Gulf Oil Corporation.

In the meantime, the business of banking was changing. The private bank was giving way to the joint-stock bank. In 1902, the Mellon family followed this trend by abandoning T. Mellon & Sons for the federally chartered Mellon National Bank. By now the Mellon financial institutions--including Mellon National, Union Trust, Pittsburgh National Bank of Commerce, Citizens National, and City Deposit--controlled deposits of $47 million, a full one third of all Pittsburgh deposits.

The financial clout of the Mellons, together with their willingness to take calculated risks and to see an industrial firm through the inevitable difficult times, built a far-flung empire. Moreover, as the tide of this empire rose, the earning capability and security of thousands of other families who were employed in the Mellon enterprises--finance, real estate, steel, railroad equipment, oil, coal, and aluminum--rose with it.

Citibank

In 1811, the First Bank of the United States, the creation of the first Secretary of the Treasury Alexander Hamilton, was about to lose its charter. The institution had been granted permission by the federal legislature to operate for 20 years beginning 1791. In proposing the institution, Hamilton stressed the need for a uniform currency and a strong banking system to promote the new country's economic development. Accordingly, the new bank received the bulk of federal deposits and its notes were legal tender throughout the country. By 1805 the First Bank of the United States had branches in New York, Baltimore, Boston, Charleston, New Orleans, Norfolk, and Washington.

At the same time, the joint-stock banks chartered by state banking authorities received almost none of the federal government's deposits. They operated as unit banks without branches, and their notes were not legal tender. Worse yet, the Bank of the United States would not accept their notes unless they were convertible into specie--gold or silver. These factors had the effect of limiting the growth of state-chartered institutions. State banks were no allies of that first federal banking institution.

The populist, agrarian members of the nonbanking sector did not hold the Bank in high esteem, either. Much of the stock in the Bank was held by European investors and America was on the verge of going to war with England. There were even questions about the constitutionality of such an institution from states' rights advocates.

When Congress did not renew the charter of the First Bank of the United States in 1811, this set the first precedent against nationwide branching and for the state regulation of the banking industry. It also left New York City to operate without the largest bank among the six. To replace this institution, the state authorities granted a charter to City Bank, capitalized with $2 million, the same capitalization of the largest joint-stock banks in New York at the time. Beginning in June 1812, the new bank operated in the same building that had housed the First Bank of the United States.

City Bank would operate as did the other joint-stock banks, like a credit union for its merchant-owners. The bank was to be:

> a common fund, for the purpose of making loans on commercial paper for the benefit of all, by a division of profits, and for the accommodation of each as funds may be required.

The merchant-owners paid themselves no interest on their deposits. Their compensation came in the form of liquidity and access to reasonably priced credit when they needed it. Both deposits and notes (loans) were payable on demand, requiring careful management. Credit to the merchant-owners would rotate. Each shareholder could borrow money during a part of the year. However, during the rest of the year, the shareholder could have no other loans outstanding and his funds remained on deposit--available for lending to the other shareholders according to their turn.

Unfortunately, war erupted in 1812, forcing the merchant-owners of City Bank to finance the government instead of trade, providing a $200,000 loan directly to the government to enable it to pay interest and principal on the federal debt. In return City Bank was designated a federal depository, receiving one third of the government's balances held in New York.

After the war, the fortunes of City Bank soured. The Second Bank of the United States was granted a 20-year federal charter in 1816 and became (as had been the First Bank of the United States) the federal depository. Also, the internal operations of City Bank had not been managed as they should. Just a few of the shareholders actually received loans and, instead of the loans being repaid, they were rolled over, with no recognition of the borrowers' inability to repay. The bank's earnings declined, its stock price fell, and by 1825, a change in ownership and management was necessary.

The bank's growth was constrained. New York state banking law prohibited loans in excess of 2.5 times paid-in capital. Because of it problems, City Bank's capital declined from $2 million upon charter to $1.5 million by 1825. At this point, City Bank responded by embracing an innovative approach to boost its funding base, the kind of innovation that would become a hallmark of the institution. Profits could be increased without increasing loans. Bank notes (liabilities) were a profitable source of funding if they could be kept in circulation, because, unlike deposits, they required no interest payments. They were a form of money. Keeping the bank notes in circulation was the problem, however, because the Second Bank of the United States kept a tight rein on note circulation. City Bank overcame this problem by maintaining correspondent accounts with banks around the country, like the Medicis had done centuries before. These correspondent accounts guaranteed the acceptance of City Bank notes in those institutions and vice versa. Correspondent balances became a trend in New York as the city became the country's leading commercial and financial center. Country banks found that they could sell the balances to customers who wished to make remittances to New York or even use them to purchase securities for their own accounts.

The combination of bank notes and correspondent balances achieved the desired outcome in providing City Bank with a higher funding base, but the bank's management did not recognize the vulnerability that went along with these instruments. Both the correspondent balances and the bank notes were redeemable upon demand, suggesting the need to maintain reserves of specie (gold and silver) in the asset portfolio. This lesson would be learned painfully.

In 1836, the Bank of England raised its discount rate sharply to stem the flow of gold out of that country. While the flow of gold out of England slowed, a flow out of the United States followed. This meant a flow of gold out of U.S. banks, reducing drastically their reserves or liquid assets. At the same time, the higher interest rates in Britain led to a recession in that country that caused the demand for U.S. cotton to plummet. Cotton merchants held unsalable inventories and were forced to default on their bank loans. Then, through the Specie Circular of 1836, the outgoing administration of President Andrew Jackson required that all purchases of land from the federal government be paid for in specie. The money supply tightened to the breaking point. Panic broke out in May 1837 as the public rushed to convert their deposits and bank notes to specie. Banks in New York were forced to suspend specie payments.

City Bank fared worse than the rest of the New York banks because it depended more on bank notes and correspondent deposits. It would likely have failed completely, but for suspension of specie payments *and* Moses Taylor, who became a director of the bank in 1837. Taylor had begun his business career as an apprentice for G.G. and S.S. Howland, leading merchants in Latin American trade. When he went into business for himself at the age of 26, his firm specialized in importing Cuban sugar. He soon began to trade in other commodities from Latin America, investing in his own fleet of ships.

After he became a director of City Bank, fellow directors invited him to invest in their companies. He began to branch out even further and invited his associates in the new ventures to invest in the bank. This loose confederation of merchants enabled each to diversify his own holdings and to exercise control over the executive in charge of his diversified investment—no small consideration given the lack of public information available at the time. The list of Taylor enterprises, in addition to City Bank, would include other financial institutions (Farmers' Loan and Trust Co., Manhattan Insurance, Metropolitan Insurance), a trading company (Moses Taylor and Company), utilities (Manhattan Gas Light Company, New York Gas Light Company), metals and mining operations (Lackawanna Iron and Coal Company, New Jersey Zinc and Iron Company), railroads (Delaware, Lackawanna, and Western; Michigan Central; Chicago and Northwestern; Central Railroad of Georgia; International and Great Northern), and communications (Western Union Telegraph Company).

This arrangement also provided a ready financial institution for the support of each of the entrepreneurs as well. Taylor's companies were required to keep their principal deposit accounts at National City Bank and they received short-term credit from the bank as needed. The foundation upon which Moses Taylor ran City Bank, by now renamed National City Bank, was *ready money.* On the asset side, the bank maintained high cash reserves, invested heavily in call loans (payable upon demand), and bought only the minimum amount of long-term government securities as stipulated by banking regulations (to avoid interest rate risk, since long-term bonds have more price volatility). On the liability side, the bank avoided the volatile bank notes and correspondent balances that it had relied on before Taylor. Instead, Taylor, his business associates, and the companies they controlled supplied most of the bank's deposits. He proudly boasted that City Bank was run "on the formula, not of the ordinary commercial bank, but of the richest and most conservative old time merchant, with a great holding of surplus cash."

This arrangement served him well. At the time of his death in 1882, his personal fortune was valued in excess of $33 million, three times the asset base of National City Bank. The bank itself had been converted from one on the brink of failure to one on sound financial footing. Taylor's closest associate Percy R. Pyne, who joined Moses Taylor and Company as a clerk and was later made a partner in 1849, became a director of the bank in 1869 and president in 1882 after Taylor's death. Pyne managed National City Bank in the same "ready money" mode that Taylor had begun until ill health forced his retirement in 1891.

James Stillman took over the reigns after Pyne. Stillman had entered his father's cotton brokerage firm in New York as an apprentice at the age of 16. In 1872, at the age of 22, he was made a partner of the firm, known as Woodward and Stillman. The senior partner, William Woodward, focused on the cotton trade and Stillman oversaw the finances. Before his death, Moses Taylor had asked the young Stillman to participate in several business ventures. Pyne had continued to cultivate Stillman during his tenure. When Stillman was named president of National City Bank in 1891, he continued the "ready money" policies of his predecessors, that is, until Pyne's death in 1895.

Beginning in 1895, Stillman drew National City Bank into the major league of industrial finance--investment banking. He joined with Jacob H. Schiff of Kuhn, Loeb to reorganize the Union Pacific Railroad. It was a natural match. Kuhn, Loeb could originate a deal and distribute the securities once they were issued, that is, the firm had originating and placing power. However, unlike J.P. Morgan and Company, Kuhn, Loeb did not have a commercial banking affiliate to support the large issues during distribution. Together, Kuhn, Loeb and National City constituted a complete investment banking package.

The reorganization of Union Pacific would take two years to complete. In the interim, National City Bank advanced funds to keep the railroad operating and participated in four syndicates to raise funds for bond interest payments and tax payments. This undertaking helped Stillman to elevate the image of the bank from one that serviced only Taylor-Pyne enterprises to one that served industry in general. He built relationships with firms that issued securities and with firms that bought securities from him. Because of these relationships, the deposits of the bank grew from less than $20 million in 1895 to $308 million ten years later and National City Bank became the largest bank in the country.

The Board of Directors included representatives from the American Sugar Refining, International Harvester, National Sugar, Armour and Company, and Union Pacific. One of the most important connections with an industrial firm was cemented through Stillman's personal relationship with William Rockefeller, the brother of John D. and the president of Standard Oil of New York. Standard Oil had been established as the dominating force in the U.S. oil industry long before Galey & Guffey would approach the Mellons about their Spindletop find.

In 1862, John D. Rockefeller operated a produce business in Cleveland, Ohio with his partner, M.A. Clark. The Civil War pushed up produce prices and their business prospered as a result, leaving John quite well-to-do. A long-time customer of theirs, Samuel Andrews, insisted that he had developed a superior refining method that produced a higher yield when crude oil was converted to kerosene. Because he considered the oil business inherently risky, John rather reluctantly invested several thousand dollars in the partnership of Clark and Andrews, keeping his own name out of it.

The new partnership prospered as demand for coal-oil declined and demand for kerosene increased. European demand went from 11 million gallons in 1862 to 27 million gallons just two years later. By the end of the war, John had decided to abandon the produce business and devote his full energies to oil. He and Andrews had a compatible business relationship, but the two of them preferred to continue without Clark. Of course, Clark had his own ideas about continuing in the oil business and resisted the sale of his share of the company. They agreed to let their lawyer act as auctioneer over the disputed partnership interest. At the appointed time and place, Clark opened the bidding at $500. Rockefeller immediately bid $1,000. The bidding continued, increasing in intensity. Finally, Clark bid $72,000--Rockefeller countered with $75,000 immediately. Clark had had enough. The business belonged to Rockefeller.

The new firm was named Rockefeller and Andrews. John realized that development of the export market for their oil products would be crucial. He started a separate firm in 1867 in New York to act as sales agent--William Rockefeller and Company. The Rockefeller brothers would dominate the oil industry by the end of the century and the two companies would become Standard Oil of Ohio and New York.

A friendship developed between William Rockefeller and James Stillman when they served together on the board of directors of Chicago, Milwaukee, and St. Paul Railroad in 1883. Soon National City Bank was the primary bank for the Standard Oil empire. The ties were so close that Stillman could telephone Rockefeller and instruct him to send Stillman $5 million because some good investments were soon "coming along." With very little questioning, a check for $5 million would be on Stillman's desk in a day or two. But the relationship went beyond business. Two of Stillman's daughters married two of Rockefeller's sons. One of the offspring of these matches, James Stillman Rockefeller, would later serve as the bank's president (1952-1959) and chairman (1959-1967).

After the turn of the century National City Bank had become a veritable financial department store. Not only did it act as investment advisor for major corporations, but it also participated in 20 percent of the new issues of corporate and government bonds (domestic and foreign) from 1921 through 1929. To distribute these bonds, National City Company, the holding company that owned National City Bank, opened offices across the country in 51 cities. Through a program of consumer education, these offices helped customers to understand the basics of bond buying, the way a client could identify a good bond buy based on individual circumstances, and the benefits of diversification.

This consumer-oriented finance was not investment banking in the Morgan sense of the word. National City Bank had matured into a financial institution that had all the components of investment banking--originating, banking, and placing power. The added dimension of delivery of financial services to consumers was to become a lasting characteristic, years after the name National City Bank was changed to Citibank. National City Bank performed the customary function of helping an issuing firm structure a new issue and then literally delivered the securities to the households of America, making the flotation far more efficient.

Conclusion

Thus, at the turn of the century, U.S. banks were poised to take the lead in international banking circles. That they are now being dwarfed by banks in other countries is a direct result of events during the 20th century. After a careful survey of the current banking systems of the United Kingdom, Germany, Japan, and China it may be possible to develop banking policies and practices that will reverse this trend during the 21st century.

Selected References

Chernow, Ron. *The House of Morgan: An American Banking Dynasty and the Rise of Modern Finance*, New York: Simon and Schuster/Touchstone, 1990.

Cleveland, Harold van B. and Thomas F. Huertas. *Citibank 1812-1970*, Cambridge, Massachusetts: Harvard University Press, 1985.

Corti, Count. *The Reign of the House of Rothschild*. London: Victor Gollancz, Ltd., 1928.

Dower, John W., Editor. *Origins of the Modern Japanese State: Selected Writings of E.H. Norman*, New York: Random House/Pantheon Books, 1975.

Flynn, John T. *God's Gold: The Story of Rockefeller and His Times*, New York: Harcourt, Brace and Company, 1932.

Ghose, T.K. *The Banking System of Hong Kong*, Singapore: Butterworth & Company, 1987.

Green, Edwin, *Banking: An Illustrated History*, New York: Rizzoli International Publications, 1989.

Kindleberger, Charles P. *A Financial History of Western Europe*, London: George Allen & Unwin, Ltd., 1984.

McElderry, Andrea Lee. *Shanghai Old-Style Banks (Ch'ien-Chuang, 1800-1935: A Traditional Institution in a Changing Society*, Ann Arbor, Michigan: Center for Chinese Studies, The University of Michigan, 1976.

Morris, Jan. *Hong Kong*, New York: Random House/Vintage Books, 1989.

Morton, Frederic. *The Rothschilds: A Family Portrait*, New York: Curtis Publishing Company/Atheneum, 1962.

O'Connor, Harvey. *Mellon's Millions: The Biography of a Fortune*, New York: The John Day Company, 1933.

Ravage, Marcus Eli. *Five Men of Frankfort: The Story of the Rothschilds*, New York: Dial Press, Inc., 1934.

Whale, P. Barrett. *Joint Stock Banking in Germany: A Study of the German Creditbanks Before and After the War*, London: Frank Cass and Company, Ltd., 1968.

ERRATA FOR 'BANKING ALLIANCES'

Index

acquisition 57, 121
Agricultural Bank of China 135
Allfinanz 98, 99
Allgemeine Zeitung 115
alliances 108
All-Japan Automobile Industry Union 109
American Banking Association 166
Antimonopoly Act 112
antipollution 115
apprenticeships 90
arbitrage 76
Article 65 107
Asian dollar market 70
Asian NIC 145
authorization 78

bancherius 5
bank 5, 23, 172
bank commercial 147, 173
bank deposit 63
bank failure 48, 167
bank, joint-stock 17, 18, 44, 45
bank loan 68
bank, merchant 34, 57–59, 73, 93
bank, national 156, 158, 160
bank, nationally chartered 162
bank, network 98
bank note 31, 42, 46, 59, 105, 156, 157
Bank of China 28, 131, 136, 142
Bank of Communications 28
Bank of England 7, 27, 47, 56, 72, 73, 76
Bank of England, Governor of 62, 67
Bank of Japan 106, 114, 119, 124, 125
Bank of Seoul 148
Bank of Sweden 7
Bank of Tokyo-Mitsubishi Bank 112
bank, regional 162
bank, universal 73
banker, merchant 59, 62, 74, 76

banking 40, 44, 64, 80
Banking Copartnerships Act of 1826 17
banking industry, consolidated 98
banking regulation 61
banking system 105
banking system, joint-stock 29
banking system, national 156, 157
banking system, private 29
banking, commercial 165
banking, corporate 140
banking, Japanese 35
banking, network 99
banking, private 40
banking, relationship 1, 36, 37, 67, 154, 155, 172
banking, universal 85, 94, 97, 98
bank-lending 77
banks, unit 45
Barclays 75
Barings 8, 9, 12–18, 77
BDI (Bundesverband der Deutschen Industrie) 96
Bethmann Brothers and Rueppell & Harnier 11, 19
Big Bang 58, 72, 73, 75, 98
bills of exchange 6, 9, 10, 24, 57, 85
Board of Trade 108
bond issues 38, 109
bond trading 12
bonds 31, 34, 35, 37, 50, 63, 125
bonds, corporate 174
bonds, long-term 48
bonds, municipal revenue 174
British Department of Trade and Industry 72
British East India Trading Company 25, 32, 139
British Stock Exchange 71
broker 73
Buderus 18
business 98
buyout 93

California gold rush 15
call loan 48
Capital Adequacy Directive of the European Union 77
capital 75
capital market 168
Carnegie 38
cartel 32, 58, 106
cash reserves 48
Cathay Pacific 140
Central Bank Committee of Governors 63
certificates of deposit 68
ch'ien chuang 24, 25, 27, 28
chaebol 146, 147, 148
Chairman of the Board 88
Chamber of Assurance 7
Chambers of Commerce and Industry 95

Chartered Bank 138
Chartered Mercantile Bank of India, London and China 138
charters 105
China 12, 129
Chinese banking 25
Cho Heung Bank 147, 148
chonin 29
chung-p'iao 24, 27
Citibank 2, 34, 50
City Bank 46, 47
City, the 55, 58, 59, 62, 67, 85, 70, 74
Civil War 15, 130
Clapp, George 42
class distinctions 89
Clayton Antitrust 154
clearing bank 56, 58, 62, 71, 72, 73, 75, 93
clearing system 56
coal 62, 84
coal mine 59
codetermination 89
cold-calling 73
collective ownership 134
Commercial Bank 148
commercial paper 174
Commerzbank 85, 98
commodity exchange 7
communist 129
Competition and Credit Central policy 70
competition 33, 121
Comprador 27, 34
Comptroller of the Currency 159
concentrations of capital 32
conflict of interest 166
conglomerate 103
consent 89
consumer funds 97
consulted 89
contract, combination or conspiracy 154
contracts to exchange 70
conversion 67
convertibility 156
corporate and government bonds (domestic and foreign) 50
correspondent balance 46
credit 137
credit crunch 69
creditbank 84,
crises of confidence 155
cross-shareholding 126
currency 6, 23, 27, 64–68, 72, 91, 139, 173, 182
currency exchange 19, 110
currency exchange market 66
currency exchange rate system, pegged 118
currency exchange services 138
currency exchange transactions 167
currency swaps 70

currency, hard 28
currency, liberalizing 110
currency, uniform 45, 157

Daewoo Group 148
Dai-Ichi Kangyo 112
Dai-Ichi Kangyo Bank 112
daimyo 29, 31, 39
decentralization 133, 162
decentralized bank 204
dedicated capital 169
default 41
demand 21
democratization 107
deposit 45
deposit insurance 165
deposit interest rate 165
deposit rate 68, 69
deregulation 72, 98
destructive competition 37
Deutsche Bank 1, 23, 85, 92, 93, 94, 98
discount rate 124, 163
diversification 73
diversified 141
division of labor 142
domestic borrowing 28
Douglas 107
Douglas Amendment
Draper, William Undersecretary of the Army 107
Dresdner Bank 85, 86, 98
due-on-demand checking 56
Duncan, Sherman and Company 35
duties 135

East India Company 9, 13, 25
economic development 83
Economic Planning Board (EPB) 143
education 105
educational 90
embargoes 131
EMS (European Monetary System) 80, 81
endaka 118, 119, 124
equitable subordination 171
equity, corporate 174
Eurobond (long-term instrument) 70
Eurocommercial paper 70
Eurodollar 65, 69
Eurodollar market 66, 69
Euroequity (common and preferred stocks) 70
Euromarket 72
European Asian Bank 93
European Atomic Energy Community 63
European Central Bank (ECB) 64
European Coal and Steel Community 63
European Common Market 63
European Economic Community (EEC) Treaty 63

European Monetary Cooperation Fund 64
European Monetary Institute (EMI) 64
European Monetary System 64
European Monetary Union 65, 66
European System of Central Banks (ESCB) 64
European Union 64, 65
exchange 156
exchange bank 7
exchange controls 72
exchange rate 65, 136
Exchange Rate Mechanism 65, 66
Exchequer 7
Executive Board (Vorstand) 88
expansion 117, 120
expansion of trade 140
export-import bank 109, 132
export market 50
Export Trading Company (ETC) Act 174
exporting dollars 68

Fang Chieh-t'ang 24
FDIC 125
federal charter 46
federal deposit 45
Federal Deposit Insurance Corporation 158, 166
federal depository institution 46
federal funds market 136
Federal Insurance Corporation 155
Federal Reserve 118, 136, 164–166, 173, 174
Federal Reserve Act 163, 172
Federal Reserve Board 162
Federal Reserve System 154, 155, 162
Federal Trade Commission (FTC) 171
feudal 29, 37
feudal lord 29, 31, 106
feudal system 130
feudalism 29
Finance Ministry 125
financial crisis 69
financial executives 169
financial institution 147
financial requirements, long-term 97
financial service 140
Financial Services Authority 78
financial system 155
financing, long-term 62, 98, 168
financing, short-term 61
First Bank of the United States 44, 45, 156
First National Bank 161
fit and proper 73
Five Articles Oath 104
fixed interest 55
fixed rates 55
flow of credit 154
foreclose 40
foreign currency 137

foreign direct investment, marginal 68
Foreign Direct Investment Program (FDIP) 68
foreign exchange 136
foreign exchange services 138
foreign exchange transactions 132
foreign investment 116, 131
free banking era 158
Frick 42
FSA 79
FTC investigation 171
Fuji Bank 112

Galey & Guffey 43
German banking 23
German Deutsche Bank 37, 75
German universal banks 85
Germany 83
gilt-edged bonds 41
Glass-Steagall 166, 167, 168, 172, 173
Glass-Steagall Act 2, 5, 67, 107, 154, 165, 172, 175
GNP 87, 110, 115, 175
gold 38, 159, 164
gold convertibility 118
gold prospecting 43
gold standard 38, 39
Gould, Jay 36
government 143, 149
government bond 31, 105
government finance 37
government loan 33
government securities, long-term 61
goyokin 32
grain exchange 7
Great Depression 155, 165
gross domestic product (GDP) 65, 168
gross national product 110, 145, 164
Grover, President 38
Guarantee Fund 17

Hanil Bank 147, 148
Hart-Scott-Rodino Act 171
Hausbank or House Bank 98
Hawley-Smoot Tariff Act 164
high-leverage potential 157
holding company 44, 126
Hong Kong 116, 129
Hongkong and Shanghai Banking Corporation 138, 141, 142
Hope and Company 9, 13
hostile takeovers 91
house bank 83
House of Bardi 6
House of Barings 76
human capital 90
Hunt 53
Hutchison Whampoa 141
Hyundai Group 147

imported 164
income 97

Income Doubling Plan 111, 113
income tax 60
independent 162
individual 134
Industrial and Commercial Bank of China 135
Industrial development 32, 91
industrialization 106
inflation 115, 159
inflation rate 65
informed 89
ING Group 76
initial offering 50
insolvency 155
institutional investors 170
insurance 166
interbank market 136
intercorporate stockholdings 154
interest 165
interest coupons 12, 19
Interest Equalization Tax (IET) 67
interest rate 37, 39, 65, 66, 68, 97, 117, 119, 136, 164
interest rate ceiling 167
intermediary activity 27
international banking center 142
International Monetary Fund 60
international relations 104
international trade 131
investment 19
investment banker 57
investment banking 50, 165
investment management 140
investments, short-term (CDs) 88

J.P. Morgan and Company 34, 153, 161
J.P. Morgan's relationship banking 170
Japan 12, 28
Japan Development Bank 109
Japanese industries 33
Japanese model 149
Jardine Matheson 139
jobber 58, 59, 70
joint venture 146
joint-stock companies 32, 107
judgment bond 40

keiretsu 2, 4, 98, 99, 103, 111–115, 118, 119, 121–123, 126, 154, 155, 170, 172, 175
Kleinkredit 97
Knickerbocker Trust Company 160
Kohl, Helmut 96
Korea First Bank 147, 148

Labor Party 59
labor union 107
Landgrave, the 11, 19, 20
Landgrave, William 11, 18, 84
large-firm model 91
large-scale investments 143

Leigh-Pemberton, Robin 62
lending 61
letter of credit 40, 168
leveraged buyout 121
liberalization 71, 90, 110, 144, 145
liberalized conditions 133
liens 40
Ligonier Valley Railroad 41
Limit 174
limited liability corporations 84
Lincoln, Abraham 39
liquidity 22, 45, 168
Lloyds of London 58
loan 31, 32, 55, 57, 124, 132, 135, 149, 156, 164, 165
loan, long-term 61, 171
loans, short-term 70
London and Scottish Committee of Bankers 56
London Futures and Options Exchange 58
London International Financial Futures Exchange 58
London Stock Exchange 79
Lucky-Goldstar Group 147

Maastricht Treaty 63, 66
MacArthur 107
Market aware 78
Medici 6
medium of exchange 30
Meiji Restoration 109
Mellon 2, 12, 34, 40–42, 44, 49
merchant 30
merger 57, 73, 75, 121
minimum commission system 72
Ministry of Commerce and Industry 108
Ministry of International Trade and Industry (MITI) 108, 110, 111, 114, 115, 116, 119, 143
Mitsubishi 2, 4, 103, 112
Mittelstand 83, 95, 98, 99, 174
Mittelstand model 94
modernization 104, 133
monetary control 56
monetary convergence 65
monetary policy 63, 66
monetary standard 38
monetary unification 106
money 30, 31, 38, 46
money crunch 38
money market 137
money market mutual funds 167, 168
money supply 38, 159
money trust 154
money trust and cartel 39
monobank system 131
monopoly 132, 147, 154
moral suasion 67
Morgan 12, 34, 35, 39, 48, 67, 76, 159, 161, 171, 173, 174

mortgage 41
mortgage-backed securities 174
most favored nation 33

National Bank Act of 1863 158
National City Bank 49, 50, 64, 161
national debt 157
National Income Doubling Plan 110
National Westminster 75
nationalized 59
negotiation 95
network 75
new joint stock companies 84
New York Stock Exchange 161
niche market 94
non-resident holding 55
nontradeable debt 65
note, promissory 24, 27, 40, 63
notes 45, 58

Office of Fair Trading 72
Office of the Comptroller of the Currency 158
oil 69, 114
oil venture 43
OPEC 69
opium trade 26
Opium War 26, 32, 130, 139
Oppenheim 10
Organization for Economic Cooperation and Development 110
Oriental Banking Corporation 138
overdraft 56
overdraft loan 61
overseas investment 62
overseas operations 97
oversubscribed 60, 140

panic 160–162, 164
Panic of 1873 41
partnerships 59, 72
Peabody 35
pension 31, 171
People's Bank of China 131, 135
People's Construction Bank of China 131
People's Republic of China 130
Perry, Commodore Matthew 104
Pittsburgh National Bank of Commerce 42
placing power 50
1985 Plaza Accord 118, 124
political system 87
prefecture 31, 33
primus inter pares or first among equals 88
private capital 32
privatization 60, 61
privatized 55, 106
productive purposes, long-term 172
protected domestic market 182
providers of capital 170

Pujo Hearings 153
Pyne, Percy 48

quota, mandatory 133

ready money 48
recession 124, 164
recession of 1920-1921 38, 163
regulate 78, 136
regulation 68, 79, 110, 155, 171
Regulation Q (RegQ) of the Federal Reserve 68, 167
regulatory structure 74, 77
requirements 96
reserve requirement 69
reserves 38, 84, 158, 159
restructuring 75, 124
rice riots 30
risk-based approach 78
risk, calculated 44
risutora 124
Rockefeller and Andrews 50
Rockefeller, John D. 49
Rothschild 8, 9–12, 17, 18, 20–22, 39, 76

S.B. Hale and Company 16
safety and soundness 4
sales contract 154
Samsung Group 146
samurai 29, 30, 31, 34
scarcity 133
Second Bank of the United States 46, 157
securities 40, 46, 55, 57, 58, 61, 67, 105, 166
Securities and Exchange Act, (Japanese) 107
securitized asset 219
senior management responsibility 78
separation of commercial and investment banking 167
separation of power 166
Shanghai 24
shareholder 31, 41, 45
shareholder, corporate 171
shares 33, 36, 60, 92
Sherman Antitrust Act 154
shogunate 29
silk 105
silver coinage 38
Singapore 116
single capacity rule 71, 72
Single European Act 63
Sino-Japanese War 140
solvency 27
South Korea 116
Special Economic Zones or SEZs 134, 135, 149
specialization 87, 88, 95
specialized 92, 136
specie (gold and silver) 45, 47, 60, 158

Specie Circular of 1836 47
sprecher 88
standard 78
Standard Oil 49, 50
state banks 45
Steel 62
Stillman, James 48
stock 41, 85, 88, 124, 125, 141, 164, 170
stock broker 59, 70
stock brokerage 140
stock exchange 7, 58, 59, 62, 63, 70, 72, 73, 79, 86
stock market 86, 125
stock market crash 165
stock speculation 164
stock, corporate 171
stockholding, intercorporate 194
strategic industries 33, 34
strike 107
subscription method 85
subsidies 33, 106, 108, 110
Supervision 76
Supervisory Board (Aufsichtsrat) 88, 98
Swire Pacific 140
syndicate 50
system of single capacity 72
system of true competitively priced commission 72
Taiping Rebellion 130
Taiwan 116
tariff 164
tax code 216
tax exemption 171
taxes 37
Thatcher, Margaret 55, 60, 70
Third World country 60
Tokyo Stock Exchange 122
Tory Party 59
trade 27, 28, 30, 142, 154
trade associations 95, 96
trade deficits 118
trade embargo 138
trade finance 9, 35
trade surpluses 116
trade union system 88
trading 77
trading company 140
tranche 60
Transfer of Regulations or Law on the Factories 33
Treasury 38, 157
Treasury bills, short-term 167
Treaty of Nanking 26, 30
Treaty of Rome 63, 66
treaty ports 26
truly competitive market 74
trust (or cartel) 32, 38
trust-busting 154

two-tiered board system 88
two-tiered financial system 66

U.S. dollar 66, 68
U.S. Federal Reserve 175
U.S. House Banking and Currency Committee 153
U.S. Treasury bills 68
U.S. Treasury Department 158
underwriter 60
underwriting 28
unfair competitive practice 4
unfair pricing 154
unfair trading system 122
uniformity 158
union 109
Union Pacific Railroad 48
United East India Company 7
United Kingdom 55, 66
universal banks 83, 86, 92
users of capital 170
usurpers 30, 31

viability, long-term 61, 113, 132, 162
volatility 48, 157
Voluntary Foreign Credit Restraint Program (VFCRP) 67
vote of no confidence 88
voting trust 37

Wall Street 39, 160, 161
window guidance 114
Wisselbank 7
works council 89
World War II 140

Yom Kippur War 114

zaibatsu 32, 34, 43, 106, 108, 111, 126

Ziegler, Philip. *The Sixth Great Power: A History of the Greatest of All Banking Families, the House of Barings, 1762-1929*, New York: Alfred A. Knopf, 1988.

2. International Leadership in the United Kingdom

Introduction

The banking system of the United Kingdom, much like the banking system of the United States, has historically kept the functions of commercial banking and investment banking separate. Unlike the United States, however, the London bankers controlled the entire U.K. banking system from a tiny square-mile area called "The City," while the clearing banks (the British equivalent of commercial banks) developed nationwide branch networks.

Within the City, the close proximity of the heads of major banking institutions encouraged the development of an almost cliquish group of financiers. Each had its own role in the carefully orchestrated financial system with fixed rates of compensation for loans and securities services. Strict controls on the use of sterling-denominated financial instruments by non-British residents precluded any real interference by foreign firms. Only the most desirable clients could gain access to the inner circle. The exclusivity of the City shut out British entrepreneurs in many regions outside London and it often appeared that the interests of British industry were not well served.

Indeed, the City was often vehemently denounced for ignoring England and investing overseas to the detriment of the entire economy. Under the administration of Prime Minister Margaret Thatcher, a free-market advocate who took office in 1979, many state-owned properties were privatized and the financial system was revamped. Gone were the restrictions of non-resident holdings of sterling-denominated deposits and securities, the fixed interest and fee structure, and the strict lines of demarcation between investment and commercial banking. "The Big Bang" of 1986 and the events that led up to it forever changed the relationship of banking and industry in the United Kingdom. There are useful lessons for the United States in the successes and the failures of the dramatic transition in the United Kingdom during the 1980s. While the industry/banking relationship in Britain is still not as close as in Germany or Japan, it has progressed considerably beyond that in the United States.

Clearing vs. Merchant Banks

Clearing banks in the United Kingdom are banks that accept transactions account deposits (checking account deposits) from individuals and businesses and settle the payment of checks written throughout the country. This is accomplished by just a handful of banks that dominate the market and form the Committee of London and Scottish Bankers: Barclays, Lloyds, Midland, National Westminster, the Bank of Scotland, the Royal Bank of Scotland, and Standard Chartered. Over two-thirds of all deposits, however, are controlled by the first four banks on the list. These private banks virtually own the U.K. clearing system, in contrast to the United States where the Federal Reserve System (created by an act of Congress) performs this function. Furthermore, because the head offices of the banks are all in London, four private banks in the United Kingdom virtually control the country's money supply.

With this much influcence over the financial system, misuse of this privately held power could threaten the viability of the U.K. economy--a matter of no small concern to the government. For many years, oversight of this clearing system was accomplished through the Bank of England, originally a private bank with special privileges from the government but later nationalized in 1946 as the official central bank. The Bank of England has never operated as a regulator in the U.S. sense of the word, however. Even today, when compared to the United States, there are relatively few written regulations. Policies are implemented through "gentlemen's agreements" which are essentially agreements to comply with the wishes of the Bank of England and other bank regulators in exchange for favors as needed in the future. This kind of negotiated monetary control is possible because of the close physical proximity of the Bank of England and the head offices of the clearing banks in London. Such on-going dialogue is in sharp contrast to the more adversarial relationship between banks and bank regulators in the in the United States.

Because the clearing banks' liabilities are due-on-demand checking account deposits, their assets are often equally liquid short-term loans to business. The most common type of loan that is extended to industry is the overdraft, that is, the right of a bank customer to write checks over and above the balance in the customer's account. In the United States, overdrafts are either paid by the customer immediately or charged to a credit card account. In the United Kingdom, overdrafts continue to be carried on the bank's books and the customer pays interest on them, causing them to become in essence short-term loans. While the loan portfolios of clearing banks have become more diversified over time, a large proportion is still devoted to such short-term financing, funded primarily by customer deposits.

It has often been said that clearing banks live on their deposits, while merchant banks live on their wits. *Merchant banks* have small, professional staffs that cater to industry. Their offices are in London, they have no branch network throughout the United Kingdom, and are funded primarily by their own capital. In addition, they accept longer-term deposits that are not subject to withdrawal upon demand (similar to certificates of deposit in the United States). One of their first activities was to facilitate trade by accepting bills of exchange. Before the mergers that added new names to the list after 1986, some of the most important London merchant banks were: N.M. Rothschild & Son; Baring Brothers & Company; C.J. Hambro & Son; Kleinwort, Sons & Company; Lazard Brothers & Company; Morgan, Grenfell & Company; and Seligman Brothers.

Acting as a securities underwriter or investment banker, a merchant bank will often hold a client's new securities in its asset portfolios until they can be sold to the public. Merchant banks can be exposed to potentially large losses if the price of the securities declines before they can all be sold upon initial issue. In addition, merchant banks are among the principal managers of pension funds and other investment pools.

Giving advice concerning mergers and acquisitions (M&A) and actually facilitating business combinations on behalf of their clients is another important service provided by merchant bankers. But banking firms can be successful in M&A only if they can help their clients identify the "right" company for their clients in terms of long-term strategic positioning, possible cost-saving aspects, and feasible financial arrangements. This is not always a gentile activity and requires that the bankers involved be able to adapt quickly to change and operate effectively under sometimes hostile circumstances.

The two cultures of clearing and merchant banks are thus contrasting, just as the cultures of commercial and investment banks in the United States. That the two have begun to coexist in the United Kingdom is even more surprising when one considers the structure of the securities industry before the Big Bang.

An Archaic System in a World Class City

The City is sometimes regarded as independent from the rest of the country. The sub-divisions of the City include the banking industry, the legal and accounting professions, and all market-related organizations--including the Stock Exchange, Lloyd's of London (insurance syndicate), the London Futures and Options Exchange, and the London International Financial Futures Exchange. It operates under its own, often unwritten, rules and regulations, tolerating government interference only when absolutely necessary.

Before the Big Bang, one of those government rules was the rule of "single capacity" as regards the functions in the Stock Exchange. Under single capacity, a *broker* receives orders for securities transactions from the public, either individuals or institutional investors. The broker may not execute the order, but must turn it over to a *jobber* (called a *specialist* in the United States), who buys and sells based on broker orders. After an issue has been sold through a merchant bank, the jobber holds a portion of the securities in its inventory to "make a market" in them. In this process, the jobber stands ready to buy or sell the securities to help maintain an orderly market--one in which all "sell" or "buy" orders can be quickly and efficiently filled. However, the broker is strictly prohibited from buying and selling securities; while the jobber is not permitted to deal with the public. Brokers' compensation is commissions on customers transactions, while jobber profits depend on the prices at which they buy and sell securities. Before the U.K. markets were liberalized, brokers' commissions were fixed guaranteeing them healthy profits because there was no competitive pressure to reduce fees and/or increase service to customers.

This cozy arrangement was not restricted to stock brokers, however. The clearing banks formed a cartel that set both the lending and borrowing interest rates that were used in the City's money markets. Before deregulation, decisions were commonly made in this way--through a consensus of opinion often based as much on personal contacts as on sound business considerations.

For example, lunch became almost a rite of passage. The typical merchant bank has more than a dozen dining rooms with in-house catering to entertain clients, potential clients, businessmen, financial journalists, politicians, and heads of foreign governments. Anyone who may be of use to the firm will be invited. During these lunches, deals are structured and relationships are formed. Better that this business be conducted within the bank's own walls, instead of in public establishments, so that the utmost secrecy could be maintained with respect to any future business ventures. Even the guest lists were protected from public scrutiny. "We had him in for lunch" was recognition that that individual had indeed "arrived" and was part of the inner circle.

Perhaps predictably, this system created implicit rankings by class, with a merchant banker occupying the highest rung on the ladder. Stock brokers, who served the needs of wealthy individuals and important institutional clients, stood on the next rung. Jobbers, as far as stock brokers were concerned, were no better than tradesmen, buying and selling for a living. The best stock broker was not even in the same league as the most insignificant merchant banker. The most experienced and wealthy jobber was looked down upon by the lowliest stock broker. Thus, artificial class distinctions and rules of conduct dictated London financial operations.

The City was able to insulate itself from the realities of the real world because of restrictions on the participation of outsiders. Both brokers and jobbers could only operate as partnerships and only members of the Stock Exchange were eligible for partnership. Neither banks, not even merchant banks, were permitted to be members of the Stock Exchange, nor were insurance companies. Furthermore, a nonmember could own no more than 29.9 percent of any member firm. Thus, there was little competition and functions within the City were all maintained separately--clearing banks, merchant banks, jobbers, and brokers.

The Reform Movement

While the City remained preoccupied with its elitist tendencies, the rest of the country fell into an economic abyss. After the devastation of World War II, many U.K. industries had been nationalized--the coal industry in 1947, railways in 1948, steel in 1951. Later, the aerospace and automobile industries were added to the list. Then the oil embargos in 1973 and 1979 quadrupled the price of crude oil, sending shockwaves through virtually all oil-importing countries and forcing inflation rates to unbearable levels.

In the United Kingdom, coal mine employees brought work to a standstill as they held out for higher wages to keep pace with inflation. Coal deliveries stopped, power was available only for brief periods during the day, and the country was forced to a three-day work week. When the demands of the coal workers were met, inflation roared full steam ahead--reaching 27 percent by June 1975. With the country's economy in disarray, the conservative Tory Party was voted out of power in the same year and the Labor Party took office. But even the Labor Party could not stop worker strikes or break the inflationary spiral. There were more demands for job security from the nationalized industries and the country faced severe financial problems that were graphically illustrated in 1976 by the request of the United Kingdom for a loan from the International Monetary Fund, as if it were a Third World country.

Privatizing Major Industries

In 1979, Margaret Thatcher of the Tory Party was elected as Prime Minister. Her platform was to take difficult steps whether they were popular or not. After her election she continued to stand firmly on that platform, reducing income taxes to give the populace incentives to work, challenging the unions, placing people in positions of influence within government-owned companies that would take the necessary steps to restore profitability, and pushing for privatization.

During the 1980s the U.K. government privatized a number of companies including British Aerospace, British Airways, British Telecom, Cable & Wireless (the overseas telephone company), Britoil, Enterprise Oil, British Petroleum, British Gas, and Jaguar Cars, raising over £22 billion pounds in the process. While the offerings were generally oversubscribed, that is, there were more bids for shares than shares available for purchase, the public sales were not without disappointments. In the case of a radioactive chemicals company, Amersham, the issue was 22 times oversubscribed. When the price escalated quickly in the aftermarket, there were disconted rumblings that the government was "giving away" the country's assets. When Britoil (part of the government's stake in the North Sea oil fields) was offered, the government deliberately took a firm stance on the minimum price at which the shares could be offered--so firm that the offer was substantially undersubscribed.

The government persevered, however, generating £3.9 billion in the 1984 British Telecom public offering. This time, an international syndicate of underwriters was organized and the government took extraordinary measures to pique the interest of the general public. Those individuals who bought shares would receive "bonus" shares at the end of the year for their loyalty to the country and even a discount on their telephone bills. This was a golden opportunity to own a piece of British industry, something that very few individuals had ever had the opportunity to do.

The British Petroleum issue sold well, but the trading of shares in the initial aftermarket was not what had been hoped for. Shortly after issuance, the U.S. *tranche*, or series of shares designated for the U.S. market, was quickly resold for a profit in the U.K. market. This pattern did not bode well for the international distribution of U.K. securities to be offered in the future. A broad and deep international market in these securities could not be developed if all the shares were immediately dumped back into the United Kingdom.

In the 1986 sale of £5.4 billion of British Gas shares, the government specifically required that the underwriters who were responsible for the U.S. tranche guarantee that the securities would remain in the United States. As a result, distribution of the British Gas shares was much more successful.

Although there were starts and stops in the British privatization program, the net effect is that the government raised well over £20 billion pounds. U.K. and foreign investors who had never before owned stock now did so and the privately owned firms were free to be restructured and to become more competitive.

Scrutinizing the Financial Sector

As the United Kingdom struggled to regain economic viability, there was real concern in some quarters about the extent to which the financial system supported the country. It was often said that bank lending by U.K. banks to industry was much shorter term than bank lending in Germany and Japan and the Stock Market did not make up the difference in this lower level of financing. In the face of this criticism, the banks often countered that overdraft loans that were not quickly repaid actually constituted long-term loans.

The problem remained, however, that bank overdrafts are secured by the assets of the firm and are thus limited by the size of the company's asset base. This in itself is a short-term perspective on lending because short-term loans are always repaid from liquidity (or asset base) while long-term loans are repaid from profitability of the projects being financed. As long as a lender considers only present circumstances and not future possibilities, such a financial arrangement is self-limiting. The effect is more insidious in that such short-term financing inspires managers to invest for short-term profits, often to the detriment of long-term viability.

Part of the problem seemed to be the culture of business and bank managers. Both seemed to be too far removed from the realities of manufacturing and competition. Business managers often were trained in the arts with an initial goal of perhaps becoming civil servants, only to be thrust into industry relatively unprepared.

For their part, the bankers were often no better prepared, having pursued a classical, rather than technical, education. Many times, the privilege of inherited wealth created even less incentive to understand the needs of entrepreneurs and industry in general. The City was an insulated fortress psychologically and physically separated from the rest of the country. The clearing banks had nationwide branches but provided no long-term financing. The merchant banks facilitated long-term finance, but maintained no regional offices and often had little appreciation for the needs of small- and medium-size industry.

With a sometimes-condescending attitude toward industry, merchant bankers in the City seemed more comfortable investing in the United States, a true capitalist country, rather than in Britain. A U.S. entrepreneur, it was thought, would fight and work to make an investment pay off. These were qualities that could not be so easily found in the United Kingdom. And besides, overseas investment was a tradition. England developed as a trading and commercial country before the Industrial Revolution. Many fortunes were made by Brits who invested in government securities and overseas ventures such as state bonds in the United States and railroad stocks. In fact, a merchant banker would sometimes accept a lower rate of return for a U.S. project than an U.K. project because the U.S. project had a higher probability of success and, thus, less risk. Ironically, the cost of capital for a British project was higher than for a comparable American project.

The merchant bankers reconciled this obvious paradox by shifting the responsibility--it was up to the clearing banks to provide start-up capital for businesses. Yet so much of the clearing bank lending was tied to a firm's existing asset base, constraining the amount of funds that a new business could raise. This deficiency of financing was addressed in 1984 by Robin Leigh-Pemberton, Governor of the Bank of England, when he challenged the status quo in an unusually candid statement. He asserted that the City should be "not only responsive to industry's needs but it has also got to positively promote industrial development and change." In an address before an audience of Stock Exchange members, Nigel Lawson, Chancellor of the Exchequer (head of the British Treasury department) was even more blunt when he charged that it had been "notoriously difficult to raise even very small sums of equity--say between £20,000 and £50,000." In 1985 the Secretary of State for Wales, the Right Honorable Nicholas Edwards, addressed the "huge chasm" between the City and the industrial areas of Britain. As he saw it, the City regarded Wales as a country overly dependent on declining steel and coal industry with few prospects for future viability:

> It is the entrepreneur who has to try to bridge the gap going to the City to offices away from the action to explain in an alien and sometimes hostile climate the potential for the project.

It is safe to say that many did not believe the City fostered economic development for the small- and medium-sized companies within the British economy. [1]

The Eurodollar Markets

While the City was seen as often unresponsive to indigenous British industry, it is ironic that London was, at the same time, the site of one of the most dynamic international financial markets--the Eurodollar markets. As noted earlier, the City was insulated from domestic competition because of the rules of membership in the Stock Exchange, the separation of functions, and fixed interest rates and commissions. The City also was protected from foreign competition by the government's restriction of the holding of sterling deposits by non-residents since 1957. In the same year, countries in Western Europe liberalized bank trading in U.S. dollars to facilitate the formation of the European Common Market. This led to a market in dollar-denominated financial instruments--bank deposits, promissory notes, and bonds--called the Eurodollar market.

The Monetary Goals of the European Union

The European Economic Community (EEC) Treaty of 1957, also called the Treaty of Rome, united Belgium, France, Italy, Luxembourg, the Netherlands, and Germany for the purpose of coordinating monetary policies and action for their mutual benefit. In 1967 the EEC joined with two other European industrial associations (the European Coal and Steel Community and the European Atomic Energy Community) and became the European Community (EC). The United Kingdom, Ireland, and Denmark joined in 1973, followed by Greece in 1981, and Portugal and Spain in 1985. Austria, Finland, and Sweden became members in 1995.

The 1987 Single European Act set the goals of liberalizing capital movements, abolishing cross-border restrictions in the provision of financial services, and removing obstructions to the free movement of goods and services throughout the member countries by December 31, 1992. The 1992 Maastricht Treaty outlined the final stage of European integration. The goal of Maastricht is

---

[1] The statements of Leigh-Pemberton, Lawson, and Edwards are taken from: Hilton, Anthony. *City Within a State*, London: I.B. Tauris & Co., Ltd., 1987, p. 140.

to create a single European currency and to coordinate monetary policy for the 15 member countries through one central bank. As a result of this closer coordination of policy, the European Community became the European Union.

Effective November 1993, the Maastricht Treaty outlined an important framework for transition from *monetary system* to *monetary union*. The treaty stipulated January 1, 1994 as the date for commencement of Stage 2 of monetary union. During Stage 2, the *European Monetary Institute (EMI)* replaced the Committee of Central Bank Governors (which had presided over monetary coordination). The EMI was located in Frankfurt, Germany and, among other things:

- Took over the administration of the European Monetary Cooperation Fund (which issued Ecus, European Currency Units) and the accompanying financing mechanisms.
- Monitored the operation of the EMS (European Monetary System).
- Facilitated use of private Ecu.
- Oversaw development of the Ecu clearing system.
- Was consulted by national authorities on monetary policy and helped draft legislation on the eventual convergence of all currencies into one currency.

All EU central banks were members of the EMI. The organization was intended to strengthen the coordination of the member states' monetary policies in preparation for full monetary union. A *European System of Central Banks (ESCB)* was formed, with the *European Central Bank (ECB)* as the principal new monetary institution. At the beginning of the third and final phase of monetary union, the EMI was liquidated and the European Central Bank assumed it functions. The formation of the new system follows guidelines established by the Committee of Central Bank Governors (predecessor of the European Monetary Institute).

The European System of Central Banks and the European Central Bank are responsible for issuing and managing the single currency that eventually will replace the national currencies.

The United Kingdom, Denmark, and Sweden elected not to converge on January 1, 1999. Greece will join upon meeting the full criteria for convergence.[2] In order to converge, a member state must:

---

[2] The eleven converging countries on January 1, 1999 were Austria, Belgium, Finland, France, Germany, Ireland, Italy, Luxembourg, the Netherlands, Portugal, and Spain.

1. *Achieve a high degree of price stability.* The average one-year inflation rate before examination by EU authorities must not exceed by more than 1.5 percentage points the inflation rate of the three best performing EU members.
2. *Demonstrate sustainability of its government financial position.* An excessive government deficit can disqualify an EU country from convergence. Public deficits may not exceed 3% of GDP, while total public debt may not exceed 60% of GDP.
3. *Observe the normal fluctuation margins provided by the Exchange Rate Mechanism* for at least two years without devaluing its currency against the currency of another EU member.
4. *Demonstrate adequate control of its interest rates.* For one year prior to examination by EU authorities, the long-term government bond (or comparable) interest rate may not exceed by more than 2 percentage points the long-term government bond rate of the three best performing EU members.

These criteria have been established for monetary convergence, but one could argue that the criteria are desirable goals in a national policy making context. Domestic price stability, adequate control of government finance, proper management of the external value of domestic currency, and a reasonable interest rate environment are conditions in any event for which every sovereign state strives.

In December 1995, the EU heads of government met in Madrid, reaffirming January 1, 1999 as commencement of European Monetary Union. The leaders decided that the name of the new currency would be the *Euro*. Those countries that are members of the monetary union beginning in January 1999 were asked to issue their tradable, government debt in Euros to create a reasonably large pool of financial instruments denominated in the new currency. Nontradeable debt may continue to be denominated in the national currency during the transition period. Commercial banks have the option of accepting deposits and opening transactions accounts in the new currency prior to the mandatory change-over date of 2002.

Euro currency and coins will begin circulation on January 1, 2002. Until that time, national currencies will circulate but their exchange rates are irrevocably fixed in terms of other national currencies and in terms of the Euro.

The United Kingdom and Monetary Union

The role of the United Kingdom in the monetary union of Europe is an interesting contrast to that of Germany and France, which have always maintained strong public support for coordination of European monetary policy. The objectives of monetary union were frustrated when the United Kingdom and Denmark withdrew from the Exchange Rate Mechanism in the fall of 1992, delaying completion of Stage 2. For reasons related to the German reunification in 1990, Germany had maintained high interest rates both to attract capital and control inflation. This caused the value of the deutsche mark to remain high vis-à-vis other EC currencies. The cost of maintaining agreed upon parities--in terms of both market intervention and maintenance of high interest rates--was too high and the United Kingdom and Denmark pulled out. For a period of time, currency exchange markets were in turmoil and serious doubts arose as to the feasibility of a true monetary union in Europe.

Since that time, German interest rates have fallen, easing some of the pressure on other European countries to maintain high interests to the detriment of their national economies. Also, the Exchange Rate Mechanism was "temporarily" modified in August 1993 such that most member countries were required just to maintain their currencies within 15% of parity (above or below) instead of within 2.5% of parity. Only Germany and the Netherlands remained subject to the original fluctuation bands. This modification effectively returned the member currencies to floating rate status until converging under the guidelines of the Maastricht Treaty. The role of the United Kingdom in this episode illustrates the country's strong focus on autonomy—even in the context of the European Union.

The Off-Shore Market in U.S. Dollars

The troubling 1992 episode in European currency markets illustrates the challenges to EC monetary integration that existed even before the 1957 Treaty of Rome. While a single European currency did not yet exist, the U.S. dollar acted as a reasonable substitute in the interim. Thus, banking laws were changed to permit easy cross-border exchange of dollars within Europe, creating a 2-tiered financial system. Lending in the national currency was subject to more or less national regulation, while trading in U.S. dollars was essentially free of regulation. In the United Kingdom, non-resident dealings in sterling were severely restricted in 1957, but not transactions in U.S. dollars. Because of its tradition of international finance, London became the central location of the new Eurodollar market.

Circumstances in the United States also promoted the development of this off-shore market in dollars. During the 1960s, the United States did not suffer the international trade deficits that are so common today. In this decade, U.S. exports of goods and services exceeded imports by $40 billion. In currency markets these surpluses created a net international demand for dollars to pay for the American goods. During the same period, U.S. firms made overseas investments in capital assets of $52 billion. The excess of these capital expenditures over the demand for dollars to pay for U.S. exports essentially created a net $12 billion supply of dollars outside the United States. Since dollars were still convertible into gold at that time, there was no real incentive to convert the dollars to other currencies.

These large holdings of dollars outside the United States did lead to conversions, however, particularly by those who speculated that the value of the dollar would fall. Just as gold left the country at an alarming pace in 1895, the gold reserves of the country were again threatened. In 1895, J. P. Morgan saved the U.S. gold standard by arranging an emergency loan that brought gold back into the country to replace that which had been shipped overseas and to restore enough confidence to stem the future flow of outgoing gold. By the 1960s, the era of J. P. Morgan and bankers like him had ended with the 1933 Glass-Steagall Act. The United States no longer had *relationship banking* to help pull it out of its predicament.

Instead, legislation was passed to try to limit the amount of dollars held overseas. The *Interest Equalization Tax (IET)* of 1964 discouraged non-U.S. residents from issuing securities in the United States. The IET added one percentage point to the cost of financing for foreigners.

One year later, the *Voluntary Foreign Credit Restraint Program (VFCRP)* of 1965 "recommended" limitation of the amount of foreign lending and investment by commercial banks, insurance companies, and pension funds. It is interesting to note that this was a kind of moral suasion for financial institutions to do something that was in the best interest of the country as a whole. If this initiative had been undertaken in the United Kingdom, it would likely have been discussed rather more informally between the Governor of the Bank of England and the important institutions in the City. That the United States chose to legislate a recommendation points to a fundamental flaw in the policy making apparatus. Critical areas of financial coordination can perhaps be better accomplished through consensus-building rather than regulation. The VFCRP also asked industrial firms to improve their individual capital flows either by:

- Exporting more goods and services (which would result in some of those dollars coming back into the United States),
- Postponing marginal foreign direct investment (thereby not adding to the supply of overseas dollars), or
- Raising more funds abroad (obtaining foreign currency financing instead of U.S. dollar loans for overseas investments).

Apparently, the "recommendations" of the Voluntary Foreign Credit Restraint Program were not effective because in 1968 *mandatory* restrictions were placed on direct investment in 1) advanced European countries, 2) Australia, and 3) South Africa through the Foreign Direct Investment Program (FDIP). (More liberal investment ceilings were established for investments in developing countries.)

The net effect of these regulations was to put pressure on multinational customers of U.S. commercial banks to finance their foreign operations outside U.S. markets. Loan rates that banks could offer foreign borrowers were not as competitive as they would have been otherwise. Thus, banks' corporate customers were generally encouraged to seek overseas financing and foreign borrowers were given disincentives to look for financing in the United States. As a result, the demand for bank loans in the United States declined dramatically.

At the same time, U.S. commercial banks were subject to Regulation Q (Reg Q) of the Federal Reserve, which placed ceilings on deposit interest rates, including large, negotiable certificates of deposit (CDs) that had become a popular short-term investment for industrial companies with a temporary excess of liquid assets.[3] Unlike their nonnegotiable counterparts, negotiable CDs could be sold on the secondary market before maturity. The ability to sell negotiable CDs to another investor before maturity, thus avoiding early withdrawal penalties, made them instruments that were as flexible as U.S. Treasury bills (which enjoyed a healthy secondary market) but carried a higher rate of return. The Reg Q ceiling on the deposit rate that banks could pay on negotiable CDs had not been a binding constraint until 5 years after its 1961 introduction.

U.S. government expenditures during the 1960s for domestic social programs and the Vietnam War dramatically increased the borrowing requirements of the U.S. government. This increased demand for funds caused Treasury interest rates to climb, which bank deposit rates were limited by Reg Q ceilings. By 1966, when a large amount of negotiable CDs were due to mature, it appeared doubtful that they would be renewed because the Treasury bill rate was

[3] Reg Q ceilings on negotiable CDs were removed in 1970.

higher than the Reg Q ceiling for negotiable CDs. If the banks that had issued these negotiable CDs were asked to pay them off instead of roll them over, the 1966 "credit crunch" would be the equivalent of a "run" on the largest banks in the United States. A solution *had* to be found!

The solution was the Eurodollar market and London was the place. The overseas branches of U.S. banks were not subject to Reg Q. It was not necessary to maintain reserve requirements (liquid assets held by the Federal Reserve) against these overseas deposits or to pay deposit insurance premiums on them. Vast amounts of U.S. dollars were being held abroad. By offering competitive deposit rates in their London branches, U.S. banks could replace those deposits that were not rolled over in the domestic market. It would then be a simple matter for the London branches to lend the money to the domestic parent.

Thus, a financial crisis was averted and a new financial market in London was born. Banks not only replaced deposits lost from maturing domestic CDs with Eurodollars, but they also used the Eurodollar to raise funds with which to offer more competitively priced off-shore loans. The loans were made to those foreign borrowers that U.S. regulations had attempted to discourage. The Eurodollars were also used to provide financing for U.S. multinationals that were being pressured not to take dollars from the United States and then invest them overseas.

When the crude oil crises of 1973 and 1979 caused the price of oil to quadruple and profits of oil-exporting countries to reach unprecedented levels, OPEC oil ministers could not reinvest the new found wealth fast enough in their home countries. Surpluses were invested in safe, easily marketable financial instruments such as U.S. government securities and bank deposits. Eurodollar deposits were particularly attractive because of the higher rates available. An added attraction was the reduced likelihood that the U.S. government would freeze these dollar-denominated assets in London in the event of a political dispute. During the Iranian hostage crisis under the administration of U.S. President Jimmy Carter, Iranian assets within the United States (including bank deposits) had been blocked from withdrawal. Investing in the unregulated Eurodollar market provided a measure of assurance that this would not happen to other OPEC countries.[4]

Through the London Eurodollar market, U.S. and other banks with branches in London could easily and efficiently settle international transactions in U.S. dollars. U.S. and non-U.S. multinational industrial corporations could invest

---

[4] OPEC is an acronym for Organization of Petroleum Exporting Countries.

in U.S. dollar short-term investments (CDs) and obtain competitively priced short-term financing (loans). OPEC profits could be more safely invested. As the market continued to develop, *Eurobonds* (long-term instruments) and *Euroequities* (common and preferred stocks) also emerged. Firms began to offer the multinational equivalent of a bill of exchange as *Eurocommercial paper*. *Currency swaps*, or contracts to exchange currencies today with the stipulation that the transaction will be reversed in the future, became a part of the unregulated London Markets.

As the activity increased, other cities in Europe became sites of Eurodollar markets: Paris, Frankfurt, Amsterdam, Zurich, Basel, Geneva, Milan, and Vienna. The term "Eurodollar" must be loosely interpreted because such markets are not limited strictly to Europe. Tax havens such as the Cayman Islands and the Bahamas are also sites of virtually unregulated Eurodollar activity. The *Asian* dollar market is centered in Hong Kong, Singapore, and Tokyo. Yet as widespread as the activity is, London remains the primary location and retains the distinction of home of the Euromarkets.

Deregulation and the Big Bang

The size and importance of the Euromarkets did not escape the attention of Prime Minister Margaret Thatcher. A tremendous amount of capital was being managed in currencies other than sterling. Given the poor state of the British economy, the existing problems of linkage between the City and small- and medium-size British firms, and the unparalleled size and impact of the Euromarkets, Thatcher undertook a restructuring of the financial system that was even more dramatic than the privatization of British industry.

Early Liberalization

Even before the Thatcher government took over in 1979, some indication of change in the financial markets was evident both in the way they were regulated and their functions. The Competition and Credit Central policy of 1971 brought to an end the interest rate cartel operated by the London clearing banks.

A few years before this change, in 1967, the rule that limited partnerships to 20 people was abolished. This resulted in the formation of larger firms, notably larger jobbers and stock brokers over time. The stock exchange also relaxed the rules with respect to outside ownership of these firms in 1969. If they chose to do so, firms could sell 100% of their equity to outsiders, that is, nonmembers of the Stock Exchange. This move was intended to attract capital that would hopefully strengthen the sterling markets in stocks and bonds, as their traditional influence in international finance had dwindled when compared with the Euromarkets, for example.

The amount of new capital invested in these firms, however, was not as much as had been hoped for because certain unattractive restrictions remained. No one outsider could own more than 10 percent of a partnership. [The percentage was not increased to 29.9 percent until 1982, after Thatcher took office.] This meant that no one partner--that was not a member of the Stock Exchange--could force a firm to change the basic nature of its activities or otherwise exercise significant influence over it. Furthermore, outsiders from various partnerships could not collectively exert pressure on the market through their own investment holdings that would in any way change the entire market. Lastly, the *single capacity* rule was not abolished, leaving the functions of broker and jobber separate and distinct.

These rule changes were a form of liberalization, but institutions with significant capital, like the clearing banks, were not attracted. No one bank could own a firm or even a majority interest in a firm. Even together, the banks could not effect any changes that would give them more policy-making power. The single capacity rule prohibited a bank from owning a firm, or even owning part of a firm, that brought a full range of financial services under one roof.

The net effect of these rules was that British Stock Exchange firms in London were smaller and not as well capitalized as their American counterparts. The staff of the largest British firms, such as Cazenove, Scrimgeour, or Capel, numbered approximately 400 at the end of the 1970s, compared with 40,000 at Merrill Lynch.

At the same time, clients were more often large, institutional investors that expected more sophisticated advice and services. Such investors held three-quarters of all equity securities and a large share of government securities. Research, computer, and telecommunications facilities were necessary in order for brokers to remain competitive and adequately service these new clients. The capital base of small jobbers was often inadequate to take on the large transactions required by institutional investors. In the absence of large amounts of new capital from outside, merger of existing firms helped the British to realize economies of scale in providing research support and to create firms whose capital base was sufficient to handle the large blocks of securities that institutional investors traded.

After the 20-member limit on partnerships was removed in 1967, the number of firms declined significantly as a result of consolidations. By the end of the 1970s, 103 brokerage firms were all that remained of the 303 that operated in the previous decade. The 108 jobbers had consolidated into only 14 firms.

The Big Bang

Until the Thatcher administration, changes in the rules that governed the city were minimal. Mergers among the firms were merely stop-gap measures that did not address the fundamental structural problems of the market. As the first step in a program of meaningful deregulation, foreign exchange controls were removed in 1979. Soon the portfolios of British insurance companies and pension funds contained large investments of foreign securities. It became apparent to the government and the Bank of England that London could conceivably become the leading financial center in Europe once again. The Euromarkets were already developing and British firms apparently had an appetite for international diversification. London was already the link between Tokyo and New York that permitted 24-hour a day trading. There was no reason why the same pattern could not be repeated in the area of securities.

In the foreign currency markets, the major British participants were the clearing banks. But, as noted earlier, there was little incentive for these institutions to become seriously involved with the securities industry. The British system obviously needed revamping. In 1983 the government (The Office of Fair Trading) sought to bring a case before the British Department of Trade and Industry against the Stock Exchange that would bring an end to the minimum commission system. The issue was settled in an agreement between the government and the Stock Exchange to end the practice by year-end 1986. Perhaps this would make the British Exchange more competitive internationally.

This alone, however, would not be enough. The system of single capacity had to go. If it remained in the presence of deregulated commissions, competition among the 100 firms that remained could intensify, forcing more mergers. As the number of brokerage firms declined, the maintenance of a system of true competitively priced commissions would become less likely and collusion to set fees more likely. The only reasonable solutions were to open the doors of membership to all those who qualified and to eliminate the single capacity rule. In order to be eligible for membership, an applicant firm must demonstrate that:

1. It is *fit and proper* to carry on the business as indicated by the proposed line of business and the applicant's financial position, expertise, and past record.
2. It has *adequate* capital to run the business. The capital requirements depend on projected annual expenditures, volume of business, and the extent to which the firm trades on its own account.
3. It complies with certain rules in the *conduct of its business* that relate to advertising, unsolicited approaches to individuals (cold-calling), published recommendations, written agreements with customers, investment advice offered, and disclosure of material interests in other firms.
4. It holds *clients' money* in separate bank accounts from those of the firm.

These rules for admission were based solely on operational competence and integrity. Together, the changes would make the U.K. system more competitive and attract capital from the domestic banking industry and overseas firms.

It was decided in 1983 that all of these changes would occur at one time--a Big Bang scheduled for October 27, 1986. The announcement of the revamping of this centuries-old system also contained the clear message that banks were considered, indeed, a legitimate source of capital. Government, the Bank of England, and the Stock Exchange collectively wished to strength domestic securities firms with banking capital before allowing foreign firms access to membership.

With this announcement, the merger wave began in earnest. The clearing banks had already begun to establish merchant banking subsidiaries. After 1983, in preparation for the Big Bang, these diversification efforts extended to acquisition of jobber and brokerage firms. The major clearing banks are becoming "universal" banks that offer a full range of financial services. The financial system changes in the United Kingdom have made it possible to merge the activities of commercial and investment banking and to offer world-class service to all clients.

While the banks benefit from an expanded universe of permissible activities, it will ultimately be the British people who benefit most from these changes. A banking system with nationwide branches as is the case of the clearing banks, has a built-in distribution network for securities brokers. Merchant banks are skilled at structuring corporate deals that result in new securities issuances. Jobbers make markets in these securities once they have been issued. When it is possible to bring all these functions together, as it is now in the United Kingdom, the financial infrastructure of the country is better prepared to support economic development. Furthermore, the presence of the Euromarkets in London adds a strong international dimension to the availability of financial support for industrial growth.

Important Lessons

While the regulatory structure has been put in place, it is important to understand the magnitude of a change like the Big Bang and the integration of financial services that accompanied it. The City was once insulated from the rest of the world, but must now compete according to rules that, in some cases, it is only now learning.

Merging Different Cultures

One of these new rules is that several cultures must be managed under one roof. The *first lesson* is that if one is to succeed in a truly competitive market, the class distinctions between brokers, bankers, and jobbers has no place. At the same time, it is not always easy to adjust to a new way of thinking. When brokers and jobbers belonged to partnerships, they had a stake in the business. As employees of banks, they now work with someone else's money. Investment banking means attending to clients' needs to the best of one's ability, while commercial banking is conducted at arm's length. Meshing these two psychologies is extremely important.

Barclays, the large clearing bank, has formed a particularly effective alliance, Barclays de Zoete Wedd--with broker de Zoete Bevan and jobber Wedd Durlacher. In a recent survey of merchant bankers, this merged firm was ranked among the top ten firms in the industry. With respect to specific attributes, Barclays de Zoete Wedd was ranked seventh in quality of service; sixth in quality of management and community responsibility; fifth in value as a long-term investment; fourth in ability to attract and retain top talent and capacity to innovate; third in quality of marketing; and first in financial soundness. Barclays presents a strong example of the potential for synergies between merchant and commercial banking when the two cultures are managed properly.

Managing Branch Networks

A *second lesson* from the U.K. banking system is the importance of managing branch networks. The nationwide networks of clearing banks make it possible for them to have close contact with industry throughout the country and to distribute a now wider range of services. Opening an office near firms virtually guarantees a large share of their banking business. There also appears to be a connection between the number of branches and total market share, especially if the branches are clustered. For example, Barclays is strongest in Wales and in the eastern portion of the country, while National Westminster dominates in the southern and middle regions.

There is a limit to the desirability of these networks, however. In the United Kingdom there is one bank branch for every 4,500 people. In Germany and Japan, also countries that have nationwide branching systems, the population per bank branch is approximately 9,800 and 8,800, respectively. In response to profit pressures, clearing banks are reducing the number of branches. During the restructuring of the 1980s, the clearing banks closed one-fifth of their branch offices. The cost of the marginal facilities was too high when compared with the revenues that they generated. In other words, the United Kingdom was "overbanked."

This phenomenon has some implications for the United States, where the population per bank branch is roughly the same as that in the United Kingdom. In an age of telecommunications and expanding services to industry, brick-and-mortar facilities play a decreasingly significant role in successful banking. If banks do not have the ability to engage in fee-generating services such as investment banking and insurance, there will be an incentive to maintain cost-ineffective branches that at least offer some possibility of retaining market share.

Capital vs. Skill

A *third lesson* from the U.K. experience is that capital alone is not sufficient to guarantee success. From 1984 to 1986, the period of mergers just before the Big Bang, banks spent £1.5 billion to buy more than 100 London stockbroker firms. Eighty percent of this amount represented goodwill, that is, amounts over and above the book value of the acquired firm's equity. Not all of these acquisitions have been successful.

Morgan Grenfell, the British merchant banking descendant of the House of Morgan, left the securities business after a loss of £39 million in 1988 and was purchased by the German Deutsche Bank. The Kleinwort Benson Group took a

£33 million loss in 1990 on one large transaction that virtually wiped out its entire profits for that year.

Prior to the Big Bang, conventional wisdom was that capital was good and more capital was better. After several disappointing episodes, however, the focus has turned to *people*. It is the skill or "wits" of the merchant banker that will determine the degree of success of securities undertakings. When several facets of financial services are merged, the ability of the firm to understand all aspects of business is critical. It is not enough to be a narrowly focused specialist in one area. The successful banker will understand financial markets, dynamics of industrial sectors, and even issues of political importance.

Adequate Supervision: The Case of Barings

The *fourth lesson* offered by the United Kingdom is that even a system of mutual agreement should not neglect the function of supervision. Indeed, the safety and soundness of the entire system depends on adequate supervision. The ultimate demise of the House of Barings provides strong support for this premise.

In 1866, poorly managed investments in Argentina led to a collapse of the venerable institution. Reliable information was not forthcoming from the Argentinean market. The bank's financial distress was relieved through a £8 million bail-out led by the Bank of England, with participation by the Morgans and the Rothschilds. After the crisis was averted, the old partnership was disbanded, personal Baring fortunes were lost, and the reorganized operation was considerably downsized.

Ironically, it was again poor information management that led to the ultimate collapse of Barings in 1995. Nicholas William Leeson was a trader in the Singapore office of Barclays where he customarily invested in futures contracts pegged to the Nikkei-225, a major index of Japanese stocks, on both the Osaka futures market and the Singapore International Monetary Exchange. The basic objective of his trading was arbitrage--that is, taking advantage of differences in price of the instruments traded in the two markets. As basically defined, arbitrage is not particularly risky. However, Leeson began to take "bets" that the Nikkei-225 would increase by taking one-sided (long) positions in futures contracts on the index. That is, Leeson bought futures contracts. The falling index created losses that Barings could not sustain. The assets of the firm were sold in order to cover the losses.

Barings was purchased by ING Group of the Netherlands. The transaction transferred the rights to the Barings name to ING, along with Baring

Brothers & Company, Limited and Baring Securities Limited. The new companies--as wholly owned subsidiaries of ING Group--are Barings Bank Limited and Barings Securities International Limited. The ING Group also acquired Baring Securities (Japan) Limited and Baring Futures (Singapore) Pte. Limited.

The haunting question is "why" this would have occurred. It is exceedingly clear that Leeson overstepped acceptable trading limits and administrative powers.

- In the span of three weeks, he bought enough futures and options contracts to amass a $27 billion "bet."
- When the Japanese stock market did not move in the anticipated direction, Leeson sold put and call options to raise cash to meet margin calls from his long Nikkei-225 positions.
- When losses mounted to $700 million, too high to cover with option writing, the margin calls were met by Barings. Apparently, the London office was given fraudulent information that the funds were necessary to cover a client position until funds were deposited.
- Leeson was permitted to be both trader and manager, often settling his own trades. This was in violation of Osaka Exchang e regulation and industry practice: traders must always be kept separate from back-office operations.
- In the final tally, the losses amounted to $1.2 billion.

The internal controls within Barings were grossly inadequate. Certain measures could have averted the crises:

- There were no informal communications links with the exchanges.
- There were no random checks by internal auditors.
- There was no inquiry by Barings management as to the reason that trading volume was soaring.

Under the new Capital Adequacy Directive of the European Union, special risk-management units are required to perform those functions sadly not performed in the case of Barings. This episode will long be an example of why such controls are necessary in European banking or any financial services regulatory structure.

The New Financial Services Authority and Future Directions

The Financial Services Authority is the umbrella organization that now oversees the financial services sector of the United Kingdom. The structure of the Authority underscores the importance of close coordination between regulators and financial service providers. In this single agency, the banking, insurance, and securities industries of the United Kingdom will be regulated.

The style and process of regulation of the FSA are based on the following:

- ***Risk-based Approach***. The FSA will adopt a flexible and differentiated risk-based approach to setting standards and to supervision, reflecting the nature of the business activities concerned, the extent of risk within particular firms and markets, the quality of firms' management controls and the relative sophistication of the consumers involved. The FSA will ensure that appropriate distinctions are made between the regulation of wholesale and retail business, reflecting the varying expertise of consumers and their relative need of protection.
- ***Senior Management Responsibility***. The FSA will look to the Boards and senior management of regulated firms to ensure financial soundness and proper conduct of their business in accordance with regulatory requirements, by acting with prudence and integrity, by developing and operating effective governance structures, systems and controls, and by ensuring that staff are competent.
- ***Promoting a commitment to high standards***. The FSA will seek to promote throughout regulated firms and markets recognition of, and compliance with, the standards expected of them.
- ***Consistency in authorization***. The FSA will adopt a consistent and coordinated approach to authorization of firms and individuals across the range of business it regulates.
- ***Enforcing standards***. Where expected standards are not met, the FSA will use its intervention and enforcement powers to secure, as appropriate, remedial action and discipline.

The role of practitioners in the industry is also emphasized in the FSA.

The FSA will seek to ensure that its staff is "market aware" since the FSA staff will be close to the markets that they regulate. In addition, the FSA sees that the practitioners have an important role in the regulatory process. Specifically, practitioner input will help FSA:

- Formulate sensible policies and improve FSA decision-making.

- React promptly and appropriately to new products or practices and to market intelligence.
- Practice efficient, cost-effective, proportionate and practicable regulation, in the interests of regulated firms, markets and their customers.
- Avoid unnecessarily inhibiting innovation or impeding firms in serving their customer.
- Engender industry confidence in the fairness and quality of the FSA's exercise of powers.
- Help to secure the understanding and commitment of the regulated community, and thereby to achieve an industry culture of high standards.

FSA will implement this practitioner input by several means:

- As a matter of routine, consulting publicly on significant proposals for regulatory change, and, whenever possible, with interested parties at a formative stage.
- Maintaining close working relationships with trade associations, interest groups.

A high level practitioner group is to provide feedback on the impact FSA is having on the financial services industry. The group will be composed of senior individuals drawn from the regulated industry, and of a caliber that would command wide authority. This high-level group would meet periodically with the Chairman and members of the Board of FSA.

Given the history of regulation in the United Kingdom, the FSA is a natural outgrowth of a long tradition of cooperation between financial services and the official entities charged with overseeing them.

Future Indications

It is often said that the stock market is a leading indicator of a country's economic vitality. If this is true, the economic future of the United Kingdom appears bright. There are definite indications that British industry will realize long-term benefits from privatization and financial service liberalization.

In total, the market capitalization of all British firms listed on the London Stock Exchange exceeds the combined total of the markets of Paris, Milan, Frankfurt, and other German regional markets. The London Stock Exchange is the largest and most important in Europe.

A number of recently privatized companies and banks are listed on the London Stock Exchange and also have international investment following: British Airways, Enterprise Oil, British Aerospace, British Telecommunications, British Petroleum, British Gas, and Cable & Wireless. These once state-run companies are now active participants in the world of international, private capital.

The banking firms of Barclays, National Westminster, and Lloyds are among the top British firms. British banks enjoy a wide scope of activities, and have the ability to branch not only nationwide but throughout the Single European Market. Clearly, there have been challenges associated with blending the cultures of investment and commercial banking, while at the same time participating in the privatization of major British industries. Nevertheless, British banks have been correctly positioned to grow and prosper in the future.

Selected References

"Bank Branches: Hidden Jewels," *The Economist*, January 9, 1993, pp. 71-72.

Deane, Marjorie. "British Banking Blues," *International Management*, June 1991, pp. 40-41.

Department of Trade and Industry and the Central Office of Information. *Europe 1992: The Facts*, London: Author, 1989.

Dermine, Jean, Editor. *European Banking in the 1990s*, Oxford, United Kingdom: Basil Blackwell, Ltd., 1990.

Green, Edwin. *Banking: An Illustrated History*, New York: Rizzoli International Publications, Inc., 1989.

Grilli, Vittorio. "Europe 1992: Issues and Prospects for the Financial Markets," *Economic Policy: A European Forum*, vol. 4, no. 2 (October 1989), pp. 388-411.

Hemming, Richard and Ali M. Mansoor. *Privatization and Public Enterprises*, Washington, D.C.: International Monetary Fund, 1988.

Hilton, Anthony. *City Within a State: A Portrait of Britain's Financial World*, London: I.B. Tauris & Co., Ltd., 1987.

Horovitz, Jacques Henri. *Top Management Control in Europe*, New York: St. Martin's Press, 1980.

Keith, Peter. "EMU Bears a German Mark: The Bundesbank Wields Its Might at Maastricht," *Harvard International Review*, Summer 1992, pp. 38-39, 52.

Melcher, Richard A. "Britain's Rather Good Show," *Business Week*, July 13, 1992, pp. 50-108.

Mullineux, A.W. *U.K. Banking After Deregulation*, London: Croom Helm, Ltd., 1987.

Nickel, Karen. "Stock Trading Without Borders," *Fortune*, December 2, 1991, pp. 157-160.

Reich, Robert. *The Work of Nations: Preparing Ourselves for 21st Century Capitalism*, New York: Vintage Books/Random House, 1992.

Smith, Roy C. *The Global Bankers*, New York: Truman Talley Books/Plume/Penguin, 1990.

"A Stormy Passage to Profit (Eurotunnel)," *The Economist*, April 30, 1994, p. 73-74.

Ziegler, Philip. *The Sixth Great Power*, New York: Alfred A. Knopf, 1988.

3. Dedicated Capital in Germany

Introduction

Throughout the 20th century, German banks have provided financing for an economy whose population is roughly one-quarter that of the United States, but which, by the 1980s, consistently challenged U.S. export productivity. The German system illustrates how a country that has been confronted by extremely difficult economic circumstances can create an environment of consensus-building, focus on technical competence, make solid long-term investment decisions, and achieve one of the highest standards of living for its citizens. While names such as Daimler-Benz and Siemens come to mind when the topic of German business is raised, it is the small- and medium-size companies, the less well known *Mittelstand*, that differentiate the German business landscape from that of the United States. These companies have perfected the science of customer-oriented engineering and have avoided concentrating on short-term outcomes for their survival. At the center of this system are German banks, providing debt and equity financing, technical assistance, and strategic guidance. All elements of the banking system--the large banks, the savings, and the cooperatives--are now evolving into "universal banks" that can offer every financial service for every customer. Furthermore, the support of the banking system extends beyond domestic matters, as "house banks" make and keep commitments to help their business clients expand internationally. Indeed, on the political front, without the support of the banking community, especially the big banks, the monetary unification of East and West Germany would have been almost impossible.

Setting the Stage for Economic Development

Interestingly, the Germans were not considered promising candidates for economic domination in any sense of the word during the mid 1800s. The country had not yet been unified and was considerably slower than the United Kingdom to industrialize. It possessed relatively little in the way of natural resources, much of which was in the form of coal reserves in the Ruhr region (northwest region of the former West Germany, where the cities of Essen and Dortmund are now located) and in what would later become East Germany.

But Germany possessed another resource that facilitated its industrial growth--a population with a strong work ethic, a virtual obsession with science, and a strong educational focus. In fact, the world's first graduate schools, complete with doctoral degrees that required original research, were in Germany. U.S. universities followed this model for graduate education, beginning with Yale University in 1861. Thus, Germany is often considered the birthplace of modern science and this tradition has been upheld throughout the 20th century.

After German unification in 1871, there was generally more capital available in Germany than was put to productive use. Those with resources often elected not to invest in entrepreneurial ventures, but chose the safer, albeit less profitable, avenue of investing in various government securities. Landgrave William, the German prince whose financial dealings were the foundation upon which the Rothschild dynasty was built, is a notable example. The German creditbanks were formed to address this deficiency in finance for industry. These banks were to gain the confidence of those with funds to invest and to guide the investors to sound industrial projects in need of financing. An example can be found in the charter of one of the first such institutions. The objective of the new creditbank was: [5]

> to bring about or participate in the promotion of new companies, the amalgamation or consolidation of different companies, and the transformation of industrial undertakings into joint stock form; also to issue or take over for its own account the shares and debentures of such newly created companies.

These new banks would help create new joint stock companies (limited liability corporations), orchestrate mergers and acquisitions of existing firms, transform partnerships into corporations, underwrite stocks and bonds, and become shareholders in new companies.

---

[5] This is part of the original statutes of Bank für Handel und Industrie (see Whale, p. 12.).

This was not to suggest that the creditbanks were forgoing any of the other banking activities that were common at the time. The first annual report of another creditbank spoke to the breadth of that institution's banking mission:[6]

> Its (the bank's) organs at home and abroad shall facilitate the export trade and the thousand other relations between German industry and the money market. It has the right and duty to transfer the capital which one industrialist has temporarily to spare to another who is at the same time in need of it, and by this continual interchange to stimulate and increase industrial activity.

It is clear that the concept of *universal banking* (providing all forms of banking services) had early origins in Germany.

The 1870 charter of the Deutsche Bank, today Germany's largest bank, stated that the bank was "to carry on banking transactions of every description, in particular to further and facilitate the trading relations between Germany, the other European countries and overseas markets. [7] All three of the large German universal banks--Deutsche Bank, Dresdner Bank, and Commerzbank--began operations during this period. They facilitated overseas trade by first accepting bills of exchange and later establishing branches in overseas locations in Latin America and Asia.

In terms of promoting specific companies, the large universal banks followed one of two approaches. The first was for the bank to offer to the public the stock of a firm, while also purchasing some portion of the stock for its own account. Through this subscription method, both the promoters and the public helped bring the new company into existence. This is equivalent to the method used in England and, later, in the United States. The second method was for the promoter of the firm to buy all of the stock initially and then, at a subsequent date, sell stock to the public.

Some of the first German firms, such as the railroads, were promoted using the subscription method. Later offerings, however, were brought to market using almost exclusively the second approach because of certain aspects of German law with respect to securities issues and stock exchange listings.

- Each new joint stock issue had to be fully subscribed and at least 25% paid before a company could come into existence. Furthermore, in order for the issue to be permitted to go forward, the full subscription

---

[6] This is a quotation from the first annual report of the Darmstädter Bank (see Whale, p. 14).

[7] See Whale, p.16.

had to be completed within the time period specified in the prospectus (document provided to the public with all relevant details of the offering).

- When a joint stock company was formed to take over an existing private firm (usually a partnership), the new corporation was required to operate for a full year and release financial statements before its shares could be publicly traded on the stock exchange.

These rules were put in place to ensure a certain amount of orderliness in the German stock market and to discourage undue speculation in new shares that did not yet have a tract record. But the rules also made it necessary for large blocks of stock to be purchased rather quickly and, in the case of the incorporation of former partnerships, held for a considerable length of time. The larger banks with substantial resources to commit were an integral part of this system, with the second method of company promotion--banks buying shares to be subsequently offered to the public--becoming the standard method of German industrial stock issuance. Although such investments by banks generally were not made for long-term purposes, these universal banks became very large shareholders in German industry almost from the beginning of that country's industrial development.

Also, almost from the beginning, the banks did not hesitate to exercise a certain amount of influence over the industrial firms. In 1900, Dresdner Bank reacted to certain plans of one of its industrial clients, the North West German Cement Syndicate, with which the bank disagreed. The bank informed the company:

> On this ground we are regretfully obliged herewith to withdraw the credit granted to you; accordingly we ask you to make no more further drafts on us and at the same time politely request that you will repay the balance due to us, at the latest by the end of the month. [8]

Of course, if West German Cement relented, not only would the current loans not be called, but the company would be able to receive new loans. This example helps to illustrate the extent to which German banks have done more than simply protect their own financial interests; they also have acted to guide the direction of German industry.

The extent of German bank intervention in industrial policy is sometimes criticized, particularly by U.S. observers who are more accustomed to an arms-length relationship between banking and industry. At

---

[8] See Whale, p. 53.

the same time, it is difficult to argue with the success that German industrial firms have enjoyed as a result of this close relationship. It is even more difficult to argue with this success when one considers the extremely difficult economic obstacles that banking and industry have had to overcome during the last four decades.

A Post War Economic Miracle

Western Germany now boasts per capita GNP that is roughly the same as that of the United States. However, at the end of World War II, the German economy was in total disarray and factories were being dismantled to satisfy reparations requirements. The most immediate problem was how mass starvation could be avoided. Starting from this dismal position, the German people reassembled the country's manufacturing infrastructure through a system of specialization that reduced the competition between companies. They were not competing with each other as much as they were competing with the rest of the world. Companies, both large and small, built world-class manufacturing capacity with the help of German banks.

Reforming the System After the War

In 1945, Germany was a desolate place to live, with housing and food in short supply. Productive capacity had been destroyed by Allied bombing during the war. Eight percent of manufacturing facilities that had been spared from the bombing was being dismantled to satisfy war reparations, especially by the Russians. In total, 15 to 20 percent of Germany's industrial plant and equipment were lost. The most important industrial center, the Ruhr region, suffered the greatest loss--a full 25 percent of manufacturing capacity. Clearly, rebuilding Germany would require the coordination of efforts of all sectors of the economy--government, labor, management, and banking.

The *political system* that emerged from the 1949 German constitution gave the country more political stability than would have been possible under a purely democratic government. It was recognized that growth in the business sector could not be achieved if the government were allowed to be destabilized as it had been. Under the new system, a minority party could not gain a foothold into the Parliament unless it won 5 percent of the popular vote. The President, elected by popular vote, was given primarily ceremonial duties. Most power rested with the Chancellor and he could receive a vote of no confidence in Parliament only if there was also simultaneous agreement as to the Chancellor's successor. This system provided the kind of stability that Germany needed to rebuild its economy.

The *trade union system* was revamped to give it more power. Before the war, there were over 200 unions that the Nazi government dissolved and replaced with its own union. The pre-war unions had been too splintered to resist. After the war, this condition was remedied by forming one central umbrella union organization with 16 individual unions. Each of the 16 represented a specific industry--all skills, grades, and areas of specialization. The new structure was strong enough to exercise control over its members and to present a united front to management. In fact, the unions are an important part of the oversight of industrial firms in Germany through their participation in Supervisory Boards.

The *management* of German companies is characterized by a two-tiered board system: the Executive Board (Vorstand) and the Supervisory Board (Aufsichtsrat). The Executive Board is the primary decision-making body, consisting of full-time salaried executives of the firm. A typical Vorstand has a chairman and eight other members--from Production, Finance, Industrial Relations, Purchasing, Public Relations, Legal Affairs, Marketing, and Product Development. The Chairman of the Board is *primus inter pares* or first among equals. As *Sprecher* or Speaker, he is more a spokesperson than a chief executive in the U.S. sense of the word. The Executive Board acts as a unit and decisions are made jointly through a process of consensus-building. The result is that decisions are embraced more enthusiastically than they would be if forced by the will of one chief executive.

It is also interesting to note that product development and production occupy full board positions, unlike comparable firms in the United Kingdom or the United States. The actual processes of design and engineering are emphasized to a great extent because German firms strive to perfect the manufacturing process, with a focus on scientific excellence that has been long been a tradition in that country.

Seats on the Supervisory Board are equally divided between shareholder representatives and, since the end of World War II, employees. All major financial decisions are subject to the consent of this Supervisory Board. Because banks own such a large share of corporate stock, the seats allocated to shareholders on the board are largely occupied by bank executives. Thus, German banks have direct influence on any major financial undertaking of the company. This is decidedly unlike the U.S. case in which banks may not own stock of industrial firms and certainly may not occupy their board seats. Moreover, the German banks wield more influence than that is implied by bank ownership of stock. In many cases, shareholders place their stock in industrial firms on deposit with banks and give those banks the power to vote the shares. Banks then hold the combined influence of loans granted to a firm, shares of stock held directly, seats on the Supervisory Board, and shares of stock held on the behalf of others.

While the extent of the power of German banks has been an alien concept in the United States during the last 60 years (after enactment of the Glass-Steagall Act), the benefits are real. German industrial firms have a reliable source of long-term funding. This makes it possible to make long-term decisions while avoiding the tyranny of short-term profits that shareholders, who are less intimately involved with the company, sometimes demand.

In the German system of *codetermination*, labor, management, and banks work together for the betterment of the firm. Within each company of more than five employees, a *works council* (elected by the workers) must be organized and maintained. Codetermination rules were put in place after World War II to reduce the likelihood that the company could be taken over by a totalitarian management team, as was suspected to have occurred during the war in some cases. Although they are officially nonunion, the works councils are closely tied to the country's organized labor movement. The works council must *consent* to the appointment of workers to new positions, internal transfers of workers, transfers between wage groups, filing newly created posts (internally), dismissals, and even the beginning and ending of the work day. The works council has the right to be *consulted* in the decisions that relate to closing plants, opening new plants, or transferring workers between plants. The works council must be *informed* about the economic performance of the company--sales, investments, and profits.

Insights into the German Company

The codetermination system has some interesting effects. There are fewer class distinctions that can be found in the British system, for example. Labor leaders and management executives cannot be distinguished by outward appearance; workers and managers alike carry briefcases, drive the same kind of cars, and eat together in the company canteen. In terms of the substance of work and decision making, meetings are attended by all ranks of employees--from clerks to managers who report directly to the Executive Board. The skilled workers actively participate in any discussion with respect to the purchase of new equipment, for example, and their comments are listened to by the engineering Ph.D.s in attendance.

The mutual respect of lower level employees is not accidental. Germany has a very strong vocational education program that prepares workers for specific jobs after their basic education in the public school system. More than 500,000 companies offer apprenticeships in over 400 "officially recognized" professions. This training is not mandated by law, but all of the larger companies and most of the smaller companies provide it. There are separate facilities for these apprentices--workshops, classrooms, a gymnasium, and recreational facilities. If a company is small, it will often share facilities with other companies. Each apprentice receives an education not only in the specific job that he or she will perform, but also learns how that job fits into the larger picture of the final product and the firm's performance as a whole. For example, a future car mechanic learns everything from the engineering concepts of a car to the environmental risks associated with car fluids and components. The overall approach of a German firm is that there will be no weak links. Every employee will be an educated and competent member of the company.

This focus on educational competence is perhaps better understood when the composition of the German management teams is examined. The predominant training of German managers is in the area of engineering, law, and economics. Given the country's tradition of scientific excellence, it is perhaps not surprising that engineering has been the most common field of study for German managers for many decades. Shortly after World War II, 36 percent of all managers were engineers by training, 19 percent were lawyers, and 17 percent had studied economics. By the 1970s, these percentages for engineers, lawyers, and economists were 61, 22, and 14 percent, respectively. Thus, German business is increasingly more likely to be run by an engineer, in many cases one with a Ph.D. in his field. The technical quality of products receives a great deal of attention and it is felt that quality can only be maintained when the work force has a high degree of technical competence.

Not only does the German firm place a high value on the development of human capital, but the actual number of employees is a source of pride. The number of jobs that a company provides is as important as its sales volume or profitability. When *Allgemeine Zeitung*, one of the leading German financial newspapers ranks firms each year, the criteria used for the ranking include sales, profits, and number of jobs. The headline of a story describing the current year's ranking could easily celebrate the number of new jobs that the company provided as the most noteworthy facet of its performance for the year. The attitude is quite different in the United States where such results would hardly be considered worthy of so much attention.

The general feeling is that German managers and workers will sink or swim together. It is more than a matter of profits; it is also a matter of self-esteem. When managers are asked what makes them proud of their firms they are likely to respond, first, with answers about the quality of their product and, then, in terms of the number of orders and exports, and, last, in terms of profits, turnover, or market share. This spirit of pride extends beyond the firm itself. German firms are considered national assets, to remain in the hands of Germans if at all possible. Because German banks hold so much stock in industrial firms, a company's shares are more likely to be in "friendly" hands than is the case in the United States. This makes hostile takeovers more difficult in Germany than in either the United States or the United Kingdom. (Of course, German companies do have foreign shareholders, a trend that began to accelerate during the 1970s when the wealth of Arab oil-exporting countries mushroomed overnight. In fact, a healthy merger and acquisition business currently is developing within Germany. However, by and large German firms are owned by Germans.)

Thus, a stable German government provides a conducive climate for industrial development. The focus of the German firm is on product quality, with the goal of technical perfection. Decisions within the firm are made with the consent and advice of workers, managers, and bankers. This system has been an important element in fostering firms, both large and small, that have undeniably achieved international competitiveness.

Two Forms of Development

There are essentially two models in which German firms have developed--both of which depended on the support of the banking community. The large firm model is to be distinguished from that model which gave rise to a number of small- and medium-size firms, or *Mittelstand* companies.

The Large Firm Model

The development of large companies was concentrated in the Ruhr Valley, in the northern state of Westphalia, and in the old trading cities of Hanover, Kassel, Nuremberg, Augsburg, and Munich. These were generally poor agricultural regions in which there was not even a handicraft type of business infrastructure. This necessitated the construction of all the stages of production within the company itself. Of course, these firms required massive amounts of resources to develop such networks; close relationships with the large universal banks made this growth possible. The firms originally produced large machinery such as locomotives or steel-making equipment and later diversified into other areas of machinery manufacture to ensure continuity of revenues and stability of employment.

Unlike the U.S. and British counterparts, however, these large German concerns did not rely solely on mass production of their manufacturing output. The European markets were so dissimilar that producing one type of machinery that could be successfully marketed in all European countries would have severely restricted their market share. As a result, these firms consistently adapted technology so that they also might occupy specialized market niches. This meant that the large German companies needed to be able to produce high-quality products in short runs. It also meant that employees must be skillfully trained so as to be adaptable to any changing product specifications. These large firms, then, thrived by being able to reorganize quickly.

From an outside vantage point, fast changes that are required by a market niche strategy could be disquieting. If a company's financial backing is more removed and widely held variety, shareholders can become impatient with what seems to be a lack of stability in some product lines. On the other hand, when the shareholders are involved in the decision making process and understand the dynamics of the industry and the market in which the firm operates, it becomes less necessary to chart those courses that involve predictability of outcome and easier to select the alternatives that will benefit the firm as a whole. As major shareholders of German industry, the larger universal banks have provided the more focused type of financial backing.

It should be noted that the large holdings by German banks of the shares of their industrial clients is partly attributable to rescue efforts of these companies during the inter-war depression and immediately after World War II. However, these rescues do not explain the full extent of equity ownership by banks. These universal banks are as comfortable as shareholders as they are as lenders.

Deutsche Bank is the largest German bank and the largest shareholder. A partial list of its holdings (and industries) includes: Daimler-Benz (automotives), Allianz (Europe's largest insurance company), Munich Re (world's largest re-insurance company), Karstadt (trading company), Philip Holzmann (construction), Heidelberger Zement (construction materials), Hapag Lloyd (shipping), and Metallgesellschaft (industrial group). In addition, managers of Deutsche Bank occupy more than 400 seats on the Supervisory Boards of other German groups.

The philosophy of the leadership of this bank clearly has had a substantial impact on the evolution of German industry. Until the 1980s, Deutsche Bank rarely made investments outside West Germany and did not even use its own name for the Berlin subsidiary. The bank had always adopted a long-term perspective, but the executives, who had run the bank were (perhaps understandably) cautious. Modest outside investment was usually accomplished through subsidiaries or consortium (joint-venture) banks.

Beginning in 1986, the goal shifted from preparing Deutsche Bank for the Single European Market and the 1990s to preparation for the 21st century. The bank became entrepreneurial once again, taking large risks. In 1986, Deutsche Bank bought the English merchant bank, Morgan Grenfell. Despite the fact that the price for the acquisition stunned the London financial community, it had a minimal effect on the bank's balance sheet. In fact, the bank financed the purchase by selling part of its bond portfolio. Earnings automatically improved because Morgan Grenfell's profit after tax exceeded the after-tax yield of the bonds that had been sold. The bank has further diversified by establishing its own life insurance subsidiary, by buying the management consulting firm of Roland Berger, and by buying 80 percent of the prestigious private Berlin bank Grunelius (founded in 1824).

In overseas purchases subsequent to the Morgan Grenfell buyout, Deutsche Bank bought out its partners' shares in European Asian Bank (a consortium bank) and extended the branch network to India, Indonesia, and Japan to keep pace with the expanding opportunities in this region. It acquired Banca d'America d'Italia (Bank of America's 105-branch Italian subsidiary) and the Vienna-based private bank Antoni Hacker. Deutsche Bank also continued to expand its overseas ownership of securities firms by purchasing Canadian stockbroker McLean McCarthy, and 50 percent of Australian broker Bain and Company. By the early 1990s, the bank had a presence in 30 foreign countries through a network of more than 325 branches, subsidiaries, and representative offices.

In extending its universal banking practices to international operations, Deutsche Bank still must achieve a certain level of maturity. Even before the purchase of Morgan Grenfell, the London subsidiary (Deutsche Bank Capital Markets) did not always work well with Frankfurt headquarters, perhaps because the London operation frequently operated in the red. As has been the case in the combination of U.K. merchant banks with U.K. clearing banks, the blending of the two cultures of investment and commercial banking is not always easy.

Nevertheless, Deutsche Bank remains committed not only to merging the two cultures of investment and commercial banking, but also to have a major presence in the insurance industry to tap into this base of savings and income-enhancing possibilities. Its stakes in Allianz and Munich Re are indications of this intent. With its commercial and investment banking operations, insurance holdings, and management consulting subsidiary, Roland Burger, Deutsche Bank now reaches beyond the domain of universal banking into the realm of *Allfinanz*. Every conceivable financial service can be found within the Deutsche Bank organization.

The Mittelstand Model

While the large firms tended to develop in the Ruhr region and in traditional trading centers, the growth of smaller firms was concentrated primarily in Baden-Württemberg--in the southwest region of the country--and in the Rhineland, west and south of the Ruhr region. In these regions, there was a preindustrial infrastructure of craft skills. As a result, there was not as much pressure for a company to grow quickly in such a way as to provide all of its vertical needs (for example, raw materials, supplies, and packaging). Most firms remained small or medium-sized and usually family-owned. Since these firms did not incorporate all facets of production within their own operations, capital costs were correspondingly lower. The large universal banks were, therefore, not the initial source of financing. Instead, the companies pooled funds within the community, forming cooperative banks, similar to credit unions. The depositors in these institutions were owners of the cooperatives and received loans when needed, in exchange for leaving their funds on deposit to be borrowed by other members of the cooperative at other times. Only when the firms began to export their goods did they begin to use the services of the universal banks.

These small companies could not become at all involved in mass production. Niche markets and flexibility were vitally important to their survival. Trained workers were perhaps even more important for them than for the bigger companies, and sincere respect for skilled labor was no less a part of the operation of these firms.

However, there was a more significant difference. A larger firm has its administrative mechanism within the company, including decision making with respect to product, pricing, and expense control. In the case of smaller German firms, the maintenance of orderly markets, the proper distribution of technical knowledge, the correct allocation of materials, and the balance of competitive forces were accomplished through the relationships among firms and government entities. By their nature, these craft-based, general-purpose machinery firms were flexible in terms of their product output. If they had been allowed to compete to the full extent, they could have driven each other out of business. Instead, they agreed to operate within their acknowledged fields of specialty, coordinating their lines of business with other enterprises within their community. The process essentially involved balancing the individual interest of the firm with the long-term interests of the industry and the community as a whole. As the industrial infrastructure of these regions grew, they began to attract larger companies that wished to take advantage of the wide product selection that was concentrated within a small geographic area.

To maintain a good negotiating position in terms of its claim on a particular specialty, each firm was compelled to remain technologically up-to-date. A number of institutions were formed (and still operate) to help accomplish the coordination of technology transfer and the risk sharing implicit in this specialization scheme. Trade associations and the Chambers of Commerce and Industry provide a forum for the negotiations, help coordinate joint research projects, and ensure that local universities are properly equipped for the necessary research. Public research institutes pool separate resources of many individual firms and provide technical information on a continuous basis that would not be available if each company sought to gather the information on its own. Over time the responsibility for these public research institutes has been assumed by the government, but they continue to play a central role in the applied research and in training technicians and engineers.

Trade associations in the United States tend either to operate defensively in an attempt to limit government intervention (that is, regulation) or to lobby for special favors from government (through legislation). German trade associations make a much more strategic contribution to the country's industrial policy and direction. A significant contribution of German trade associations has been provision of funds for research and development. Another important role has been fostering stable, long-term relationships between smaller companies and local banks.

It is from this environment that the *Mittelstand* companies grew. Mittelstand companies arose primarily from the individual or family-owned businesses in the craft tradition. Because of the tradition of specializing within a particular product line, these businesses are usually fairly stable. More often than not they are run by an individual rather than by supervisory and executive boards. In fact, 80 percent of them are privately held. They are the small- and medium-size businesses of Germany--defined as those companies that have less than 500 employees and annual sales of less than DM100 million. Together, Mittelstand companies are responsible for one half of total German output and employ two thirds of all German workers. However, *Mittelstand* is more a spirit in Germany than a statistical definition. In fact, some owners of companies with thousands of employees and over DM1 billion in sales still claim to be part of the Mittelstand.

Although relatively small in size, the Mittelstand have a significant role in national policy making. The BDI (Bundesverband der Deutschen Industrie) is an umbrella group of various industrial trade associations. The permanent administrative committee of the BDI includes the heads of large public companies (such as Volkswagen and Siemens), but the president of the BDI is always a representative of a Mittelstand company. The government routinely consults the leaders of the BDI on matters that involve the business community or government/business policy. On a less formal basis, former Chancellor Helmut Kohl consulted with the heads of various trade associations every few weeks to discuss current topics. For example, during the period prior to unification, Kohl met with trade association representatives from the Mittelstand to determine the measures that would be necessary to spur investment in Eastern Germany.

Mittelstand companies complement the large German corporations and have contributed much to the high standard of living enjoyed by residents of Western Germany. Their growth, as well as that of the larger companies, has been facilitated to a great extent by the German banking system, which itself continues to evolve.

The Growth of Universal Banking in the German Economy

Shortly after World War II, the large universal banks in Germany concentrated on rebuilding the economic infrastructure. The large banks, more than the civil authorities, drew up plans and estimated financial needs of reconstruction. Savings banks, regional banks, and cooperative banks served the relatively meager needs of families and small businesses. Immediately after the war, families required housing finance for the most part because of the devastation. Small business had modest requirements for inventory and other capital because the firms in this sector continued to concentrate on the developing domestic market.

But by the end of the 1960s, three major developments helped to pave the way for the expansion of universal banking activities.

- Individual incomes had risen to the point that the housing needs of families had been largely satisfied. Individuals now needed more long-term vehicles for investment and new forms of consumer credit.
- The regulation of interest rates ended in 1967. Since the 1930s, loan and deposit interest rates had been tied to the discount rate (rate charged by the central bank to banks that borrow from it). Interest rate regulation had provided banks with a built-in spread (difference between rate earned and rate paid for funds). After 1967, rates were permitted to find their own level.
- As German industrial companies expanded their overseas operations, German banks were forced to become more involved in international banking activities.

These three developments meant that there were increasing long-term financial requirements from the individual sector, that competition among banks would necessarily increase because bank services no longer would be priced the same, and even the smaller companies (by now the Mittelstand variety) would require more extensive financial services.

By the second half of the 1950s, the government had begun to allow banks to expand their individual client business. For example, the public needs test for a new branch was dropped. This meant that it was no longer necessary for a bank to prove that there existed a "public need" for a proposed new branch. Predictably, the branch networks of all banks increased significantly. Many of these new branches were created by buying existing financial institutions, causing a consolidation in the financial services industry. In 1959, a loan for personal use (the Kleinkredit) was introduced and soon followed by a wide variety of consumer banking products. In the late 1950s, savings banks introduced checking accounts to handle the volume of wage and salary payments now originating from the consumer sector. Within ten years of their introduction, checking accounts were used by 80 percent of the working population.

As a result of this expansion of consumer funds, commercial and savings banks had a greater volume of liquidity to manage. That the expansion was in the form of consumer deposits meant that the funds were more stable, that is, less subject to rapid withdrawal. Savings banks, regional banks, and credit cooperatives began to offer Mittelstand (and even larger companies) loan and other financial services on a competitive basis.

Today, more than 75 percent of all German banking institutions are involved in universal banking. Virtually all forms of services can be obtained by a consumer or a business at either a branch office or at headquarters. These services also include insurance, a practice that is prohibited for U.S. banks with only rare exceptions. Insurance products enable banks to offer individuals a wider variety of long-term investment options at rates that may be more attractive than the rate paid on savings accounts. As noted earlier, the concept of *Allfinanz* is rapidly being realized in Germany. Insurance companies and banks have signed contracts to cross-market the products of their individual companies. The more consolidated banking industry can offer all these products in efficient branch networks throughout the country.

Other changes are also emerging as Deutsche Bank, Dresdner Bank, and Commerzbank have been joined by other universal financial institutions. There is a trend toward the "network" approach to financing. The traditional German banking model involves the *Hausbank* or House Bank that provides all financial services for a client company. In the network model, several banks join together informally to provide funding for a network of several industrial firms. Network bank representatives sit on the Supervisory Boards of network industrial firms. In turn, network industrial firm representatives sit on the Supervisory Boards of network banks. This is very similar to the Japanese *keiretsu* arrangement in that there are interlocking relationships between a range of firms and financial institutions.

The network model provides the Mittelstand company with long-term financing that is, at the same time, more flexible since a number of banks are included in the network. In fact, network banks work to build strategic links between smaller companies that will benefit their respective developments while enabling them to compete more effectively than would otherwise be the case. This approach to industry consolidation and deregulation has enabled German banks to avoid some of the painfully speculative adjustments that were experienced during the Big Bang in the United Kingdom and the 1980s deregulation of the savings and loan industry in the United States.

The universal banking system and now the network banking system of Germany have evolved as a response to the need for both industrial and consumer finance. Government has been supportive by encouraging coordinated specialization among firms and by funding research institutes.

Conclusion

No description of German industry can be complete without reference to the German banking system. With relatively little in the way of natural resources, Germany grew by focusing on the quality of production and a skilled work force. Neither of these factors could have been adequately developed if short-term profits were the ultimate goal. Long-standing relationships with their house banks relieved companies of the immediate pressure to show a profit. Instead, they concentrated on long-term viability of product and process. The Mittelstand companies had the added advantage of coordinated specialization--a system that recognized that German companies did not compete as much with each other as they did with the rest of the industrialized world.

Understanding these strategies and maintaining a long-term perspective, German banks provided universal banking services, that is, both commercial and investment banking. The practice is now expanding into the concept of *Allfinanz* (or all finance) in which comprehensive insurance services are added to the list. The system is being strengthened further through "network" banking, by which groups of industrial companies affiliate with groups of banking firms--through loans, equity holdings, and board seats. The network arrangement is very similar to the Japanese *keiretsu* and illustrates the development of banking and industry relationships in countries with unquestioned manufacturing capabilities. The United States would be well served to observe and understand these trends in the context of its own economic circumstances.

Selected References

"The Deutsche Bank Juggernaut Will Keep on Rolling," *Euromoney*, January 1990, pp. 33-44.

Fahrholz, Bernd. "Buy-Outs in Germany," *European Management Journal*, vol. 9, no. 1 (March 1991), pp. 60-64.

Glouchevitch, Philip. *Juggernaut; The German Way of Business: Why It Is Transforming Europe--and the World*, New York: Simon and Schuster, 1992.

Katzenstein, Peter J. *Industry and Politics in West Germany: Toward the Third Republic*, Ithaca, New York: Cornell University Press, 1989.

Lawrence, Peter. *Managers and Management in West Germany*, New York: St. Martin's Press, 1980.

"The Long Wait for Rich Pickings," *Euromoney*, August 1990, pp. 51-59.

"Need the Money? Change the Tune," *Euromoney*, October 1990, pp. 36-41.

"Pass the Parcel (Franco-German Finance)." *The Economist*, January 9, 1993, pp. 69-70.

Porter, Michael. *The Competitive Advantage of Nations*, New York: The Free Press, 1990.

Reier, Sharon. "Krupp's Blitzkrieg," *Financial World*, December 10, 1991, pp. 26-28.

Savic, Bob. "Big Three See No Setback in Asia," *Asian Finance*, September 15, 1991, pp.97-100.

Simon, Hermann. "Lessons from Germany's Midsize Giants," *Harvard Business Review*, March-April 1992, pp. 115-123.

Smith, Eric Owen. "Equity Stakes: Are U.K. Banks Following the German Pattern?" *Banking World*, June 1991, pp. 28-30.

"Strained Relations Among West Germany's Big Banks," *The Economist*, September 1, 1990, pp. 67-68.

Templeman, John, Richard A. Melcher, and William Glasgall. "A Challenger for Germany's Heavyweight Banking Title," *Business Week*, August 12, 1991, pp. 36-37.

Wever, Kirsten S. and Christopher S. Allen. "Is Germany a Model for Managers?" *Harvard Business Review*, September-October 1992, pp. 36-43.

Whale, P. Barrett. *Joint Stock Banking in Germany*, New York: Augustus M. Kelley, Bookseller, 1968.

4. Formal and Informal Ties in Japan

Introduction

When the emperor was restored to power in the Meiji Restoration, Yataro Iwasaki, the 20-year-old son of a samurai family decided to leave his home in Osaka to find his fortune in Tokyo. Before leaving, he climbed Mount Moyken, the mountain behind his home, one last time and carved a message on the staircase to the Shinto shrine:

> Business nationwide is awaiting my skills. If I fail to become a great success, I swear that I will never return to climb this mountain.[9]

That was 1868 and the young man was the founder of what is now one of the largest, most diversified business organizations in the world--the Mitsubishi *keiretsu*. The outgrowth of Iwasaki's business ventures is now composed of 160 companies with 500,000 employees. In addition, there are over 700 "related firms" (primarily suppliers) that are dependent on the group. The 38 most powerful Mitsubishi companies generate sales that represent more than 7 percent of Japan's annual gross national product.

From the start of the Meiji Restoration in 1868, the Japanese began to form the first true international conglomerates with banks at the center of the groups. The Japanese government needed the help of companies to speed the country's modernization process. Companies needed the help of the government to facilitate their business undertakings. Both the government and the firms needed banks to finance the country's growth. There was never a doubt as to how their relationship would develop.

---

[9] See Kearns, p. 157.

Japan had been humiliated by the ease with which the West had penetrated their society in the mid-1800s. If national dignity was to be restored and the country was to regain control over its own destiny, Japan needed to be united for a common purpose and quickly brought up to world standards of competitiveness.

The emperor set forth The Five Articles Oath--a document that would help Japan set a deliberate course for world power. [10]

Article One:	All matters were to be decided by public discussion.
Article Two:	The Japanese people, from the emperor down to his least subject, would share one heart and would unite in an effort to achieve common objectives.
Article Three:	The central government and local warlords would share the same path. The court and commoners were equal.
Article Four:	Japan would eliminate outdated customs.
Article Five:	Japan would be receptive to knowledge and expertise from whatever source it came. Japan would send students to the United States and Europe, and would invite foreign experts to come to Japan and disseminate their knowledge to the Japanese.

Japanese society was to be characterized by unity of purpose and would seek the best and brightest from the West to help the country advance toward modernization. Government and business would walk "the same path." While the path to such unity contained many obstacles, the Five Articles Oath reveals much about the behavior of government, industry, and banking in Japan--then and now.

Early Modernization

In order to advance economically, it was widely felt that Japan must abandon its absolute concentration on Confucian studies and expand the horizon to the science and logic of the West. Since it was Commodore Matthew Perry who forced the issue of more open international relations, the United States was seen as the country that could provide the most valuable lessons. In 1881, when the

[10] See Chu, pp. 90-91.

government selected several hundred students to study in the West, over half were sent to the United States. Moreover, a government mission, begun in the same year, traveled to the United States in its quest for Western knowledge before going to Europe.

The Japanese who visited were astonished by the extent of public education in America. They came to realize that if they were to cultivate generations of Japanese that would adhere to the tenants of loyalty, justice, humanity, and decorum, they must all be properly educated. Basic education was made compulsory for everyone in Japan. Higher education was reformed to more closely resemble the U.S. model, including the more practical studies of agriculture, engineering, and medicine.

The growth of industry also could not be left to chance. The government attempted to organize merchants and other wealthy men into companies that would serve the state's industrial policies. However, the spirit of cooperation among them had not yet developed, forcing the government to initiate some of the first industrial factories, including modern cotton-spinning mills. Soon family silk farms led to the development of a silk export trade, with silk remaining the primary export of Japan until the 1930s. Thousands of young women worked under less than ideal conditions in new textile factories that were, in some cases, little more than sweatshops.

Heavy industry followed. There were government railroads, coal mines, steel mills, and shipbuilding facilities. But there were problems with the heavy industrial sector. Here, too, working conditions were difficult. Moreover, the government-run facilities were not always efficient.

In 1872, the banking system had been transformed into one that resembled the U.S. system. National bank charters enabled institutions to issue bank notes (liabilities) that were backed by government bonds (assets). As was true in Europe and the United States, these bank notes circulated as money and were originally convertible into gold or silver. Then, in order to stimulate more growth in the economy (as well as more demand for government securities), the government permitted national banks to convert their notes into government securities. This, of course, provided more money for the government to finance industry. But the easy money policy sparked inflationary fires that were not corrected until the Bank of Japan (the country's central bank) was created in 1882, the currency unified, and a large privatization program initiated.

Government industries were sold to the those merchant families that had provided financial support during the Meiji restoration--notably Mitsui,

Mitsubishi, Sumitomo and Yasuda. At this point, industrialization began to accelerate. The new industrialists capitalized on the educational reform and massive investment that had been undertaken by the government. The work force was educated, skilled, mobile--and low-cost. The government sold the businesses at modest prices and provided subsidies to ensure continued operation.

The former Japanese feudal lords (who had been financially compensated for not resisting with the Meiji Restoration) provided a strong base of private capital. In addition, the Bank of Japan had been given the sole authority of note issue and effectively became the mechanism through which funds were made available to the newly privatized industries. The Bank of Japan was selective in its attention, providing services and support primarily for those large "city" banks with ties to the merchant families that had purchased companies from the government and that were engaged in what the government considered strategic industries. These banks were located primarily in Tokyo, Osaka, Kyoto, and Yokohama. They received low cost loans from the Bank of Japan that were collateralized by (relatively illiquid) common stock in the favored industrial firms.

As a country with few natural resources, the industrialization of Japan depended in large measure on other countries for inputs for the manufacturing process. International expansion, in one sense or another, has been always been a part of Japanese industrialization. The large *zaibatsu*, as the industrialized merchant families came to be called, developed into major holding companies that pursued an agenda of expansion both domestically and overseas. At the same time, the government became increasingly militaristic in defending its right to expansion, annexing Korea and capturing Manchuria in northeast China. Eventually, Japan's involvement in World War II ended in its ultimate defeat and the forced reorganization of its economic system. Nevertheless, no amount of reorganization would break the ties that bound Japanese government, business, and banking.

Breaking Up the *Zaibatsu*

The *zaibatsu* were blamed for having provided armaments and finance during the war. During the U.S. occupation, the cartels were ordered disbanded and all the executives of the *zaibatsu* removed from office. Entire factories were moved from Japan to other Asian countries that had been overrun during the war. As a result of wartime bombing and postwar in-kind reparations, by the end of 1946 the industrial infrastructure of Japan was in shambles and there were 13 million people unemployed. The occupation forces also encouraged the formation of a strong labor union movement to act as a counterbalance against big business. The occupation consistently refused to intervene against planned strikes and worker slowdowns. Article 65 of the Japanese Securities and Exchange Act was introduced as the equivalent of the U.S. Glass-Steagall Act, separating commercial and investment banking. The Japanese economy was to be "democratized" in the American sense of the word. All of these checks and balances would presumably prevent Japan from developing companies that, because of their size and strength, were a threat to world peace.

For its part, the labor movement initially welcomed the new freedom of speech that it enjoyed. The working conditions in many of the factories and mines had been unacceptable for some time. A railroad workers' strike was barely averted in the fall of 1946 when the government capitulated to the wage demands of the workers. Only a few months later, however, the labor movement organized a general strike with strong political undertones. Unlike the U.S. labor movement, the Japanese labor movement had developed decidedly Marxist tendencies before the war. The objective of the general strike after the war was to bring down the Japanese government and to engage in a kind of class warfare against the business sector that in the past had been so contemptuous of workers' rights. Clearly, this was *not* the kind of loyalty that would later characterize the Japanese work force.

While the Allied forces sought to encourage the labor movement, it became clear that this was more than just a dispute over working conditions. General Douglas MacArthur, the Supreme Commander of the Allied forces, moved to order the strike canceled as too disruptive to the public peace and order. However, it soon became clear that if the occupation continued in the direction in which it was headed, Japan would be a prime target for Communist takeover.

The focus of the occupation changed. Democratization was less important than helping Japan regain its economic strength and independence. There was the clear threat of Communism and the burden of Marshall Plan aid to Japan continued to grow. William Draper, Undersecretary of the Army, was assigned to help develop policy that would spur real economic development. As a former investment banker from Wall Street, he and other U.S. banker/businessmen urged that the breaking up of Japanese business be reversed and inflation curbed. The Japanese government had printed money to pay wartime commitments, procurement contracts, and production loans. If, before the war, the commodity price index were set at 100, then its level would be measured at 1,800 in 1946;

5,908 in 1947; 14,956 in 1948; and 24,336 in 1949. There was too much money in circulation and too few goods and services.

Joseph Dodge, president of the Detroit Bank, was sent to Tokyo as President Truman's personal representative to implement the new occupation policy to help Japanese businesses help themselves. Dodge followed a balanced budget approach to curb inflation by insisting that the government stop subsidies to key industries and curtail the preferential lending programs that had raised production levels in coal mines and some manufacturing areas. He urged the government to abandon deficit financing and even run a surplus.

Without the subsidies and other preferential treatment, Japanese industry collapsed. Thousands of firms went bankrupt, dismissing hundreds of thousands of employees overnight. The Japanese National Railways alone terminated 100,000 employees. The inflationary spiral was broken by 1950, but the economy did not rebound until the United States became involved in the Korean conflict and placed special procurement orders in Japan of almost $600 million in 1951. Orders totaling $800 million were placed in 1952 and again in 1953.

Reestablishing Powerful Alliances

Yoshida Shigeru continued to serve as Japanese Prime Minister for two years after the occupation ended in 1952. During the occupation, he complied with the U.S. initiatives, but he never agreed with them. He believed in the basic tenets of the Meiji Restoration and the collaboration of business and government. Strong business ties had been disrupted by the occupation, but the government bureaucracy had not been because the Allied needed channels through which to operate.

As a career diplomat, Yoshida had always been opposed to the military aggressions that led the country into war. He was determined that a strong bureaucracy would prevent that from reoccurring. In 1949, Yoshida's cabinet established the Ministry of International Trade and Industry (MITI). MITI was the consolidation of the Board of Trade and the Ministry of Commerce and Industry, that is, one large central government mechanism that would control the economic direction of the country. When the occupation ended in 1952, MITI took over all the controls that General MacArthur had used to run the economy--an economy that the bureaucrats in MITI intended to "jump start."

The disassociation of the *zaibatsu* companies had been accompanied by the dismissal of all the top executives. The orders of the occupation forces stated that all "standing directors" of major Japanese companies would be removed. The Japanese bureaucracy interpreted this to mean that only managing directors and those in higher ranks need be purged. Thus, there remained many other well-trained managers that could now be moved to the top ranks of their companies. This in itself created a sense of opportunity and optimism within management ranks.

The labor front did not appear as promising--at least not right away. Still attempting to eliminate the conservative government, in 1953 the All-Japan Automobile Industry Union planned a strike on all three automakers, Toyota, Nissan, and Isuzu (not unlike a United Autoworkers Strike in the United States). Toyota and Isuzu settled quickly, but Nissan chose to fight. Nissan workers were locked out during a five-month-long strike. In the end, Nissan signed a contract with a second, company-approved union. The new "enterprise union" was one union to which all employees of the company belonged. There were no ties with industry unions. This was a major victory for management--one that had been supported strongly by the company's banks and even the other automakers. Workers were deeply shaken and left the All-Japan Automobile Industry Union in large numbers, fearing for their livelihood. This and other failed strikes during the 1950s helped to foster labor-management harmony in Japan. During the 1960s workers willingly worked within the framework of the enterprise union in exchange for job security, information sharing, and steady pay increases.

The cooperative mechanisms between government, industry, and labor were beginning to solidify. The next phase was a period of high growth in which the unification ideals of the Meiji Restoration were largely realized.

The High Growth Years

The cooperation between labor and management was an important factor in the increasing levels of productivity that began in the 1960s, but it is by no means the primary factor because Japanese government played a pivotal role. Ikeda Hayato served as Finance Minister for Japan after the war and, in 1951, created the Japan Development Bank, the Export-Import Bank, and other instruments of financial and industrial policy. The Japan Development Bank raised money through bond issues; the Bank was also given access to surplus funds accumulated from government budget surpluses and from a tax-exempt postal savings system. These funds were directed to industry for investment in manufacturing infrastructure. The Export-Import Bank provided financial support for the export of the manufactured goods and the import of necessary raw materials. In addition, in 1956 Ikeda introduced an unprecedented tax cut that stimulated both investment and consumer spending.

When Ikeda became Prime Minister in 1960, one of his first official acts was to help MITI to establish mechanisms that would protect targeted industries such as electronics, steel, and automobiles. The bureaucracy that Yoshida structured would now be used to nurture the businesses considered most important to Japan's future. MITI would offer these industries tax breaks, research and development support, and export subsidies.

The Income Doubling Plan

Ikeda drafted a blueprint for growth and development that he called the National Income Doubling Plan. The first plan objective was for the gross national product (GNP) of Japan to double in the ten years ended 1970.

By the late 1950s, Japan had greatly expanded its export of manufactured goods to the United States. On the other hand, its imports were composed primarily of food, fuel, and raw materials. Japan's industrial trade was thus composed of imports of materials that were used for manufacturing and exports of finished manufactured goods destined to developed countries, especially the United States. However, the United States faced large trade deficits that were threatening the value of the dollar--to which the values of all other currencies were tied. The available choices were for the United States to either slow its demand for foreign goods or to boost its own exports. The United States chose the latter. European countries that traded with the United States agreed to make it easier to import U.S. goods through liberalization of foreign currency exchange laws and by reducing their own subsidies for exports.

As a new member of the Organization for Economic Cooperation and Development, Japan had to do the same. [11] Trade with the United States had thus far favored the strong, established companies in Japan. Smaller and expanding businesses had difficulty obtaining the foreign currency to import the capital goods needed for investment. Liberalizing foreign currency provisions and import regulations would actually help these smaller enterprises. These provisions became part of the Income Doubling Plan.

---

[11] The Organization for Economic Cooperation and Development is an association of the major industrialized countries of the world.

The Plan contained other considerations as well. The regions of Japan that had benefitted most from economic expansion after the war were primarily along the Pacific coast--Tokyo, Yokohama, Osaka, Kobe, Nagoya, and the northern area of the island of Kyushu. The result had been excessive development of essentially four regions with underdevelopment of inland regions. The third objective of the Income Doubling Plan was to promote development in inland regions, through large scale industrial projects and the necessary infrastructure to support them.

In a somewhat related way, the fourth provision of the Plan was to improve social welfare in Japan in an attempt to bring the country up to the standards of other industrialized countries. As a result, National Social Insurance and Pension programs were developed, similar to the social security program in the United States.

It should be noted that the provisions of the Income Doubling Plan did not contradict the MITI policies of protecting targeted industries. In liberalizing imports, the industries that had been targeted for "nurturing"—steel, automobiles, and electronics—continued to receive government protection from excessive foreign competition. The government had set the stage. Industry and banking then worked together to spur even greater economic development.

The New Keiretsu

The U.S. occupation forces had disbanded the *zaibatsu* and dismissed its major executives. To further promote the democratization of business, banks were prohibited from holding more than 5 percent of the stock of any industrial corporation. But this was not the end of the associations among Japanese firms. The former holding companies were not reconstituted. Instead, one company bought a small percentage of the stock in each of the other companies in the former *zaibatsu*. Each of the other companies in the group did the same. The cumulative effect of these cross-shareholdings was that as much as 70 percent of the stock of a company was held by other related firms. In some cases, companies belonged to more than one such group. The new *keiretsu* satisfied the letter, if not the spirit, of the laws established during the U.S. occupation.

The modern *keiretsu* of Mitsubishi (160 companies), Mitsui (120 companies), and Sumitomo (130 companies) are directly descendant from the old *zaibatsu* of the same name. Fuyo (150 companies) is the offspring of the Yasuda *zaibatsu* of the 1960s. The Dai-Ichi Kangyo *keiretsu* (90 companies) is of even more recent vintage, having assembled all the necessary components in 1974--a bank, general trading company, accompanied by various business enterprises. Dai-Ichi Kangyo is an example of *keiretsu* that do not have pre-war ties. The Sanwa *keiretsu* (29 companies) is another example, having formed in the 1960s. In addition, Sanwa is distinctive in that it is more open to new firms joining its ranks than some of the older groups. Other, smaller *keiretsu* with the basic components of bank, trading company, and industrial enterprises have also formed since the war. Nevertheless, the largest are the six noted above with combined sales that currently represent 25 percent of total sales generated by all Japanese companies.

In 1953, very soon after the end of the U.S. occupation, the Antimonopoly Act raised the limit that banks could own in one industrial company from 5 percent of its stock to 10 percent. This spurred immediate increases in the investments by banks, particularly in companies located in Tokyo and other heavily industrialized areas.

Each *keiretsu* has a main bank that is either the lead firm or shares this role with a trading company. A general trading house supplies the members with raw materials and sells the finished products of the manufacturing firms on domestic and international markets. There are long-standing relationships between the industrial members of the *keiretsu* and the trading company. These relationships are negotiated, but ultimately depend on the decisions made by the trading houses and the main banks. This is not to suggest that there is no competition in Japan. In fact, the *keiretsu* engage in vigorous competition with each other. But, within a *keiretsu*, a general spirit of cooperation prevails between the industrial firms, the trading company, and the main bank.

In addition to the main bank, a *keiretsu* often contains other financial firms. The Mitsubishi *keiretsu* includes Bank of Tokyo-Mitsubishi Bank, Mitsubishi Trust and Banking, Meiji Mutual Life Insurance, and Tokio Marine and Fire Insurance. The financial members of the Sumitomo and Fuyo groups have similar designations. All those in the Sumitomo group carry the Sumitomo name. The main bank of the Fuyo group is Fuji Bank, while the other financial members have retained the Yasuda name. The Dai-Ichi Kangyo *keiretsu* is led by Dai-Ichi Kangyo Bank and the group includes two life insurance companies (Asahi Mutual Life and Fukoku Mutual Life), one fire and marine insurance company (Taisei Fire and Marine), and a joint venture leasing company (Century Leasing System). The Sanwa group has a similar mix of financial firms that do not share the same name: Sanwa Bank, Toyo Trust and Banking, Daido Mutual Life Insurance, Nippon Life Insurance, and Orient Leasing. All these large financial firms stand ready to support the members of their respective *keiretsu*.

Some of the more familiar industrial names in these six *keiretsu* include:

Keiretsu	Familiar Industrial Members
Mitsubishi	Mitsubishi Motors, Kirin Brewery
Mitsui	Toshiba Corp., Toyota Motor Co.
Sumitomo	NEC Corp.
Fuyo	Nissan Motor Co., Canon, Hitachi
Dai-Ichi Kangyo	Fujitsu, Isuzu, Hitachi
Sanwa	Sharp Corp., Daihatsu Motor Co., Suntory

Not all *keiretsu* are as large as these six. Nor are all the related firms accounted for in the formal group. The initiative in the Income Doubling Plan that addressed the need to more evenly modernize the country spurred growth within the small- and medium-size companies that were not a part of the formal cross-shareholdings of stock. These smaller firms acted as suppliers for the formal *keiretsu* firms. During the 1960s many of their large *keiretsu* clients invested in them, boosting the productivity of the smaller firms and, ultimately, the productivity of the *keiretsu* firm that used their output. Indeed, some of the smaller firms grew to worldwide recognition in their own right--including Panasonic, Sony, Honda, and Pioneer.

Coordination of Government, Industry, and Banking

All elements of the Japanese society united behind the Income Doubling Plan. The work force saw their standard of living increase by measurable degrees. During the 1950s, the consumer goods that workers obtained as rewards for their labor included radios, motorbikes, and sewing machines. During the Income Doubling 1960s, the list broadened to include refrigerators, washing machines, and television sets. During the 1970s, standards of living increased to include air conditioners, color televisions, and automobiles. Thus, labor cooperated with management to achieve whatever was best for the firm. Having white- and blue-collar workers in the same enterprise union also fostered a deep sense of loyalty.

Throughout this high-growth period, Japanese companies relied heavily on bank financing. A company's main bank, which often also held shares in the company, was focused on long-term viability instead of quarterly profits. Shareholders in general and, specifically, the banks and related companies were more interested in the perpetuation of the firm and remained content to receive low dividends so that needed capital investment could continue.

In terms of the loans that were provided to industrial *keiretsu* members, the *keiretsu* banks were consistently "overloaned" in the sense that the demand for investment capital during this high growth period always exceeded the banks' deposit and capital base. The Bank of Japan made up the shortfall in capital investment needs. These needed funds may have come from the Bank of Japan, but the "window guidance" that accompanied the funds originated with MITI. Those industries that had been targeted for growth received loans with preferential terms through their *keiretsu* banks, which, in turn, received funds from the Bank of Japan.

This system led to a close coordination of the entire economic system. It was both *necessary* and *possible* for the government to control the rate of growth in the economy. It was necessary because the Japanese economy depended on its exports. If a recession occurred in other industrialized countries, especially in the United States, the demand for Japanese exports also slumped. On the other hand, growth in the industrialized West translated into a growth stimulus in Japan.

It was possible to orchestrate such adjustments through the Bank of Japan connection. When conditions warranted, the Bank of Japan ordered the *keiretsu* banks through "window guidance" to reduce their loans. This had the effect of reducing the expansion plans of the companies in the group. (It should be noted that when excess capacity represented a serious threat, MITI generally stepped in to coordinate an orderly restructuring of the industry.) When the *keiretsu* firms cut back production they also reduced orders to the smaller firms with which they subcontracted. Thus, the interconnections of government, banking, and industry made it possible to react very quickly to changing economic circumstances.

The results of Ikeda's Income Doubling Plan speak for themselves. With the entire country united behind the Plan, Japan's 1970 GNP rose to a level that was 2.7 times the 1960 level. By the mid-1960s, Japan's GNP was the third highest in the world.

International Expansion

The economic cohesion that had developed during the 1950s and 1960s was seriously threatened by the first oil price shock in 1973. The Yom Kippur War between Arabs and Israelis resulted in restriction of crude oil supplies from Arab oil-exporting countries and a quadrupling of oil prices. As noted above, Japan was heavily dependent on fuel and raw material imports to support its manufacturing sector. Oil represented 90 percent of Japan's energy supplies and

99 percent of its crude oil was imported from the Middle East. Thus, close to 90 percent of its total energy needs were filled with oil from the Middle East.

What had been a climate in which the group took precedence over all else degenerated into an environment of everyone for himself. As all prices escalated, purchasing power evaporated. Everything was in short supply. There were runs on banks and savings institutions. Producers exploited the situation by deliberately withholding supplies of products to inspire panic buying, inflated prices, and extraordinary profits. Companies and *keiretsu* that had been engaged in fierce competition colluded to extract extortionary profits from the consumer. The government was clearly caught off guard by these developments and, at first, did not react at all.

When consumer price inflation reached 26% in early 1974, wage demands by labor reached equally lofty levels. Worker loyalty had been seriously strained by the price gouging to which the average consumer was subjected. Since the inflation was believed to be a short-term aberration, companies were reluctant to increase the wage base to such an extent. That would only mean higher prices of goods and perhaps lay-offs when inflation cooled.

Supplies of raw materials were also an issue. Economic planners began to wonder how the country's future raw material needs could be satisfied. At the rate of growth of current raw materials consumption in the early 1970s, it was projected that by 1980, Japan alone would require 30 percent of the world's raw material imports in order to manufacture its high value-added products.

At the same time, antipollution activists picketed factories and in a rare move for the Japanese sought remedies in court. Some urban areas had become virtually uninhabitable because of the pollution. A court settlement in 1973 actually gave compensation to victims of a crippling bone disease that had caused over 1,000 deaths among those who resided near chemical plants in Kyushu.

The results were perhaps predictable. With a decrease in real purchasing power, a higher cost of production, and disruption in the flow of supplies, raw materials, and fuel, real GNP fell in Japan for the first time since the end of the war. The mood was clearly pessimistic. To make matters worse, the value of the yen had increased relative to the U.S. dollar, making Japanese products more expensive in the United States, Japan's key export market.

The government was forced to react, this time decisively. MITI published in 1974 its first "long-term vision" for Japan. The plan addressed Japan's need to move away from dependence on raw materials imports, to counteract the effect of a strong yen, and to reduce the level of industry-related pollution in the country.

According to the vision, Japan would become a *headquarters* nation. Its processing, converting, and assembling facilities would be located around the world. MITI had advised that the country move away from energy-intensive and labor-intensive industry for some time. The answer was to develop the robotic, advanced electronics, and high-technology industries.

Japan: The Control Center

Future growth in Japan would come from overseas investment--not just exports. The government and business would focus on information resources, not just raw materials. The trading companies would become control centers for the exchange of information, as well as supplies and finished products. More money would be devoted to foreign investment. After all, establishing manufacturing plants in the largest export markets could counteract rising criticism of Japan's growing trade surpluses. For example, when Japanese products are made in Japanese plants in the United States (so-called "transplants"), these products do appear as imports in U.S. trade statistics.

When MITI released its vision statement, some of Japan's major companies had already begun to expand their manufacturing facilities overseas. Sony's San Diego plant had been producing television sets since 1972. In 1974, Matsushita opened a Quasar TV production facility in Chicago. Honda had plans to produce motorcycles in Marysville, Ohio.

But the countries of Southeast Asia represented the most promising regions for this global "division of labor." Here the most challenging problems that faced the companies at home could be satisfactorily resolved. The cost of labor could be reduced because wage rates were a fraction of those in Japan. Since many of these countries had abundant raw materials in their own right, the problem of importing raw materials was also alleviated. Shifting production to these locations meant that some of the most difficult pollution problems in Japan could also be shifted offshore.

To a large extent, the Newly Industrialized Countries of Asia--Hong Kong, Singapore, Taiwan, and South Korea--were the initial beneficiaries of Japanese offshore investment initiatives. Labor costs were low and governments were generally receptive to the entry of Japanese technology and jobs, especially Hong Kong and Singapore. In the 20 years ended 1970, Japanese investment in plants and equipment in the four countries amounted to $179 million. In the *five* years ended 1976, new investment totaled $1.5 billion. In the next five years, the amount of new Japanese investment more than doubled to over $3 billion. This investment not only helped further the Japanese agenda of moving production offshore, but also set the stage for explosive economic growth in these countries. During the decade of the 1980s, per capita GNP in the four Asia NICs grew at real rates (that is, after adjusting for inflation) that ranged from 6 to 10 percent per year.

The newest frontier of Asian expansion by the Japanese is in countries that have abundant natural resources as well as a low-cost labor pool. Before the entry of Japanese industries, Thailand exported primarily rice and rubber. Today, the capital city of Bangkok is dominated by the presence of major Japanese companies, including Mitsubishi, Mitsui, Matsushita, Citizen, Nikon, Nissan, Fujitsu, NEC, and others. The industrialization of Thailand began in earnest in the 1970s--when MITI developed its "headquarters" strategy. Recently, Japanese companies have invested in Thailand alone at the rate of $1 billion per year. Japan is Thailand's major investor and trading partner. Thailand's role in the Japanese economy has gone beyond that of a new export market. With Japan as control center, Thailand now manufactures goods that can be exported to other countries. Japanese headquarters maintain tight control on the Thai managers and the workers receive extensive training in new skills and technologies.

This scenario is being repeated in Indonesia and Malaysia as well. All three countries offer natural resources. Oil, tin, rubber, and timber exports to Japan pay for their imports of Japanese computers, cameras, machine tools, and high-tech products. Japanese factories in these countries represent an increasingly appealing employment alternative, as people in the labor force leave villages in the countryside to perform many of the labor-intensive jobs that have been transferred from Japan.

It should be noted that the industrial firms of Japan have not expanded alone. In fact, the entire *keiretsu* system--trading company, bank, industrial members, major suppliers--establishes offshore operations to support the effort. This is no less true when Japanese business and banking greatly expanded its investment in the United States.

Expanding Into the United States

While there were early investments by Sony, Matsushita, and Honda during the 1970s in the United States, these activities accelerated considerably during the 1980s. During this decade, the United States experienced unprecedented trade deficits. U.S. imports from Japan constituted one of the primary problem areas, with the annual deficit with Japan averaging $50 billion. Also, high U.S. interest rates during the early 1980s continued to attract foreign capital to the United States despite the trade deficits, resulting in a strong dollar vis-à-vis the currencies of U.S. trading partners. The strength of the dollar made exports relatively more expensive and imports relatively less expensive, only aggravating the trade situation. The Federal Reserve maintained its tight money policy during the early 1980s to ensure that the episode of high inflation (experienced in 1980 and 1981) would not be revisited. But the recession that ensued as a result of the tight money climate, along with the high prices of imports, prompted the U.S. Treasury department to take action against the Fed's position.

The 1985 Plaza Accord between the United States, the United Kingdom, Germany, France, and Japan set the stage for a devaluation of the dollar that would make U.S. products less expensive overseas. These countries would intervene in the currency markets to help correct the dollar's overvaluation. In the face of such a strong international coalition, the Federal Reserve relented and began to ease monetary policy, including lower interest rates. As one of the countries in the agreement, Japan had no choice but to agree also to assist in correcting the overvaluation.

Of course, as the dollar weakened, the yen strengthened. Japan had entered the era of *endaka*, the strong yen. Immediately after the war, the U.S. occupation forces had pegged the exchange rate at ¥360 to the dollar. After gold convertibility of the dollar and the pegged exchange rate system were abandoned in 1971, the yen strengthened. In 1985 before the Plaza Accord, the exchange rate was ¥260 to the dollar. After the Accord, the dollar collapsed. Within three years, the U.S. dollar was worth no more than ¥125.

Officials in the United States were satisfied that the trade deficits would reverse and that the market share that had been lost to the Japanese would be reclaimed. They were mistaken. U.S. automakers raised their prices, anticipating that the Japanese would be forced to raise theirs. They were also mistaken. In fact, in some cases, Japanese manufacturers drastically reduced prices to maintain market share until they could set up more offshore production facilities.

At the exchange rate of ¥260 to the dollar, a $10,000 sale yields ¥2.6 million. At ¥125 to the dollar, the same sale yields only ¥1.25 million. The U.S. government and U.S. manufacturers expected Japanese manufacturers to raise their (dollar) prices in order to maintain their (yen) profit margins. Instead, the *keiretsu* banks provided financial support to help make up the difference in profits that resulted from the thinner margins. The territory that had been gained through product development and competitive pricing would not be lost to the tyranny of quarterly profits.

The government was supportive by helping to restructure those industries that were depressed, by supporting high-technology industries, and by adjusting monetary policy (interest rates) and fiscal policy (government spending). The Finance Ministry, the Bank of Japan, and MITI cooperated to keep interest rates low and to relax previously tight money policies. Land and property values were allowed to sky rocket and companies were permitted to borrow against these high values. Small- or medium-sized companies that found it difficult to operate in the high-yen environment were encouraged to establish off-shore production facilities in Southeast Asia or other low-cost labor regions.

In the wake of *endaka*, Japanese manufacturers sought ways to increase productivity. From 1986 to 1991, Japanese companies invested the equivalent of *$3.2 trillion* in new plants and processes. In addition, the initiative of international expansion that had begun in 1974 took a new twist with the United States as the target. As was true in Southeast Asia, the *keiretsu* system has been maintained in the expansion of Japanese companies in the United States. The Toyota plant in Georgetown, Kentucky is a good example. As noted earlier, Toyota is a member of the Mitsui *keiretsu*, but has connections with Sanwa Bank, and a number of other Japanese firms either through cross-holdings of stock or close ties in the production process. The Georgetown facility has been constructed to be the mirror image of a Toyota operation in Japan. The *Ohbayashi Construction Company* (partially owned by Sanwa Bank) controlled construction of the facility. Japanese engineers took their orders from Japan, staying in close touch through frequent faxes between Tokyo and Georgetown. The robots in the factory are manufactured by *Kawasaki*, the metal press by *Komatsu*, the forklifts by *Toyota*.

Beyond the boundaries of the Georgetown facility, the presence of other Japanese companies is evident. The trading company, *Mitsui and Company*, has been established to fulfill the normal responsibilities of a Japanese *keiretsu* trading company. *Trinity Industrial Corporation* is an early transplant to Georgetown that makes paint-finishing equipment. Thirty percent of Trinity's stock is owned by Toyota. Within an hour's drive of Georgetown, *Kentucky Franklin Precision Industry* sells auto engine parts. Franklin is owned by Aisan Industry, in which Toyota has a 24.5 percent interest and another Toyota affiliate (Automatic Loom) has a 22.1 percenter share. *Central Light Alloy Company* sells aluminum wheels in Paris, Kentucky; 60.4 percent of its stock is owned by Toyota. *Ichikoh Industries* in Shelbyville, Kentucky supplies rear- and sideview mirrors. In Japan, the primary customers of Ichikoh are Nissan and Toyota, which purchase 58 and 16 percent of its output, respectively, and own 22.4 and 8.6 percent of its stock.

Sumitomo Metal, Japan's third largest steel producer, and *Nippon Steel*, the world's top steel producer, supply 40 percent of the steel used in the Toyota plant in Georgetown. The remaining 60 percent of the steel is obtained from Armco, Inland, (the financially troubled) LTV, and National Steel companies. All of these U.S. firms have been adversely impacted by Japanese competition and more efficient, low-cost domestic mills. The use of steel from these companies is quite willingly disclosed by Toyota officials who are anxious to assure the American public that the Georgetown plant uses not only U.S. labor but also U.S. manufactured goods in its production process.

However, the appearance and the reality are not necessarily the same. *Kawasaki Steel Corporation* owns 49.5 percent of the main steel-making division of Armco Steel. *Sumitomo Metal* has invested $280 million in two joint ventures with LTV. *NKK Corporation* purchased half interest in National Steel in 1984 and later increased its share to 90 percent, becoming the first Japanese company to own a majority stake in a major (sixth largest) U.S. steel maker. Inland Steel is the third largest steel producer in the United States and is considered perhaps the best managed and most viable. Beginning in 1981, *Nippon Steel* and Inland Steel began to exchange research and technology. In 1989, Nippon bought a 13 percent share of Inland for $185 million.

Clearly, the Toyota network of companies in Georgetown, Kentucky extends far beyond the plant itself. Expansion by these companies has been facilitated by the presence in the Georgetown area of Japanese banks. Sakura Bank (the result of a 1990 merger between Mitsui Bank and Taiyo Kobe Bank), Sanwa Bank, and Tokai Bank have established representative offices in Lexington, Kentucky. Representative offices do not offer banking services in the general sense of the word, but only act as contact points between companies in the host country and banks in the home country. All decisions of any kind are made in the home country. With such a limited scope of activity, these three Japanese banks are not attempting to compete effectively with the U.S. banks in the area to serve potential U.S. clients. Sakura, Sanwa, and Tokai banks are in Georgetown, Kentucky for one reason only--to support the Japanese companies that are a part of the U.S. version of the Toyota group.

In Kentucky, the Japanese have constructed 57 plants, most serving the auto industry. The Toyota facility represents a $1 billion investment. Other Japanese plants in the state bring the total investment to almost $3 billion, most of it since the Plaza Accord in 1985.

The process of Toyota's expansion in the United States is not unlike the expansion of other automakers and other industries. For example, Sony

Corporation purchased CBS Records ($2 billion), Columbia Pictures ($3.4 billion), and Guber Peters Entertainment Co., producers of commercially successful motion pictures. These acquisitions enable Sony to complement its full range of hardware in the electronics field (VCRs, audio cassette and CD players) with offerings of software that will, in turn, increase demand for the hardware.

Kubota Ltd., the largest Japanese manufacturer of agricultural equipment and a member of the Fuyo *keiretsu* decided to diversify in the early 1980s. Seeking to fill a niche in a high-technology area, Kubota targeted the market of mini-supercomputer workstations. This was a major departure from its normal line of business, but the company did not venture into the field alone. Canon and Hitachi, also members of the Fuyo group, provided guidance and technical support. Beginning in 1986, Kubota purchased minority stakes in promising start-up firms in California's Silicon Valley near San Francisco. These acquisitions included 38 percent of Ardent Computer (graphics-based minicomputers) for $32.5 million, 20 percent of MIPS Computer Systems (advanced computing instructions) for $20 million, 8 percent of Exabyte (tape drives) for $6 million, 100 percent of Akashic Memories (hard disks) for $15.5 million, and 4.6 percent of Synthesis Software (software vendor) for $750,000. Kubota obtained some of the most talented new firms in Silicon Valley for less than $75 million. With the technical assistance of industrial members of its *keiretsu* and the support of the group's financial institutions, Kubota shipped its first highly advanced minicomputers from its plant in Tokyo within three years of developing its plan for diversification.

Penetrating the *Keiretsu*

The *keiretsu* is a well connected group of firms that provides support for other members of the group. The competition between different *keiretsu* is often keen, however. Also, the ability of an outside firm to penetrate the group is sometimes limited.

T. Boone Pickens is a Texas businessman who is most widely recognized as head of Mesa Petroleum. Pickens also became involved in the M&A (merger and acquisition) and LBO (leveraged buyout) frenzy of the 1980s in the United States. He often portrayed himself as an advocate for shareholders' welfare in that he put pressure on management to improve returns to shareholders either by changing management teams or by selling off whole units of the business.

Early in 1989, Pickens disclosed that his Boone Company had purchased a 20.2 percent interest in Koito Manufacturing, Japan's largest manufacturer of automotive lighting equipment and a member of the Toyota *keiretsu*. Koito sells roughly half of its manufacturing output to Toyota Motor, but also sells to Nissan Motor, Mazda Motor, and Matsushita Electric. In turn, Toyota owns approximately 20 percent of Koito, with Nissan and Matsushita also holding stakes in the firm. Other Koito shareholders include Nippon Life Insurance, Dai-Ichi Mutual Life Insurance, and a number of other firms with less than a 3 percent stake (Matsushita Real Estate, Japan Securities Finance, Bank of Tokyo-Mitsubishi Bank, Sumitomo Bank, and Dai-Ichi Kangyo Bank).

As a major shareholder, Toyota held three seats on the Board of Directors. Pickens insisted that Boone Company, with a larger stake, was entitled to three or four seats. One of his stated objectives in seeking these board seats was to expose the collusive elements of the *keiretsu* system--in his opinion, an unfair trading system that was being introduced into the United States. His experience in this endeavor illustrates the danger of underestimating the strength of the *keiretsu* system.

Koito's president, Takao Matsuura, first questioned Pickens' motives. He noted that Pickens had been involved in "greenmail" in the United States, that is, that Pickens had purchased shares of other companies in connection with a takeover threat that he never intended to carry out. Such threats had the effect of raising the price of the stock. When the targeted company resisted the takeover, it would sometimes offer to buy back his shares--at a substantial profit for Pickens. Hence, the term "greenmail." Matsuura charged that Pickens was attempting the same ploy with Koito. In fact, Matsuura observed, Pickens had apparently purchased his stock from Kitaro Watanabe who had previously launched an unsuccessful greenmail attempt of his own. When Watanabe decided to sell his Koito shares, Pickens was anxious to purchase. But even after Pickens increased his stake to 26.4 percent, Koito continued to resist.

It became clear that this was not merely one company against another. All the corporate shareholders had an interest in keeping Pickens off the board. If Pickens' true motive was to somehow damage the *keiretsu* system, he potentially represented a greater threat than Watanabe ever could have. It seems that the government recognized this potential threat. After Pickens disclosed the extent of his holdings, the Ministry of Finance initiated several investigations into how he had obtained the Koito shares. The Tokyo Stock Exchange, notorious for its own practice of less-than-arms-length trading, investigated the possibility of improper conduct in the trading of Koito shares, including insider trading, stock manipulation, and hidden transactions with respect to purchases and sales.[12] None of the investigations revealed any irregularities. It was clear, however, that the Japanese bureaucracy was not sympathetic to Pickens or his agenda.

The storm clouds gathered with full intensity at the time of Koito's annual shareholders' meeting in June 1990. Pickens had been given no hearing at the 1989 shareholders' meeting, so he came better prepared in 1990. Before the meeting, he sent videotapes to other Japanese shareholders that depicted him as a down-to-earth Texan who sought board representation and who suggested that shareholders should receive higher dividend payments from the company. He arranged for the transportation of 30 other Koito shareholders from the United States.

They all arrived together at the Tokyo hotel that had been designated for the meeting in a show of strength and solidarity. However, the entourage was seated away from Japanese shareholders and placed under the "protection" of 20 hotel guards and 25 Koito-hired private security guards. All the while, professional hecklers shouted diatribes such as "Yankee go home," "Remember Pearl Harbor!" and "We've won the economic war!" It became necessary to replace one of Pickens' interpreters who left the meeting in tears. Matsuura, Koito's president, made no move to silence the hecklers. At one point, when Pickens was interrupted by the outbursts and turned to respond directly, Matsuura warned Pickens to stick to the topic at hand. Finally, insulted and outraged, the American entourage stormed out of the meeting having achieved none of its stated objectives.

The Koito episode shows that the *keiretsu* system is an integral part of Japanese business. Despite the fact that some of the aspects of the system appear alien to Americans, it has strong cultural foundations that are not likely to be eroded by U.S. pressure or any other external force. This cohesion will continue to protect the interests of the group even when less than ideal circumstances arise.

---

[12] Examples of scandals involving the Japanese stock market include the Recruit Scandal in which it was alleged that politicians received new share allocations before the shares were offered to the public, manipulation of bank shares by the exact same dividend being paid by all banks, the use of professional hecklers at shareholders' meetings to discourage any shareholder that may ask embarrassing questions, and companies leaking information to stock brokers before its public release for the benefit of the brokers' major clients.

Reforming the Financial System of Japan?

The Japanese economy is now faced with significant challenges. Japan has not been able to avoid the effects of the worldwide recession. Industrial production has fallen. There have been large cut-backs in the capital investment budgets of companies such as Fujitsu, Matsushita, Sumitomo Metal Industries, and Kawasaki Steel. Companies are engaging in *risutora*, or restructuring, which can take the form of reducing the number of product models that are manufactured, hiring fewer college graduates, reducing the amount of summer and winter employee bonuses, or reassigning current employees. Some middle managers in Japanese companies who thought they had lifetime employment are being encouraged to take early retirement or being reassigned to obscure subsidiaries.

The government has responded by attempting to stimulate the economy. There have been multi-billion-dollar packages of tax cuts and infrastructure building. The Bank of Japan lowered the official discount rate (at which banks borrow from the central bank) from 6.5 percent in 1991 to 2.5 percent in 1993. In 1999, the rate was close to zero.

Japanese banks have not escaped the painful economic realities. The stock market collapsed, straining bank capital just when new international capital standards are introduced.[13] To make matters worse, banks are inundated with bad loan portfolios that have been estimated to amount to $1 trillion. The dual problem of declining stock values and questionable loans has raised fundamental questions about the viability of Japanese banks.

The problems began after the 1985 Plaza Accord when *endaka*, the strong yen, compelled government officials to create an "easy money" environment to help companies offset thinner profit margins. When property values increased in this climate, Japanese banks were permitted to make loans against the higher property values. Banks, either directly or through subsidiaries, lent heavily against real estate. In the peak years of 1987 and 1988, loans collateralized by real estate represented half of all new bank financing. By 1991, total outstanding property loans amounted to ¥116 trillion (almost $1 trillion).

---

[13] Effective 1993, the international banks of OECD countries must comply with uniform capital standards. The total of Tier I capital (primarily common equity and disclosed reserves) and Tier II capital (primarily subordinated debt and revaluation reserves) must equal 8 percent of risk-weighted assets. While Tier II capital may not exceed Tier I capital, Japanese banks are permitted to include 45 percent of the appreciation of common stock (of other companies held as assets) in the calculation of Tier II capital. Stock market price declines have the effect of reducing the amount of Tier II capital.

When the Bank of Japan decided that the expansion in real estate and stock prices needed tempering, it raised interest rates in May 1989. There was little initial reaction in the stock market; the Nikkei index went on to reach 38,915 by the end of the year. But bond yields had responded to the rate increases. The message was clear--the days of easy money were coming to a close. February of 1990 witnessed a slip in the stock market. In March, the stock market went into a free fall, down almost 30 percent to 28,000. In the process $1 trillion in equity value evaporated.

When the value of the yen fell in response to the stock market collapse, the Bank of Japan raised interest rates once again to support it. This only complicated the problems in the stock market. By September, the Nikkei index stood at just over 20,000.

Also in March 1990, the Finance Ministry prohibited banks from increasing their lending for property more than they increased their lending for other purposes. As a follow-up in September, the Bank of Japan ordered the major city banks to reduce their total new lending by more than 30 percent as compared to the same quarter in 1989. Real estate lending ground to a halt. Property values fell by 10 percent, not so much because of panic selling but because transactions simply stopped. Banks have been told by government authorities not to sell property (that was provided as loan collateral) into the depressed real estate market.

Japanese banks are clearly in serious trouble—stock values have declined and many real estate loans look questionable at best. These are clearly serious issues, but the situation is not as much of a threat to the banking system of Japan as it would be to the U.S. system. In the United States, the banks would be forced to fend for themselves, perhaps by seeking formal remedies such as Congressional bail-out legislation or higher FDIC insurance premiums to cover potential bank failures. In Japan, government support is less difficult to obtain. In fact, the September 1990 ruling of the Bank of Japan that city banks reduce lending activity by more than 30 percent gave the banks a convenient reason to reduce their loan portfolios and, thus, increase their capital ratios in compliance with international capital standards.

Current problems in the banking system of Japan should not be dismissed. Nevertheless, the support mechanisms that have assisted Japanese industrial firms in the past can be used to respond to a crisis in the banking sector. In any event, it is safe to say that a banking dilemma of the magnitude that is being experienced in Japan at this time, would have far more serious consequences if it occurred in the United States.

Conclusion

The expansion of the Japanese industry has been largely accomplished through the support of both government and financial institutions. The dominance of Japanese firms in areas such as steel, automobiles, and electronics is no accident. Nor is it the result of free market, *laissez faire* government policy. Since the Meiji Restoration of 1868, Japan has focused on the need for collaboration between government, business, and banking. The holding company or *zaibatsu* structure was disbanded after World War II. But the cross-shareholding or *keiretsu* structure soon took its place. In the latter structure, generally the major decision making power rests with the trading company and the main bank in the group. Major industrial firms in diversified fields complete the formal *keiretsu* and dozens, if not hundreds, of small- and medium-size firms have long-standing supplier relations with the major firms.

The strong cultural significance of the group creates incentives for excellence within the group while encouraging competition between the groups. This attitude has been transferred to Japanese organizations that have expanded internationally. Notwithstanding the troubled loan portfolios of Japanese banks, the strong relationship between government, industry, and banking in Japan has produced world-class industrial firms and commercial banks.

Selected References

Abiru, Masahiro. "Toyota Keiretsu; Empirical Analysis," *Fukuoka University Review of Economics*, vol. 36, no. 4, 1992, pp. 619-645.

"Bricks-and-Mortar Fantasies (Japanese Banks)," The Economist, February 6, 1993, pp. 82-84.

Chu, Chin-ning. *The Asian Mind Game: Unlocking the Hidden Agenda of the Asian Business Culture--A Westerner's Survival Manual*, New York: Rawson Associates/Macmillan Publishing Company, 1991.

Eli, Max. *Japan, Inc.: Global Strategies of Japanese Trading Corporations*, Chicago: Probus Publishing Company, 1991.

Gibney, Frank. *The Pacific Century: America and Asia in a Changing World*, New York: Charles Scribner's Sons/Macmillan Publishing Company, 1992.

"How Japan Will Survive Its Fall," *The Economist*, July 11, 1992, pp.65-68.

Johnson, Hazel. *Dispelling the Myth of Globalization: The Case for Regionalization*, New York: Praeger, 1991.

Kearns, Robert L. *Zaibatsu America: How Japanese Firms Are Colonizing Vital U.S. Industries*, New York: Free Press/Macmillan, Inc., 1993.

Kester, W. Carl. *Japanese Takeovers: The Global Contest for Corporate Control*, Boston: Harvard Business School Press, 1991.

Neff, Robert and Larry Holyoke, Neil Gross, and Karen Lowry Miller. "Fixing Japan," *Business Week*, March 29, 1993, pp. 68-74.

"Overburdened (Japanese Banks)," *The Economist*, July 25, 1992, pp. 77-78

Reading, Brian. *Japan: The Coming Collapse*, New York: HarperBusiness, 1992.

Roberts, John G. *Mitsui: Three Centuries of Japanese Business*, New York: Weatherhill, Inc., 1991.

Wood, Christopher. *The Bubble Economy: Japan's Extraordinary Speculative Boom of the '80s and the Dramatic Bust of the '90s*, New York: Atlantic Monthly Press, 1992.

5. Forging Banking Alliances in China, Hong Kong, and Korea

Introduction

Upscale shops line the streets, offering a wide range of merchandise for sale including everything from Japanese cameras to Reebok shoes to Motorola mobile phones. Many of the residents of this city work in more than 6,000 factories that have located there. Less than 50 miles south, another thriving metropolis boasts an even higher standard of living, supported to a large extent by its almost 150,000 factories and 140 commercial banks. Is this the Tokyo or Osaka region of Japan? No. The city to the north is Dongguan, located in the Guangdong Province of the People's Republic of China. The city to the south is Hong Kong.

The differences between the southern regions of communist China and Hong Kong are becoming less apparent. Hong Kong is not reverting to communist economic customs. Instead, China is moving closer to the outward focus of Hong Kong. Already, Guangdong Province produces roughly one quarter of China's exports while representing less than 10 percent of its population. For some time, Hong Kong has been China's link to the West and much of its industrial development has been financed through Hong Kong banks or Chinese banks operating in Hong Kong.

South Korea has combined principles of central planning (as in China) with the technique of large business combinations (as in Japan). The government consciously adopted the model of large business combinations to promote those industries which it targeted for development. The Korean *chaebols*, the equivalent of the Japanese *keiretsu*, have been the beneficiaries of subsidized, low-cost loans--channeled through banks which were partially owned and completely controlled by the government. In 1950, South Korea's economy was labor-intensive and primarily agricultural. Less than fifty years later, Korea's exports of clothing represented more than 10 percent of the world's clothing exports; Korean exports of ships and boats were one quarter of the world total. In the interim, Korean businessmen took huge risks--risks that were backed by the country's banks and that have led to what is often referred to as an "economic miracle."

China: Breaking Economic Ties with the Past

China evolved from a long-standing feudal system to (briefly) a republic to a communist government, complete with central economic planning. While it retains its socialist foundation, the country now has a strong capitalist component.

Transition to the People's Republic of China

Before the Communist takeover in 1949, there was almost constant tension between Chinese and foreigners, and often between warring factions of Chinese. China had been forced open to the Western trade after losing the Opium Wars of the 1840s. Five Chinese ports were opened to foreign ships, Hong Kong was relinquished under a 99-year lease to the British, and China was forced to pay Britain $21 million. The Taiping Rebellion (1850-1864) against the Manchu dynasty was a popular uprising against what was seen as economic exploitation by the West. This Rebellion was suppressed only after the Chinese government obtained Western military assistance.

The frustrations of the Chinese people crystallized in a theory of governance formulated by Sun Yat-sen, born in Canton and educated as a physician. The theory was based on three principles: nationalism, democracy, and livelihood. After revolution erupted again, Sun Yat-sen was elected in 1912 as President of the new Chinese republic, ending almost 4,000 years of dynastic rule. It was a short-lived republic, however, as warlords seized power in 1916. After his death in 1925, Sun's Nationalist Party was led by Chiang Kai-shek. The Nationalists did not regain control of the country until they cooperated with the Communist Party, led by Mao Tse-tung, to oust the warlords in 1925.

This uneasy coalition fought the Japanese during World War II, but shortly after the end of the war, civil war again erupted. In 1949, the Communist Party emerged victorious and established the People's Republic of China. The objective was that the Chinese people would no longer be victimized either by foreigners or by a dictatorial ruling class. Instead, they would be independent and self-sufficient.

There were fundamental economic changes, including land reform and nationalizing business. Landlords were subjected to public trials during which the Communist government urged peasants to find them guilty of crimes against the people. After those on trial were pronounced guilty, land was redistributed to the peasants. All businesses were nationalized and became property of the state.

A strong egalitarian philosophy prevailed. China emphasized an even distribution of income and resources, perhaps more than other socialist countries. Centrally determined wage scales were maintained within narrow bands or limits. Worker motivation took the form of nonfinancial incentives—inroduced through political education in the work place. Although wages were low, the urban worker had certain important social safety nets such as old-age pensions, medical and disability benefits, highly subsidized housing, food and transportation subsidies, educational facilities for children provided by the enterprise, and employment opportunities for family members.

Embargoes imposed by western nations after the change of government and a deterioration of the relations with the Soviet Union in the late 1950s served to reinforce the inward-focused development strategy of the Chinese. There was little economic interchange with the rest of the world. International trade was kept to a minimum, foreign investment was not permitted, and external borrowing was minimal.

The central planning process determined credit allocation to both agriculture and business. These funds were made available through the new socialist banking system.

The Socialist Banking System

Modeled after the system of the former Soviet Union, the banking system of the People's Republic of China was to be a *monobank* system, that is, one in which all financial transactions are handled by one bank or by a few banks with very specialized functions. The main bank is the *People's Bank of China*, responsible for all domestic industrial and commercial credit operations, and in many cases rural credit as well. This bank also acts as the supervisory body for the specialized banks. As one of the specialized banks, the *People's Construction Bank of China* is responsible for transferring budget allocations to construction projects. The *Bank of China* is another specialized institution that is responsible for foreign exchange transactions.

For many years, these three institutions managed the credit base for China and held 99 percent of all financial assets. Enterprise managers in China prefer bank loans for the purposes of raising investment capital over other alternatives such as grants from higher-level authorities, selling excess assets, or reducing the work force. And, until recently, these loans could only be obtained through the People's Bank of China--a large institution with 15,000 offices and over 300,000 employees.

The People's Construction Bank of China was established in 1954 with the principle function of distributing state budgetary appropriations to enterprises for capital construction. The appropriations were in the form of nonrepayable, interest-free grants. Repayment took the form of remittances of profits to the central state budget authorities. The Construction Bank was also charged with overseeing the units responsible for the actual construction and with forwarding profit remittances to the Ministry of Finance. The Construction Bank played no role in evaluating construction projects before they were financed, but disbursed funds according to the central plan. Its branch network includes 2,800 offices, 29 supervisory branches, employing over 50,000.

Until recently, the Bank of China held a monopoly on foreign exchange transactions and international payments. It acts as an export-import bank, implements foreign exchange control, acts as an agent for all international loans, and manages all transactions that relate to foreign currencies and securities. The Bank of China has 100 branches in China and a number of overseas branches including Hong Kong, Macao, Singapore, Luxembourg, New York, and Tokyo.

Until 1979, the loans made available to state enterprises were primarily revolving credit to cover working capital needs. There were no loans for equipment, because these funds were provided by the state as grants (not subject to objective project evaluation). The amount of working capital loans was determined (via the budget) to support the normal rate of sales, any seasonal needs, and goods in transit. Interest rates were regulated by the government and were often lower than they would otherwise have been. All enterprise profits were remitted to the state.

There were several problems with this system. The central planning process was not sensitive to regional differences in the needs for capital investment. The managers of state-run enterprises had little incentive to improve efficiency because all profits accrued to the state. Investments in plant and equipment were "grants" not expenditures that were examined for feasibility or long-term viability. The consequences of this flawed approach led to economic reform in 1979.

Economic Reform

Under Mao Tse-tung, the Chinese standard of living had improved. Health care was more widely available, the incidence of common diseases was sharply reduced, massive food distribution programs helped to counteract the effects of famine, the adult literacy rate rose from 20 percent in 1950 to 66 percent in 1979 (three years after Mao's death), and, over the same period, average life expectancy rose from 36 to 64 years. However, much of this progress was the result of massive investments in capital goods which, in turn, were made possible by holding down wages and agricultural prices. Productivity levels were stagnant in both agricultural and industrial sectors, placing the People's Republic of China far behind other developing countries that were also in the process of industrializing. With little improvement in productivity, industrial output could continue to improve only with increasing levels of material and equipment input. This left few resources for consumption purposes. There was general scarcity of consumer goods and wages remained low.

With a lack of industrial project evaluation and so little accountability for investments of material and equipment, resources were wasted and product quality was often poor. There seemed to be a general lack of technical competence. Large-scale industrial concerns had been promoted while small-scale operations had been neglected. Moreover, the industrial sector had grown at four times the rate of the agricultural sector.

After the death of Mao Tse-tung in 1976, Deng Xiaoping (who had previously been exiled for his persistent calls for modernization) came to power and took control of the country in 1977. Under his leadership, in 1979 China embarked on the "four modernizations" in industry, agriculture, science and technology, and national defense. In general, these modernizations involved *greater decentralization of microeconomic decision-making*, especially for the managers of the productive units; *increased reliance on market incentives*, instead of planned budget allocations; and *opening the economy*, especially to foreign trade, investment, and technology.

In the agricultural sector, prices paid by the state procurement agencies increased and the mandatory quotas of agricultural products were not increased. Production above these quotas would be purchased by the state at premium prices. Over time, even these conditions were liberalized. First, farmers were allowed to sell above-quota production either to the state or on the open market. Later, mandatory quotas were completely abolished and farmers could produce whatever amount they chose and sell to whichever market they desired. Land itself remained under the ownership of the village, but long-term leases (15-20 years) entitled families to assume all production decisions about their individual plots and to retain any profits (or losses) that resulted. Within six years of the start of China's new policies, annual grain production rose from 305 million metric tons to 407 million, even though less land was cultivated. Yields of rice and wheat almost doubled. Cotton output tripled. The average income of a farmer increased 90 percent.

In the industrial sector, price reform followed a similar pattern--above-quota production could be sold for prices that moved incrementally higher, the number of goods subject to quotas was gradually reduced, and in some cases the prices for above-quota production were completely liberalized.

State enterprise managers gained more autonomy in the decision-making process--greater freedom to select among alternative sources of needed inputs, the ability to negotiate sales terms with potential buyers, and the right to determine the mix and quantity of production not subject to quotas. Enterprises have been allowed to market their above-quota production. Street markets specializing in consumer goods have been permitted to develop. State wholesale and retail establishments may select from any above-quota production sources and prices are all negotiable.

While wages are still subject to central control, managers have been encouraged to distribute bonuses based on worker performance. Bonuses are paid out of enterprise profits, creating a positive link between enterprise performance and worker compensation. More individual and collective ownership of enterprises is now possible, with this sector representing the fastest growing component of the Chinese economy. During the first six years after the new economic system was introduced, industrial output grew at the rate of almost 14 percent per year, particularly in the area of consumer durable goods.

Chinese markets have been opened to foreign investment through the introduction of Special Economic Zones or SEZs and through specified coastal cities, including Shanghai and Tianjin. [14] There are four SEZs, also located along the coast (in Shantou, Shenzhen, Xiamen, and Zhuhai), in regions from which many of the Overseas Chinese immigrated, two of which

---

[14] In addition to Shanghai and Tianjin, the 14 specially designated coastal cities include Dalian, Guangzhou, Qinhuangdao, Yantai, Qingdao, Lianyungang, Nantong, Ningbo, Wenzhou, Fuzhou, Zhanjiang, and Beihai.

are close to Hong Kong. [15] These special zones serve two purposes. They are intended to serve as special export platforms and to attract foreign investment from Overseas Chinese. They are located in relatively isolated places so as to insulate the rest of the economy from any potentially destabilizing effects.

Products made in SEZs may be exported without duties; imports used for production within SEZs or for offshore oil explorations are also duty-free. Products made within the SEZs, but sold to the interior of the country, are generally subject to normal tax law. Foreign banks are permitted to operate in the SEZs. Foreign investments of $5 million or more qualify for favorable income-tax treatment. The most favorable treatment is granted to high-technology investment, which receives a 5-year exemption.

The four SEZs are in southern provinces of Guangdong (Shenzhen, Zhuhai, and Shantou) and Fujian (Xiamen). Shenzhen has experienced particularly impressive growth--from a small fishing village in 1979 to a modern city, complete with skyscrapers and an entrepreneurial population of 2 million.

The restructuring of the Chinese economy has led to impressive gains in income. The country's annual gross national product rose from $100 billion in 1983 to approximately $400 billion today. This growth would not have been possible, however, without the assistance of a reformed banking system.

Support from the Banking Sector

While maintaining the basic structure of the banking system, with the People's Bank of China in the center, the financial system of China was refocused on the needs of agriculture and industry. *The Agricultural Bank of China* was created in 1979 primarily to provide working capital to state units involved in agricultural supply and marketing. Its scope of operation has recently expanded to extending loans to small, local industrial enterprises. It is currently the second largest domestic specialized bank with a far-reaching organization of over 200 offices in major cities and 25,000 offices in townships.

The Industrial and Commercial Bank of China was created in 1984 and is the country's largest domestic specialized bank. This institution is a spin-off of the People's Bank of China and has assumed all commercial banking activities. The deposit base of the Industrial Bank is primarily urban residents and it makes domestic currency loans to state enterprises. Its

[15] The Overseas Chinese are those who left Mainland China for either political or economic reasons and migrated to Taiwan, Hong Kong, or other regions.

functions include working capital and equipment loans for urban enterprises, and, for state enterprise and large cooperatives, cash and payroll management. These services are offered through the Bank's more than 20,000 locations.

At the same time that the Industrial and Commercial Bank of China was created, the *People's Bank of China* was reconstituted as a central bank. As such, it is now more involved in monetary policy and supervision of the specialized banks. The People's Bank now formulates and implements financial policy; controls the issue of currency; determines interest rates and foreign exchange rates; draws up and manages the credit plan; approves the establishment, merger, and closure of financial institutions; regulates the issuance of negotiable securities by enterprises; supervises the money markets; manages the state treasury; issues government bonds; handles the government's official foreign exchange reserves and international transactions. With the exception of the function of managing and drawing up the credit plan, the list of duties of the People's Bank is strikingly similar to the list of duties performed in the United States by the Federal Reserve, Comptroller of the Currency, and Federal Deposit Insurance Corporation.

The growing similarity of the system to more Westernized versions is not limited to the People's Bank. The specialized banks now enjoy more autonomy in the decision making process. They are encouraged to examine the profitability of enterprises and to otherwise evaluate the feasibility of projects that are proposed by enterprises. The specialized banks have more control over funds transfers to their various branches to accommodate differential demand for credit in various regions. In 1985, an interbank market (similar to a federal funds market) was established to facilitate the management of excess liquidity among the specialized banks.

What were previously government grants for construction and equipment projects are more often made available as bank loans, subject to loan review. This has removed the separation between the budget and the banking system, giving banks responsibility for long-term investment in a more autonomous fashion. In a real sense, the expansion of the Chinese economy has been fueled by these loans for plant and equipment, made in a more competitive environment under more decentralized control.

The Bank of China has fulfilled its function as a specialized bank in the international arena. It is the richest and most worldly of all Chinese government banks. Thirty-five percent of the nation's foreign currency flows through its hands before being transferred to Beijing. The Bank settles trade and other foreign exchange accounts between local and foreign enterprises and banks, extends credit to enterprises engaged in foreign trade, engages in joint venture investments abroad, issues foreign-currency denominated financial instruments (including bonds), and maintains accounts for Overseas Chinese.

The London branch of the Bank of China plays a role in the management of international trade through "supplier credits" to pay for imports. The branch maintains numerous correspondent accounts with other Western banks (offsetting deposit accounts). Generally, the accounts balance, that is, the amount that the London branch has on deposit with the correspondent equals the amount that the correspondent has on deposit with the London branch. However, when the government requires more foreign currency that this arrangement provides, the London branch arranges a supplier credit. This is done by having the supplier arrange credit with its own bank and the supplier's bank sets up a deposit at the Bank of China's London branch. This deposit is used by the Chinese government to pay the supplier. When there is sufficient government-owned foreign currency on deposit at the London branch, the transaction is reversed. Thus, the London branch uses the money markets to help manage China's foreign trade.

The Hong Kong branch of the Bank of China (its largest) also plays an important role in the industrial sector of China. It has acted as China's point of observation in the West since the 1949 change in government, where international trade and finance are discussed and analyzed. It also oversees the 13 affiliated banks, state-controlled nonbank enterprises, and other government investments in Hong Kong. While not publicly disclosed, these investments are said to include real estate companies, airlines, hotels, stores, gas stations, cinemas, warehouses, and factories of all kinds. Apart from these official duties, the Hong Kong branch operates as a competitive commercial bank, providing short-term financing for local merchants who purchase goods from mainland China as well as a full range of conventional banking services.

The stimulus of Hong Kong has played a significant role in the extent to which the People's Republic of China has modernized both its industrial and banking sectors and forged a stronger bond between them.

Hong Kong Industry and Banking

Sun Yat-sen, considered the father of modern political thought in China, was educated in Hong Kong before he returned to the mainland to become China's first president during the short-lived republic. Merchants and bankers of Hong Kong have played leading roles in the industrial development of the People's Republic of China. In the following discussion, Hong Kong will be shown to have played a major role in the development of China. Accordingly, Hong Kong will be referred to as if it is a separate entity rather than merely a province of China.

Hong Kong depends on the mainland for food and water. In fact, Hong Kong is China's largest export market and a major source of imports. The vast majority of foreign investment in China is by Hong Kong companies. A large share of the loans syndicated by Hong Kong banks are used to finance projects in the People's Republic.

Hong Kong as an Industrial Center

Before the communist takeover in China, Hong Kong's industry consisted primarily of ginger production, sugar refining, textiles, fishing, quarrying, and shipbuilding. Most of the banks in the colony were foreign and involved primarily in the active trade sector, providing foreign exchange services, but showing little enthusiasm for financing internal Chinese trade. They included Oriental Banking Corporation (the first British bank in Hong Kong, 1845), Chartered Mercantile Bank of India, London, and China (1853), and Chartered Bank (1853, the predecessor of the Standard Chartered Bank). The Hongkong and Shanghai Banking Corporation was established in 1865 as a locally-based bank with Hong Kong interests (British businessmen or *taipans*). As such, this bank supported the establishment of the Union Docks, the Saigon Refinery, Pier and Godown Company, Taikoo Sugar Refinery, and Taikoo Dockyards.

In 1876 there were approximately 200 large Chinese businesses and just under 300 small trading firms in Hong Kong. In just 5 years, these numbers grew to almost 400 businesses and 2,400 trading firms. Immigrant Chinese began to set up small manufacturing firms. The traditional Chinese bankers (*ch'ien-chuang*) and the Hongkong and Shanghai Banking Corporation supported these businesses.[16] Chinese-owned, Western-style banks were also soon established, such as the Bank of Canton (1912) and the Bank of East Asia (1918).

After the People's Republic of China was formed in 1949 and the trade embargo with the communist country was imposed by the United Nations, a number of powerful manufacturers from Shanghai immigrated to Hong Kong, taking their work forces, and sometimes their machinery, with them. These entrepreneurial businessmen prospered by taking advantage of the low-cost labor available in Hong Kong. The colonial government has also facilitated trade and development by maintaining a business climate that was almost completely free of

---

[16] See Chapter 1 for a discussion of the *ch'ien-chuang*.

constraining regulations. There were no restrictions on foreign investment and very few duties.

As a British base for Chinese trade, the original purpose of Hong Kong was to re-export goods, a function that remains a significant part of the Hong Kong economy today. Over half of China's exports to Hong Kong are re-exported to other countries. But Hong Kong, now with a population of approximately 6 million people and over 150,000 factories on a land mass of 400 square miles, ranks at or near the top of export rankings of developing countries in several categories:

- Leather
- Textile yarn and thread
- Plastic material
- Footwear
- Telecommunications equipment, sound recorders and parts
- Electric power machines
- Office machines
- Travel goods and bags
- Noncotton textiles
- Cotton fabrics
- Clothing
- Domestic electric equipment
- Toys and sporting goods
- Watches and clocks
- Gold and silver jewelry

The Hong Kong Trading Companies

While there are many small- and medium-size enterprises in Hong Kong, there is also a tradition of large trading houses that began with the British East India Trading Company in the early 19th century. The most prominent, modern versions of the trading company are *Jardine Matheson Holdings*, Swire Pacific, and *Hutchison Whampoa*.

William Jardine and James Matheson, the two founders of *Jardine Matheson*, met in Bombay in 1820 and established their company in 1832 in Canton, the only Chinese city in which foreigners were permitted to reside at the time. Their first enterprises included exporting tea from China and smuggling Indian opium into the country. After the Opium Wars, the company moved its headquarters to Hong Kong. Opium importation was legalized by then, but expansion of trade opportunities in other areas led the founders to abandon the politically dangerous opium activities and enter the industries of brewing, silk trading, textiles, sugar, and banking and insurance. Later other ventures included steamships (the first introduced into China), China's first railroad, and the real estate company Hong Kong Land. By 1930, the far-flung conglomerate employed 130,000 people.

Although the Sino-Japanese War and World War II interrupted operations, Jardine Matheson reopened in 1945 with an airline, brewery, textile mills, and real estate operations. Today, the holdings of the firm encompass supermarkets, restaurants, hotels, shipping concerns, auto dealerships, and financial services. The trading end of the business, that is, marketing and distribution, still represents nearly half of pre-tax profits. Nevertheless, the financial services subsidiaries are an important component, generating 15 percent of Jardine Matheson's pre-tax income. They are organized as Jardine Insurance Brokers and Jardine Fleming (corporate banking, investment management, and stock brokerage).

As a major real estate holder, Jardine Matheson controls 5 million square feet of office and retail property in the heart of Hong Kong's central business district. The company's stated objective is to reduce its reliance on the Hong Kong market. In line with this objective, Jardine Matheson sold 300,000 square feet of this property to Chinese investors for $492 million in 1992.

Like Jardine Matheson, *Swire Pacific* began as a trading company. The concentration of the predecessor firm, Butterfield and Swire, was in the areas of tea and cotton. After moving to Hong Kong in 1870, the firm expanded into shipping, creating China Navigation Company in 1872 to transport goods along the Yangtze River. With the financial backing of Hongkong and Shanghai Banking Corporation, Taikoo Sugar Refinery began operations in 1884 and Taikoo Dockyards followed in 1898.

The wars disrupted the operations of Butterfield and Swire as was the case for Jardine Matheson. As the basis of the rebuilt firm, Butterfield and Swire purchased the controlling interest in Cathay Pacific, a new Hong Kong firm with 6 airplanes (DC-3s). The firm evolved into Swire Pacific, expanding the airline and establishing airport and aircraft service companies. By the 1980s the airline was a large, profitable company. When Cathay Pacific went public in 1986 the stock offer was oversubscribed 55-to-1. The following year, the Chinese government bought 12.5 percent of the stock. In 1990, Swire Pacific and Cathay Pacific bought 35 percent of Dragonair, an airline that is 38 percent owned by the Chinese government. Almost 70 percent of Swire Pacific operating income is derived from the aviation industry.

In general, Swire Pacific is moving toward closer collaboration with the Chinese government. Two Swire subsidiaries signed agreements to build a paint factory and to operate a construction material plant in China. The company's trading division purchased the right to distribute Reebok shoes (Hong Kong's leading brand) in Guangdong province.

Other holdings of Swire Pacific include Carroll Reed International (clothing), Continental Can Hong Kong (aluminum beverage cans), Swire Bottlers (Coca-Cola distributorship), and Swire Marketing (Kentucky Fried Chicken franchise). Other products and services include audio- and videocassettes, computer marketing, electrical and mechanical contracting. life and property insurance, and real estate development and investments. Although Swire Pacific does not own a banking subsidiaries, Hong Kong and Shanghai Banking Corporation has played a critical role in the company's development.

The Hongkong and Shanghai Banking Corporation has played an even more central role in the firm of *Hutchison Whampoa*. Established in 1861, Hongkong and Whampoa Dock operated shipyards and, later, shipping container terminals. In 1880, Hutchison International began as a major consumer goods importer and wholesaler. Later, in the 1960s, Hutchison International undertook a major acquisition program and purchased drugstores, supermarkets, soft drink companies, and a stake in Hongkong and Whampoa Dock.

Without a strong financial institution as part of its group, the complex financial arrangements involved in the acquisitions fell apart in the 1970s. Hongkong and Shanghai Bank led a rescue effort, purchased 23 percent of the company's stock, and replaced the chief executive. The new CEO slashed expenses, sold 103 of the companies, and bought the rest of the stock of Hongkong and Whampoa Dock. The new firm of Hutchison Whampoa rebounded and Hongkong and Shanghai Banking Corporation sold its stake in the company to Cheung Kong Holdings, a separate Chinese company owned by the chairman of Hutchison Whampoa. Now with major holdings in the stock of Hutchison Whampoa, Cheung Kong controls this large diversified company which includes investments in real estate, container terminals, hotels, energy, finance, and telecommunications. This was the first traditional Hong Kong trading company to be controlled by the Chinese.

Greater China

Greater China is one of the fastest growing regions in the world. The southern region of the People's Republic of China, Hong Kong, and Taiwan have virtually merged in an economic sense. Each brings its own competitive advantage to this Chinese productivity triangle. China contributes land, workers, and boundless ambition; Hong Kong brings international marketing expertise; and Taiwan contributes technological know-how and financial backing. Before his death, Deng Xiaoping advocated market reforms and called this collaboration "socialism with Chinese characteristics."

The Chinese have invested over $10 billion in Hong Kong in recent years. The Taiwanese business person is no longer barred from the mainland, but now often enjoys an advantage when negotiating deals in China because of personal contacts with family and friends. Although Taiwan still prohibits direct air and shipping links to China, trade through Hong Kong is well over $10 billion.

The division of labor that results from this collaboration is difficult to compete with. For example, talking toy dolls are designed in Hong Kong and assembled in South China, complete with microchips from Taiwan. Jogging suits headed for U.S. retailers, such as the Limited, begin with velour from Taiwan that is sewn in South China and then are shipped from Hong Kong. Taiwanese companies have set up 4,000 factories in South China, primarily in the south to manufacture a wide range of products, including bicycles, handbags, and sporting goods. Hong Kong companies have 25,000 factories in China that employ 3 million workers.

It is not merely the international marketing experience that makes Hong Kong such a valuable part of this productivity triangle. Hong Kong is also an international banking center with over 140 commercial banks that engage in a full range of services, including participation in the Asiandollar Market.[17] The Hongkong and Shanghai Banking Corporation (although now headquartered in London) is the largest group with approximately 400 offices. The Bank of China group is the second largest with over 200 offices. The Hongkong and Shanghai Banking Corporation is one of three institutions whose bank notes circulate as legal tender.[18] In fact, a quarter of all Hong Kong money circulates in South China. The majority of major long-term loan syndications by Hong Kong banks are related to projects in China. With this much financial expertise and the ability

---

[17] The Asiandollar markets are equivalent to the Eurodollar markets.

[18] The other note-issuing banks are Standard Chartered Bank and Bank of China.

to mobilize funds for investment, it is little wonder that Hong Kong is sometimes referred to as the capital of South China.

South Korea: Adapting the Japanese Model

It was the conflict in Korea that provided Japan with a strong U.S. market for its products beginning in 1950. By the time the war ended three years later, Japan was on its way to economic recovery and South Korea was in shambles. The South Koreans learned many lessons from the Japanese in terms of business groups and bank-led industrial growth. But a very real sense of urgency did not allow them the luxury of arriving at the needed economic decisions through a democratic process. The government bureaucracy directed the development of industry and the allocation of bank capital.

The Economic Plan

It is fair to say that Korea has risen from extremely humble origins. Japan had invaded the country in the late 19th century and formally annexed it in 1910. In 1944, less than one half of one percent of the Korean population had 13 or more years of education and over 86 percent had *no* formal education. In 1953, South Korea was a labor-intensive, primarily agricultural country. What industry had existed was in North Korea for the most part. One of the first industries to gain momentum in South Korea was the construction industry. The United States permitted participation by Korean firms in building Korean military bases. In addition, large-scale investments in infrastructure were necessary to form a foundation for the growth of other industries.

The purpose of the Economic Planning Board (EPB) was similar to that of the Japanese Ministry of International Trade and Industry (MITI). However, the EPB went much further than the MITI in its direction of industry development because South Korea had a much weaker base upon which to build. It was clear to the EPB that the Japanese model was one that Korea should adopt.

Beginning in the 1960s, an ambitious plan for economic development and industrialization was launched. There were incentives to assure that private industry complied with the plan provisions. One of these incentives was differential access to credit. Korean firms developed as highly leveraged companies with roughly two-thirds of their liabilities in the form of short-term bank loans. In turn, the commercial and specialized banks were under government control. There were real incentives to follow the government plan because a company that somehow displeased the government could find itself without adequate financial resources to survive. Even foreign loans were authorized and controlled by the government. Those firms which complied with government plans had two distinct advantages. First, credit was available at interest rates that were substantially below market rates. Second, as long as the company followed the plan, the company was not denied access to financial resources, even if the company did not operate profitably right away. In this way, Korean banks provided risk capital for the development of the preferred industrial sectors.

The Economic Planning Board guided South Korea through three phases of development: the "takeoff" phase between 1961 and 1973, the promotion of heavy industry between 1973 and 1979, and liberalization of markets since 1979.

The *takeoff phase* was based on the philosophy that economic independence required discipline and sacrifice. Accordingly, controls were instituted to curtail the importation of consumer and other goods that were not considered necessities. In a protected domestic market, the industrial firms could then realize healthy profits by producing substitutes for goods that would normally be imported. While the government sought to reduce imports, it also wanted to encourage export activity. Incentives for exports included direct cash payments, permission to retain foreign currency earnings from exports, the privilege of borrowing currency, and some liberalization of import restrictions when the imported goods were used to produce items for subsequent export.

Support for exports also came in the form of policy loans--loans made by banks specifically earmarked for particular activities. These loans were easily obtainable at interest rates below those for other loans. As the takeoff phase progressed, banks increasingly used export performance as a qualifying criterion for credit allocation. The growth of exports during this period seemed to confirm the government's ability to orchestrate the continued economic development that South Korea needed.

The *Heavy and Chemical Industries (HCI)* phase began in 1973 and shifted the focus from basic materials and intermediate goods to heavy industry. This change was partially in response to increasing wage rates in Korea and partially in recognition that the entry of China into Western trade could erode some of the country's progress in world export markets. The model of Japan's heavy industry buildup was also a motivating factor. The targeted industries were petrochemical processing, steel, metal products, shipbuilding, machinery, and automobile production. Again, the government used bank loans to promote these industries. During the 1970s between 42 and 50 percent of all lending was devoted to these industries. The objectives of this phase were clearly realized. By 1983, these industries accounted for more than 50 percent of all Korean exports.

The HCI drive produced a world-class, efficient steel-making infrastructure. However, the initiative was overambitious in that it produced overcapacity in a number of areas, including shipbuilding, heavy equipment, and petrochemical processing. The *liberalization phase*, which began in 1979, attempted to correct some of these excesses. In this phase, the government reduced its emphasis on heavy industry, reduced its role in credit allocation decisions, and eliminated some of the interest rate subsidies, and restructured some of the distressed industries. Also as part of this initiative, the government permitted a broader scope of foreign activity by domestic commercial banks, as well as more access to the Korean market by foreign commercial banks. In addition, commercial banks were sold to private shareholders, although the government continues to be a significant influence in bank decisions.

South Korea evolved very quickly from a colonized country to a celebrated Asian NIC.[19] Among developing countries, South Korean ranks high in a number of export categories:

- Unprocessed tobacco
- Cotton fabrics
- Organic chemicals
- Road motor vehicles
- Iron and steel
- Plastic materials
- Clothing
- Domestic electric equipment
- Watches and clocks
- Toys and sporting goods
- Rubber articles
- Textile yarn and thread
- Woven noncotton textiles
- Footwear
- Travel goods and bags
- Ships and boats
- Sound recorders

---

[19] NIC is an acronym for Newly Industrialized Country.

- Telecommunications equipment

The government and the banking system led the way. These sectors, combined with the initiative of the Korean people, created a close approximation of the Japanese *keiretsu* in the form of the Korean *chaebol*.

The Chaebols

A *chaebol* is a Korean business combination that is similar to a *keiretsu* in that it is a combination of companies. But, unlike the *keiretsu*, which have a long history (including the era of the *zaibatsu*) and have developed into professionally managed companies, *chaebols* are of more recent vintage and most are still managed by families of the founders, if not the founders themselves. In addition, Korean banks are not the major firms in *chaebols*, because, before liberalization in 1979, the Korean government was the major bank shareholder. Nonetheless, the *chaebol* groups now hold significant shares of bank stock. The four largest *chaebols* are Samsung, Hyundai, Lucky-Goldstar, and Daewoo.

Composed of more than 30 firms with annual sales in excess of $40 billion, *Samsung Group* is the largest *chaebol*. The founder Lee Byung-Chull, began operating a rice mill in 1936, when Korea was still under Japanese rule. By 1938, he began to trade in dried rice and incorporated as Samsung, which means "Three stars." Here, too, the Japanese influence appears to have been strong since Mitsubishi, which means "Three diamonds," was already a powerful *zaibatsu*. After the Korean War, Samsung formed the profitable Cheil Sugar Company, organized Cheil Wool Textile (1954), and entered banking and insurance. Later, the company branched into paper manufacturing, department stores, and newspaper publishing.

With the help of Sanyo in 1969, Samsung Electronics was formed. Its initial electronics know-how came from disassembling Western products and producing inexpensive, private label versions. Beginning with black-and-white televisions, the company graduated to color televisions, VCRs, and microwave ovens for U.S. firms such as General Electric, J.C. Penney, and Sears. By the 1980s, the company was shipping electronics under its own name. During the HCI drive in the 1970s, Samsung Shipbuilding, Samsung Petrochemicals, and Samsung Precision Industries (aircraft engines) emerged. Samsung Aerospace received a contract in 1991 to co-produce F-16 fighter planes with General Dynamics in Korea. A joint venture with Motorola develops and manufactures a small, wireless computer.

Like the Japanese *keiretsu*, the Korean *chaebols* have connections with financial institutions. In the case of Samsung, these include Ankuk Fire and Marine Insurance Company, Samsung Life Insurance Company, and Kukje Securities. In addition, Samsung owns approximately 16 percent of Commercial Bank and over 5 percent each of Hanil, Cho Heung, and Korea First banks.

Hyundai Group is composed of 27 companies in the industries of automobiles, shipbuilding, construction,and electronics. Its founder, Chung Ju-Yung, began a business repairing trucks for the U.S. occupation forces. In 1947, he branched into construction after forming Hyundai Engineering and Construction. Hyundai Motor began operations in 1967 by assembling Fords. During the HCI drive in the 1970s, Chung started Hyundai Heavy Industries with the express mission of building the world's largest shipyard, although he had no prior experience in this area. With government help, a virtual monopoly in Korea, and a hard-working labor force, his ambition was realized. Mitsubishi, owing 15 percent of Hyundai Motor, collaborated in 1975 in building the first Korean automobile--the Pony. The experience of Hyundai Motor in the United States has been disappointing with sales slumping one-third since 1988, but sales in Europe continue to grow.

Hyundai's financial affiliates include Hyundai Marine and Fire Insurance Company. Also, the company owns over 5 percent in Korea First Bank, Hanil Bank, and Bank of Seoul.

Lucky-Goldstar Group is a group of 39 companies that resulted from the combination of Lucky Chemical Company and Goldstar Company. During World War II, Koo In-Hwoi made tooth powder to use instead of salt (the most common toothbrushing substance at the time). In 1947, he founded Lucky Chemical Company to make facial cream, deodorant, shampoo, and Lucky Toothpaste.

Emulating the Japanese, Koo formed Goldstar Company to make electronics goods in 1958. The first products were electric fans, but the company later moved into radios (1959), refrigerators (1965), televisions (1966), elevators and escalators (1968), and washing machines and air conditioners (1969).

During the HCI drive, Lucky, Ltd (the successor of Lucky Chemical) entered petrochemical processing in 1977. In 1984, it entered a biotech venture with Chiron, a U.S. firm. In 1986, Lucky constructed the world's largest petrochemical plant in Saudi Arabia.

Meanwhile, Goldstar (like Samsung) produced private-label electronics for J.C. Penney and Sears. The company has since invested heavily in semiconductor production and has entered joint ventures with AT&T, NEC, Hitachi, and Siemens. Its target market is office automation, and high-end consumer electronics.

The financial affiliates of Lucky-Goldstar include Lucky Insurance Company, Lucky Securities Company, and Pusan Investment and Finance Corporation. The group also owns more than 5 percent in Korea First and Hanil banks.

There are 22 firms in the *Daewoo Group*, the youngest of the four largest *chaebols*. In 1967, Kim Woo-Choong and To Dae Do combined their names and $18,000 in borrowed funds to form Daewoo, a textile exporting company. Not long after, Kim bought To's interest in the firm and, with the low-cost labor available in Korea, turned the company into a profitable clothing manufacturer. Its customers included Sears, J.C. Penney, and Montgomery Ward.

Daewoo later entered the construction business. In 1976, the government requested that Kim take over a government-owned machinery plant that had been unprofitable for 37 years. Kim accepted, actually moving into the plant for 9 months. That was the start of Daewoo Heavy Industries, a subsidiary of Daewoo Group that has been consistently profitable. Later, the government asked Kim to take over the government's 50 percent share of GM Korea. The name of the automaker was changed to Daewoo Motor and the company turned into the third largest car manufacturer in Korea.[20] Kim's experience with a shipyard that the government asked him to complete and operate was not as successful.

During the 1980s, in a series of export deals in which low-cost goods were exchanged for technology, Daewoo Group worked with Caterpillar (forklifts), Northern Telecom (telephone equipment), Boeing, Lockheed, General Dynamics, Daimler-Benz, and United Technologies (aerospace components).

The financial affiliates of Daewoo Group include Daewoo Capital Management Company and Daewoo Securities Company. In addition, Daewoo owns almost one quarter of the equity in Korea First Bank and small stakes in Cho Heung Bank, Hanil Bank, Bank of Seoul, and Commercial Bank.

There is no doubt that the *chaebols* have been the backbone of the Korean industrialization. Nor is there any doubt that their ascendancy would have been much more difficult without the Korean banking system. The country is entering an important phase in its development. South Korea must now provide comparable financial backing for small- and medium-size companies in the

---

[20] In 1992, Daewoo bought out General Motor's 50 percent stake in the joint venture for $170 million after disagreements over how to adjust to weak market conditions.

economy. Furthermore, the political and economic consequences that would be associated with a possible reunification of North and South Korea provide additional challenges. [21] Nevertheless, it cannot be denied that the partnership of government, banking, and industry has accelerated the standard of living in South Korea even faster than was the case in Japan.

Conclusion

The People's Republic of China may appear to be a paradox. It is a communist country that has tolerated and even invested in capitalist ventures. But in its own way, China is learning faster than the United States how banking and industry can and should work together to promote economic development. The country provides an example of how economic experiments can be structured (in the Special Economic Zones) to control for unanticipated developments. The vibrant productivity triangle of South China, Hong Kong, and Taiwan suggests that the economic ties that are being forged may ultimately reduce the potential political tensions in the region.

South Korea's growth has been guided by the government. Using the Japanese model, the government first encouraged exports with incentives that were directed toward specific industries, then targeted heavy industry for development. The result is that South Korea is now one of the most efficient producers of clothing, steel, ships and boats, and other major industrial classifications.

Virtually all the growth in China and South Korea was financed with bank loans. The governments of these countries have recognized that banking may be defined and structured in more than one narrow model--that it can instead be a readily accessible, flexible means of fueling economic development.

---

[21] The industrial infrastructure of North Korea has not advanced to the same extent as that of South Korea since the end of the Korean War.

Selected References

Besher, Alexander. *The Pacific Rim Almanac*, New York: HarperPerennial/HarperCollinsPublishers, 1991.

Chai, Alan, Alta Campbell, and Patrick J. Spain, Editors. *Hoover's Handbook of World Business 1993*, Austin, Texas: The Reference Press, 1993.

Elegant, Robert. *Pacific Destiny: Inside Asia Today*, New York: Crown Publishers, 1990.

Engardio, Pete, Lynne Curry, and Joyce Barnathan. "China Fever Strikes Again," *Business Week*, March 29, 1993, pp.46-47.

Engholm, Christopher. *The China Venture: America's Corporate Encounter with the People's Republic of China*, Glenview, Illinois: Scott, Foresman and Company, 1989.

Ghose, T. K. *The Banking System of Hong Kong*, Singapore: Butterworth & Co., 1987.

Gibney, Frank. *Pacific Century: America and Asia in a Changing World*, New York: Charles Scribner's Sons/MacMillan Publishing Company, 1992.

Kelly, Brian and Mark London. *The Four Little Dragons: A Journey to the Source of the Business Boom Along the Pacific Rim*, New York: Touchstone/Simon & Schuster, 1989.

Kraar, Louis. "A New China Without Borders," *Fortune*, October 5, 1992, pp. 124-128.

Lee, Sang M., Sangjin Yoo, and Tosca M. Lee. "Korean Chaebols: Corporate Values and Strategies," *Organizational Dynamics*, vol. 19, no. 4 (spring 1991), pp.36-50.

Mattera, Philip. *World Class Business: A Guide to the 100 Most Powerful Global Corporations*, New York: Henry Holt and Company, 1992.

Meyer, Richard. "Keynesian Communism," *Financial World*, April 27, 1993, pp. 46-50.

Morris, Jan. *Hong Kong*, New York: Vintage Books/Random House, 1989.

Porter, Michael E. *The Competitive Advantage of Nations*, New York: Free Press/MacMillan, 1990.

Schlender, Brenton. "China Really Is on the Move," *Fortune*, October 5, 1992, pp. 114-122.

Scott, Robert Haney, K. A. Wong, and Yan Ki Ho. *Hong Kong's Financial Institutions and Markets*, Oxford: Oxford University Press, 1986.

Skully, Michael T. and George J. Viksnins. *Financing East Asia's Success: Comparative Financial Development in Eight Asians Countries*, New York: St. Martin's Press, 1987.

United Nations. *Handbook of International Trade and Development Statistics*, New York: Author, 1989.

World Bank. *China: External Trade and Capital*, Washington: Author, 1988.

World Bank. *China: Finance and Investment*, Washington: Author, 1988.

World Bank. *Korea: Managing the Industrial Transition, Volume I, The Conduct of Industrial Policy*, Washington: Author, 1989.

6. Steps Toward Financial Modernization in the United States

Introduction

James Pierpont Morgan sat before the U.S. House Banking and Currency Committee to testify in the Pujo Hearings in 1912. By this time, the House of Morgan held 72 directorships in 112 corporations in diverse areas that included banking, transportation, and public utilities. In a spirit of true relationship banking, the House of Morgan had underwritten industrial bond issues during the previous decade that amounted to almost $2 billion--phenomenal volume for this era. J.P. Morgan was asked what really drove this system of relationship banking. Was the credit that his firm arranged based primarily on money or property? Morgan responded:

> No, sir, the first thing is character... Before money or anything else. Money cannot buy it...Because a man I do not trust could not get money from me on all the bonds in Christendom. [22]

He continued,

> I have known a man to come into my office, and I have given him a check for a million dollars when I knew that they [sic] had not a cent in the world.[23]

The cynics considered such statements to be, at best, hyperbole, but Morgan's sentiments did reflect the nature of industrial relationships at the turn of the 20th century. At that time, there existed U.S. business

[22] See Chernow, p. 154.

[23] See Chernow, p. 154.

combinations that would rival today's Japanese *keiretsu* in terms of strong industrial firms with dedicated financial backing.

But these arrangements were the object of considerable disdain. Their opponents insisted that too much power had been vested in such combinations and that they should not be permitted. The Sherman Antitrust Act (1890) declared that any contract, combination, or conspiracy that restrained trade was illegal. The Clayton Antitrust Act (1914) prohibited any action--sales contracts, intercorporate stockholdings, or unfair pricing--that tended to reduce competition.

There was also a general feeling that too much financial power lay in the hands of a few banks and that there was a "money trust" conspiracy. There seemed to be ample evidence to support this charge. Witness the fact that money panics frequently arose, precipitating runs on commercial banks and, ultimately, bank failures. The large banks in New York, Chicago, and St. Louis--the country's money centers--were blamed. First, the Federal Reserve System would end the monopoly on financial power by a few financial institutions. The flow of credit would be determined by a government agency, not by J.P. Morgan and his counterparts. Later, the Glass-Steagall Act would separate commercial banking from investment banking to limit the power of bankers in the board rooms of industrial America. While it is clear that reform of the banking system was required, it is not clear that all the reform measures were appropriate.

The United States today suffers from a lack of dedicated capital to industrial enterprises. Banks may not take equity stakes in their customers, which would increase the potential for both bank and client growth. The deficiency of this approach is reflected in the low levels of productive investment in this country relative to its major trading partners. Compounding the problems that have been created by unnatural obstacles to relationship banking is the increasing role of nonbank financial institutions, such as mutual funds and pension funds, as major industrial shareholders. These financial institutions are focused on short-term results that they report to their own shareholders. If these results fall below expectations, the institutions will often "vote with their feet" and sell the stock. When shares change hands quickly, there is more than just the exchange of abstract financial claims. The ownership of the firm actually changes. This does not encourage continuity in direction or operations. Meanwhile, the firm's bank is legally not permitted to take an active role in management decisions.

These factors work together to help encourage a short-term perspective in U.S. business. The "trust-busting" attitudes that prevailed at the turn of the 20th century are no longer appropriate. More cooperative efforts should be encouraged and the artificial barriers to a universal form of banking should be removed. Relationship banking, as can be observed in German bank-centered groups or Japanese *keiretsu*, has fostered economic development in many countries. As one of the key elements in developing and maintaining international competitiveness, collaborative efforts between industry and banking must be acknowledged and supported in the United States.

Misconceptions About the U.S. Banking Industry

The U.S. banking industry has been unjustly held responsibility for a number of economic problems that the country has experienced. Unfortunately, many of the legal and regulatory constraints to a more effective banking system are based on these misconceptions. One misconception is that large money center banks were responsible for money panics that destabilized the financial system. Another is that commercial banks were primarily responsible for the financial devastation of the Great Depression. Neither of these is true. In fact, the banking system was prevented from developing in ways that would avoid some of the money panics. Moreover, it was the Federal Reserve System, not the commercial banking system that prolonged the agony of the Great Depression.

The True Cause of Early U.S. Money Panics

Before the Federal Reserve System (1914) or the Federal Insurance Corporation (1933), money panics occurred when depositors lost faith that a bank could meet its obligations. When this faith was lost, virtually all depositors requested repayment. Under these circumstances, even sound banks could be driven to insolvency. This is because loans and securities could not be liquidated fast enough to satisfy all requests for cash. Essentially, smaller banks were more subject to these crises of confidence than larger institutions. The evolution of U.S. bank regulation almost guaranteed that the country would be subject to these episodes because a system of strong, nationwide banks was never permitted to develop.

Early Attempts at National Banking

There has always been a basic suspicion of powerful banks in the United States. For example, Thomas Jefferson (drafter of the Declaration of Independence, Secretary of State from 1790 to 1793, and President from 1801 to 1809) opposed both strong central government and a national banking system. As an advocate for the agricultural sector and for the rights of states and local authorities, he championed self-reliance, not government protection or planning, as the key to the success of America. In Jefferson's view, if the agricultural sector suffered one or more difficult years, large amounts of land would fall into the control of banks instead of farmers as a result of wide-scale foreclosures. Thus, banks should remain under state, not national, control.

On the other hand, Alexander Hamilton (first Secretary the Treasury from 1789 to 1795 and architect of the banking system) advocated a strong banking network. In 1790, during George Washington's first term as President, Hamilton conceived the idea of a national bank. It was not a central bank in the European sense; it would neither have a large number of branches nor be publicly owned.

A national bank with note-issuing power could convert the national debt into a medium of exchange if government securities could be used to collateralize or back national bank notes. [Recall that early bank notes were liabilities of the various issuing banks and were convertible into gold or silver.] If a national bank issued bank notes backed by government bonds, the government could thereby standardize the nation's currency *and* finance its operations. A strong national bank would also promote business and industry, he reasoned. As one who believed that the industrial interests of a developing country were of primary importance, Hamilton saw this as a powerful argument in favor of a national bank. President Washington accepted Hamilton's argument and in 1791 the 20-year charter of the First Bank of the United States was granted.

The First Bank of the United States accepted deposits, made loans, and issued bank notes. It carried on both private business and the official business of the U.S. government. Soon it was the country's largest bank, with branches located in all major cities and notes circulating throughout the country. The power that accrued to the First Bank because of its special relationship with the federal government was distasteful to some. The First Bank implemented a strict policy with respect to money supply growth by redeeming state bank notes, thereby forcing such banks to convert their notes into gold or silver. State banks formed a strong lobby against the Bank. In 1811, when the charter of the First Bank expired, the Jeffersonians were in office and the charter was not renewed.

In the five years ended 1816, the volume of circulating state bank notes more than doubled to over $200 million, and the state banking system was found inadequate to accommodate the nation's needs. Complete convertibility of these notes became virtually impossible, given the limited supply of gold and silver coins. The first bank failure in the United States is an example of the abuse of note-issuing powers. When a Rhode Island bank that had issued $800,000 in notes failed in 1809, it was discovered that the bank had only $45 in capital!

Without a national banking system, this kind of high-leverage potential spurred the creation of many small, unstable institutions. In 1781, the number of U.S. commercial banks was 5. By the time the charter of the First Bank of the United States expired 30 years later, the number had grown to 250. Had a national banking system been allowed to develop, the volatility in money supply and the resulting panics could have been reduced. As it was, practices like those of the failed Rhode Island bank fueled resistance to the banking industry.

During the War of 1812, a sizable national debt (in the form of government bonds) had been built up, and the money supply issued by state banks remained unstable. *The Second Bank of the United States* was chartered in 1816 to address the lack of a national currency. The Second Bank was entitled to repay the government bonds with bank notes backed by government securities, thus providing a uniform national currency. This would, hopefully, reduce the number of money panics that resulted from a variety of weak institutions that varied from state to state.

The Second Bank quickly became a powerful financial presence, holding both the federal government's deposits and a large share of private wealth. It maintained close relationships with the large money center banks in New York, Chicago, and St. Louis. Smaller state banks looked to it as a lender of last resort, or the ultimate provider of liquidity in the event of a bank run. The Second Bank even acted to restrict the money supply when it appeared that speculative lending was accelerating beyond acceptable levels.

Nevertheless, the Second Bank enjoyed little popularity. Its branches crossed state lines, giving rise to territorial disputes with state banks. Andrew Jackson, President from 1829 to 1837, was also opposed to the Bank. He considered his constituency to be the farmers and laborers of the country--people who were opening up the frontier to agriculture and mining, developing roads and canals, and building new cities and towns. These people found their futures and fortunes tied to a concentration of power and wealth in the Northeast, where the Second Bank of the United States was headquartered.

In 1832, Jackson vetoed legislation that would have kept the Bank alive. The following year, the Treasury withdrew its funds and redeposited them in a number of state banks. The Bank's charter was not renewed upon expiration in 1836, and the "free banking era" in the United States began.

From 1836 to 1863, there was virtually no federal regulation of the banking system in the United States. At the beginning of this 27-year period, there were 600 state banks. Without the presence of a stabilizing national bank, 1600 state banks emerged--all issuing their own form of money as bank notes.

It should not be surprising that many of them were not sound and that some were, in fact, unscrupulous. Specie, generally gold or silver coin, continued to be legal tender, but the sheer volume of notes that circulated often made guaranteed convertibility impossible. In some cases, bankers generated large amounts of notes that could never be redeemed. In other cases, they issued notes and then avoided all attempts to redeem the notes. Not surprisingly, many of these "free banking era" institutions failed. The reputation of the banking industry was perhaps at its lowest ebb. However, this was not because concentrations of financial power rested with too few banks. Instead, this situation resulted because control of the banking system was too widely dispersed and was not coordinated by a central authority.

National Bank Charters

The National Bank Act of 1863 introduced a new kind of federally chartered bank. Unlike the First and Second Banks of the United States, the new form of bank, the "national bank," would not branch nationwide. Nor would only one institution be formed. Instead, a newly created Office of the Comptroller of the Currency would charter national banks to operate as unit banks (one office only) within their respective states. Restricting the geographical region in which national banks could operate would presumably reduce resistance to the new institutions on the part of state banks.

At the same time, the objective of creating national banks was to restore a measure of order and stability to the banking industry. The new national banks were required to meet minimum capital requirements. Their bank notes were backed by Treasury securities and printed by the U.S. Treasury department to ensure uniformity. Moreover, national banks placed minimum reserves (liquid assets) on deposit with the Comptroller (as a percentage of bank notes and deposits).

These were much stricter standards than those which existed under many state banking laws. The framers of the National Bank Act had hoped that state banks would convert to the national charter. However, the incentives were not sufficient to encourage all state banks to convert. Thus, the basic framework of

U.S. banks emerged as a dual banking system--one in which a bank could be chartered by either the state in which it operated or by the federal government.

Unfortunately, the creation of national banks was, at best, a partial solution to distortions in the money supply. The nation's economic growth was occurring primarily in the regions outside the northeast, yet the money center banks in the northeast controlled a significant amount of the money supply. State banking authorities could not authorize operation of their banks in other states. National banks were not permitted to branch nationwide. So the money supply was not sensitive to needs for financing in the regions experiencing economic growth. However, the money center banks did not create this problem. The regulatory environment imposed the restrictions.

The money supply itself was inelastic in that it was tied to the amount of gold and government securities. The availability of gold constrained the extent to which the money supply could expand. After passage of the National Bank Act in 1863, the federal debt gradually declined, that is, the debt from the Civil War was repaid, which also constrained growth in the money supply. Then in the 1890s, the discovery of gold in Alaska and South Africa increased the supply of gold (and the money supply) so dramatically that inflation became a real threat to the economy. These shifting money supply conditions were not necessarily favorable for the U.S. economy, but they were not the responsibility of the money center banks.

Morgan's Role as a Central Banker

In fact, the money center banks worked within the existing regulatory framework to maintain an orderly system to the extent possible. The cycles were usually driven by the demand for agricultural credit. The Comptroller of the Currency required that nationally chartered banks in rural areas, so-called country banks, maintain their reserves at larger banks in 47 "reserve cities." In turn, these larger banks kept their reserves on deposit with the largest banks in the three "central reserve cities"--primarily New York, but also Chicago and St. Louis.

When the demand for loans increased in the autumn, the country banks drew down their reserves at the 47 reserve city banks who, in turn, drew down their reserves in the money centers. If the demand for loans continued to expand, the pressure mounted on the money center banks to provide needed liquidity. The House of Morgan and other money center institutions maintained large fortunes in their vaults to accommodate such needs. If even these proved insufficient, the money center banks often structured loan syndicates that mobilized idle funds on reserve at many different banks throughout the country, or even in London or Paris.

Of course, if all of these measures failed, a panic resulted. If New York was forced to say "No," somewhere in the United States a bank failed because it either could not meet a loan commitment or could not honor a deposit withdrawal request, prompting all its depositors to request withdrawals immediately. Often when one bank failed, the panic automatically spread to others. Yet it is clearly inappropriate to hold the money center banks responsible for these panics. The problem was the structure of the banking system, not the size of the banks in New York.

The watershed event came in 1907 when Wall Street itself was shaken by these structural problems. The problem began in the trust company sector. In general, trust companies tended to hold more speculative stock portfolios than other members of the banking community. While national and most state-chartered banks were not allowed by law to accept trust accounts (such as wills and estates), they could form trust company subsidiaries. In fact, J.P. Morgan and his counterparts thought so little of the management of many of these companies that they formed their own affiliated company--Bankers Trust--to be able to offer their clients sound trust services.

Knickerbocker Trust Company was the third largest trust in New York, with 18,000 depositors, and was heavily invested in copper mine stocks. When new copper mines were discovered in Alaska, the fear of a copper glut pushed down the value of United Copper by 35 points on Monday, October 21. Realizing that Knickerbocker had a major stake in United Copper, depositors lined up in front the trust company on Tuesday morning to withdraw their funds. Soon the panic spread to other trust companies.

With no mechanism in place to bring stability to the system, J.P. Morgan acted as a central banker in the truest sense of the word. He formed a committee of other commercial bankers in New York. Together, they realized that Knickerbocker could not be saved. At the same time, they were determined to protect the system. Morgan's committee met with George Cortelyou, the U.S. Treasury Secretary, in New York on Tuesday evening (October 22, 1907). The next day, Cortelyou placed $25 million in government funds at the disposal of J.P. Morgan.

As more trust companies were pressured by depositor withdrawals, Morgan's committee called together the presidents of the New York trust companies to urge them to form a rescue pool. As it turned out they did not know each other, had not worked together, and found it difficult to cooperate under these trying circumstances. Clearly, an important element of relationship banking involves bankers that can work together to resolve crises. Trust Company of America appeared to be the soundest of the group and Morgan decided to stop the trouble there. J.P. Morgan and Company, First National Bank, and National City Bank formed a $3 million pool to rescue Trust Company of America.

Nevertheless, the panic continued. Customers formed lines and waited overnight, bringing with them food, water, and portable chairs. In desperate need for cash, trust companies called in margin loans, that is, those that had been granted for the purchase of stock. Money was in such short supply that the interest rate on margin loans rose to 150 percent! Stock brokers came to Morgan in desperation for help. On Thursday, October 24, three days after Knickerbocker failed, Ransom Thomas, president of the New York Stock Exchange walked across the street to J.P. Morgan and Company. He told Morgan that unless $25 million was raised immediately, no less than 50 brokerage firms would fail. Thomas suggested shutting down the stock exchange. Morgan resisted the idea and insisted that the Exchange remain open until its normal closing time at 3:00 p.m. In the interim, Morgan called a meeting of bank presidents and obtained pledges for the $25 million by 2:19 p.m. He then sent a team of Morgan employees to the Stock Exchange floor to announce that call money (short-term loans) would be available at 10 percent. Brokers scrambled to sign up for the loans and, as the news spread, a roar of relief and gratitude rose as a salute to J.P. Morgan.

In spite of Morgan's efforts the results of the panic were devastating. Eight banks and trust companies had failed during the week. The Wall Street panic did not go unnoticed in Europe, where investors began to withdraw money from the United States. The City of New York had difficulty placing its securities there. George McClellan, mayor of New York, came to Morgan on Monday, October 28 (only one week after the Knickerbocker failure on October 21, 1907) and told him that the city needed $30 million to meet its obligations. Under J.P. Morgan's direction, the same group of New York money center bankers that had rescued Trust Company of America also rescued the city of New York.

In the span of one week in October 1907, J.P. Morgan was instrumental in saving the banking system, the New York Stock Exchange, and the city of New York. Assertions that Morgan and other New York bankers possessed great financial power are true. However, criticisms that they consistently abused this power are <u>not true</u>. In fact, Morgan acted to avert financial crises that he himself had no role in creating within a banking system that had no provision for emergency measures. The basic mistrust of concentrations of banking power is thus not justified. Those laws and regulations that are designed to constrain the size and scope of commercial bank activities are misguided and inappropriate under these circumstances.

The Federal Reserve System

The panic of 1907 revealed many flaws in the banking system and inspired the creation of a federal system of banks that would presumably correct these deficiencies. In 1913, the Federal Reserve System was crafted by federal legislators. The Federal Reserve was the first bank to carry out all the functions of a traditional central bank: performing banking functions for the government, regulating commercial banks, maintaining orderly financial markets, acting as lender of last resort, and managing the value of the dollar in foreign currency markets. In contrast to the First and Second Banks of the United States, the Federal Reserve is a decentralized and independent bank. There are 12 regional banks, each with authority over a specific geographic region.[24] The Federal Reserve Board is the policy making body in Washington, D.C.

Nationally chartered banks are required to be members of the Federal Reserve and state banks may elect to be members. Member banks contribute equity capital for the reserve bank in their district, receiving in return a fixed dividend on their Fed stock. Member banks elect six of the nine directors of their district reserve bank, of whom, no more than three may be bankers. The three reserve bank directors, who are not elected by members, are appointed by the Federal Reserve Board. All members of the Federal Reserve Board are appointed by the President of the United States.

The Federal Reserve System was designed to prevent the money panics that had plagued the country before its creation. Among other things, the district reserve banks were designated to hold the required reserves of members, were permitted to discount commercial paper (that is, buy commercial loans from member banks), and became lenders of last resort. Finally, it was hoped, local money shortages would be addressed by local monetary authorities. At least, that was the plan. The Great Depression would show that the system had not yet been refined. Perhaps even more damaging to the long-term viability of the country's

---

[24] The Federal Reserve District banks are in New York, Boston, Philadelphia, Richmond (Virginia), Atlanta, Cleveland, Chicago, St. Louis, Kansas City, Minneapolis, Dallas, and San Francisco.

financial system, much of the blame for the depression would be placed on the shoulders of the commercial banking industry.

The Great Depression: Facts and Myths

One of the instructions contained in the 1913 Federal Reserve Act was that the reserve banks should maintain credit conditions that accommodated commerce and business. The Fed is charged with maintaining adequate access to credit by expansion of the money supply, if necessary. At the same time, the Fed is responsible for not allowing inflationary spirals to develop as a result of excessive growth in money supply. There is clearly a trade-off between these two. The early choices made by the Federal Reserve with respect to these two opposing objectives had more influence over economic conditions in the United States than did the structure of the banking system.

The Recession of 1920-1921

One of the first important decisions by the Federal Reserve occurred after the end of World War I. To finance the war, the national debt had risen from $1 billion to $27 billion. By the fall of 1919, prices rose at an annual rate of 15 percent. The Federal Reserve decided to stop the inflationary spiral. The discount rate (the rate that banks pay to borrow from the Fed) rose from 4 to 7 percent over the course of a few months and was maintained at this level for 18 months. Other interest rates followed suit. In other words, the price of money nearly doubled.

The economic consequences were dramatic. Commodity prices declined by 50 percent from their 1920 peak and farmers found themselves in financial crisis. In general, business activity declined by one-third. Specifically, manufacturing output fell 42 percent. The unemployment rate increased by a factor of five to almost 12 percent. In 1919, 63 banks had failed; in 1921, the number was 506.

The Roaring '20s

The economy began to recover in 1921, although it was plagued by two milder recessions during the decade (1923 and 1926). New technologies led to a 63 percent increase in output per hour of labor. Mass markets for goods developed, such as automobiles, refrigerators, and radios. New factories were built and manufacturing production increased. The stock market reached new heights. This was the "roaring twenties." The promises of the Federal Reserve appear to have been fulfilled.

Signs of trouble began to develop, however. Farmers had not recovered from the recession of 1920-1921. There was a glut of agricultural commodities and commodity prices remained deflated. In 1920, farm families represented 15 percent of gross national product. By 1928, their share was down to 9 percent. Even factory laborers were being affected. Some of the productivity gains came from laborers working longer hours for the same pay. Other productivity gains came from improvements in technology that required fewer workers, creating a labor surplus.

In the financial markets, individual loans to purchase stock were increasing rapidly. The public was eager to buy equities and credit was easy to obtain. Leveraged investment trusts, a new form of financial institution, were formed with a little capital and a lot of borrowed money--for the purpose of investing in stocks. Both banks and investors were engaged in stock speculation and stock prices rose dramatically as a result. By the summer of 1928, the Federal Reserve was concerned about the level of speculative financial activity.

The Crash and the Depression

The bubble burst on October 24, 1929. Within a few days the stock market's value declined by one-third. On the order of $7 billion in bank loans for stock purchases became worthless. The psychology of 1907 threatened to resurface. But surely the same sort of panic would be averted, because the Federal Reserve could ease the contracted money supply by exercising the powers conferred upon it by Congress. The Fed could lower interest rates and inject liquidity into the economy to stabilize the decline.

The Federal Reserve neither lowered interest rates nor consistently pumped money into the economy. In fact, the position of the Fed was that the stock market declines were a natural consequence of the speculative activities in which the market had engaged. By mid-1930, the decision was made to *increase* interest rates to stop the flow of gold to Europe as concerned overseas investors converted dollars to gold. The higher interests only served to exacerbate depressionary conditions.

Meanwhile, in a misguided attempt to protect American farmers and producers from lower prices for their products because of foreign competition, the Hawley-Smoot Tariff Act was passed in mid-1930 to increase the price of imported goods. In some cases, these tariffs accounted for 50 percent of price of imported products. In retaliation, two dozen countries raised their own tariffs and drastically reduced their imports of U.S. goods. The reduced demand for U.S. output added to the economic woes.

The combination of difficult financial and economic conditions was devastating. Billions of dollars of bank loans were liquidated through defaults and bankruptcies by farmers and businessmen. Money disappeared on a massive scale, with the money supply shrinking by more than one-third from 1929 to 1933. Almost 10,000 commercial banks failed during the same period.

Later, the commercial banking system would be punished for the excesses of the 1920s. It is true that commercial banks became involved in speculative activities of the decade by lending money for stock with inflated prices. It is also a fact that commercial bankers foreclosed on defaulted loans during the Great Depression that followed the 1929 Stock Market Crash. It is a myth, however, that the banking system was responsible for the severity and the length of that depression. Instead, inappropriate action by the Federal Reserve and ill-advised tariff legislation prolonged the misery of this difficult period in U.S. history.

The Glass-Steagall Act

Under the administration of President Franklin Roosevelt sweeping reforms of the banking industry were initiated. The Glass-Steagall Act of 1933 was intended to rein in the practices of the 1920s and restore the banking industry to a more mundane level of activity. The principle measures in the act that pertained to commercial banks included restrictions on deposit interest rates, deposit insurance, and the separation of commercial and investment banking. While these measures may appear reasonable on the surface, they have had serious negative implications over time.

The Provisions of the Act

It was felt that bankers were prone to excessive competition when they paid interest on checking accounts. Paying interest on their deposits led them to make more risky loans to cover the cost of this interest expense. Then, during difficult economic conditions, the banks forced liquidation on their loan customers. The Glass-Steagall Act prohibited the payment of interest on checking accounts. Also, rates paid on time deposits would be regulated by Federal Reserve System. The logic was that once banks were assured a much lower cost of funds, they would be more careful in their lending practices and more tolerant of delinquent borrowers when economic conditions worsened.

Certain Congressional members that aligned themselves with the interests of the small depositor included deposit insurance in the act. As a result, the Federal Deposit Insurance Corporation was established. The FDIC fund would be established and maintained via insurance premiums paid by the banks. All depositors were protected in the event of bank failure. Even if the insurance fund proved insufficient to adequately cover all deposits, Congress would, no doubt, step in and payoff the remaining deposits. Presumably, an unconditional guarantee would eliminate the destructive bank runs that had become so common.

Interestingly, this provision was not initially endorsed by the banking community, President Roosevelt, or the Federal Reserve. The American Banking Association believed that providing the same insurance for all institutions was unsound, unscientific, and dangerous. President Roosevelt thought that the insurance would pull down the strong with the weak, placing a premium on irresponsible banking and punishing good banking. The Federal Reserve, although mindful that it had clearly not stopped the money panics that led to its own creation, saw the FDIC as an infringement on its authority. The volume of mail that Congress received in favor of deposit insurance, however, ensured its inclusion in the Glass-Steagall Act.

The insurance provision also affected the scope of activities that banks would be permitted to pursue. There was absolutely no support for insuring the securities affiliates of commercial banks. If banks were to have deposit insurance, they must restrict themselves to accepting deposits and making loans. In addition, popular arguments for the separation of powers centered around the conflict of interest that appeared to exist when both commercial and investment banking were permitted. Banks could package their bad loans as bonds, sell them to the unsuspecting public, and even lend the money to investors to buy the bonds. Joining in this conflict-of-interest chorus were smaller investment bankers that were anxious to eliminate competition from the larger commercial banks.

Upon closer examination, the removal of investment banking privileges by Glass-Steagall appears to be basically a punishment, not a true testament that commercial banks cannot or should not engage in the activity. Under the act, national banks and state banks (that were members of the Federal Reserve) were still permitted to underwrite U.S. government securities and general obligations of states and political subdivisions. [25] They were prohibited from the same activities with respect to corporate securities.

Two important factors were ignored in the analysis of the separation of commercial and investment banking. First, the banks that failed during the Depression were not large banks, but small banks. The larger banks with securities operations withstood the economic crisis much better than the smaller ones without such operations. Second, the securities houses that were *not* subsidiaries of commercial banks were just as caught up in the speculative frenzy of the 1920s as those which were bank-affiliates. There is no evidence that the episode would have been avoided even if Glass-Steagall had been enacted twenty years before.

The Effects of Glass-Steagall

The 1933 Act did not correct the basic structural problems of the banking industry. Before Glass-Steagall was enacted, the U.S. banking system was a fragmented collection of approximately 15,000 institutions governed by differing rules and regulations at the state vis-à-vis the federal level. After Glass-Steagall, the only change in the system was that it was then deprived of one of its most important functions--the ability to underwrite corporate stocks and bonds.

One might argue that the Act produced stability in the banking system that last for more than 40 years. After all, it was not until the 1980s that the system seemed to come under competitive pressure once again. Bank failures numbered less than 20 per year from the end of World War II through 1979. This number rose to over 200 in the late 1980s.

The argument that the reforms worked is only partially correct. The number of bank failures was drastically reduced. However, the banking system itself was unable to remain competitive. Under Regulation Q (the Fed regulation that governed deposit interest rate ceilings), banks were less able to compete effectively for deposits when interest rates rose beginning the 1970s. Checking accounts that paid no interest and savings accounts that paid 5 percent interest were not attractive when the rate of inflation reached double-digit proportions and safe, short-term Treasury bills yielded as much as 14 percent.

Money market mutual funds filled the gap created by these interest rate disparities by providing a means of investing in a pool of safe, short-term

---

[25] General obligations of states and political subdivisions are those which are backed by the full taxing authority of the issuer.

instruments that yield market rates. Consider the growth in these funds since 1974, when assets under management of money market mutual funds amounted to approximately $2 billion. Currently assets under management are well in excess of $800 billion. Despite that fact that, starting in 1980, bank deposit interest rates were deregulated, money market mutual funds have captured market share that the banks will probably never regain.

In addition, banks inability to offer a full-range of corporate services has led to loss of business in the corporate sector. Corporate treasurers are now more likely to invest temporarily excess liquidity in various money market instruments rather than in bank deposits. For the largest, more creditworthy industrial firms, commercial paper is a less expensive alternative to short-term bank loans. With the exception of providing a standby letter of credit to support commercial paper, commercial banks may not participate in the issuance of commercial paper under the provisions of Glass-Steagall.[26] Moreover, Glass-Steagall has prevented banks from actively participating in the long-term financing of industrial America.

The Investment Shortfall

Glass-Steagall brought an end to relationship banking as J.P. Morgan would have defined it. This law and other restrictions have contributed to a shortfall in both financial and intellectual investment in U.S. industry. Aggregate investment is below levels in many major trading partners of the United States. Capital markets, which are intended to provide long-term financing, have been taken over by a short-term focus. There is clearly a lack of dedicated capital upon which to build an economic foundation for the future.

Aggregate Investment

Productive investment as a percentage of gross domestic product (GDP) in the United States was generally less than 20 percent in the 1970s and 1980s. In contrast, in Germany and the United Kingdom, investment ranged from 20 to 30 percent of GDP. In Japan, the range was from 30 to 40 percent over the same

[26] In the absence of legislative measures, U.S. bank regulators have granted expanded powers upon special application with respect to securities activities including underwriting commercial paper; issuing, underwriting and dealing in collateralized mortgage obligations; offering brokerage services; offering and selling units in a unit trust solely on the order of and for the account of a bank customer; and making limited investments in an investment bank.

period. The relative lack of U.S. investment has led to a decline in the role of U.S. companies in critical industrial areas. During the 1980s, the United States suffered considerable erosion of world market share in the high-technology fields of fiber optics (from 73 to 42 percent), semiconductors (from 60 to 36 percent), and supercomputers (from 100 to 76 percent).

Fiber optics are the basis for advanced telephone service or ISDN (Integrated Services Digital Network). With ISDN capability, users may send different types of information over one line--voice, data, graphics, and video. Almost 90 percent of all Japanese phone have ISDN capability, while less than 20 percent of U.S. phones do. It is believed that no country without fiber optics and ISDN can be a world leader in telecommunications.

Semiconductors are used extensively in the electronics industry. Production in electronics grew three times as fast in Japan as in the United States during the 1980s. For example, U.S. color television production has all but disappeared because U.S. firms did not invest in the technology. Zenith, the only remaining U.S. manufacturer of color TVs, builds virtually all of them in Mexico.

In the field of computers, rising imports have reduced the U.S. trade surplus in computer hardware from $7 billion in the early 1980s to less than $1 billion by 1990. Moreover, the United States is falling behind Japan in the critical area such as floppy disk drives, displays, microelectronic components, and chip-making equipment. Other applications that depend on computer technology have also suffered. For example, in late 1990, Cincinnati Milacron became the last U.S. company to leave the robotics industry when it sold its robotics division to Asea Brown Boveri AG of Switzerland. Westinghouse, General Electric, and United Technologies had left the field before Cincinnati Milacron.

These are particularly troublesome developments when one considers that the Ministry of International Trade and Industry has stressed an emphasis on telecommunications, electronics, computers, and machine tools with robotics. The Deutsche Bank in Germany has also identified these areas as critical in the industrial development of that country. The United States faces a crisis in terms of the amount of capital that is being devoted to the industries of the future.

Lack of Dedicated Capital

It appears that the problems associated with this investment shortfall are readily recognized. In the 1990s, the Financial Executives Institute, an organization of America's top financial executives, conducted a poll of 2,000 of its members. Ninety-eight percent of respondents believed that the United States faced a competitive crisis. The two most frequently noted reasons for the crisis were shortsighted investors and shortsighted corporate managers.

Neither shareholders nor lenders consistently adopt a long-term perspective as do the banks in Japanese *keiretsu* and in German business groups. This condition is caused primarily by an artificial distance between the users of capital (corporate managers) and providers of capital (shareholders and lenders). Shareholders trade their stock to frequently to provide more continuity of ownership interest. Lenders are forced by regulation to take a virtual hands-off approach to management.

There is often a lack of communication that prevents investors from understanding the long-term goals and objectives of management. In some cases, shareholders hold such widely diversified portfolios that they cannot possibly keep abreast of the business activities of all the companies in the portfolio. Because of this detachment, investors frequently rely on the information that they routinely receive from the company. However, this information relates to past performance, either the last quarter or the last year, and is not reflective of future plans, challenges, or growth potential. Poor performance is often a signal to sell the stock, which depresses the price, and warns the market that the firm may be a poor investment prospect.

Early in the 20th century, there was no such lack of communication. Much of the stock of a U.S. firm was owned by relatively few individuals--for example, the Morgans, Mellons, or Fords. By mid-century, stock was more widely distributed among a broader cross-section of individuals. Today, ownership is becoming more concentrated once again, not in the hands of a few individuals, but in the hands of institutional investors, including pension funds, mutual funds, and insurance companies.

In the mid 1960s, individuals owned 85 percent of corporate stock while these three industries held 13 percent. Currently, the share held by individuals is approximately 40 percent and the share held by pension funds, mutual funds, and insurance companies is 50 percent. These are generally not investors that subscribe to J.P. Morgan's relationship banking theory. On average, they hold stock for a much shorter period than individuals. For example, the annual turnover of pension fund portfolios is more than 50 percent. This means that more than half of the portfolio is sold during the course of a year. Since these institutions hold well over $1 trillion in corporate stock, pension funds alone are responsible for over $500 billion in annual stock ownership transfers.

In fairness, current laws and regulations discourage these financial institutions from taking a more active role in management decisions. For example, the Hart-Scott-Rodino Act holds the Federal Trade Commission (FTC) responsible for regulating shareholder activity that might lead to monopolistic behavior. One of the central issues is whether the acquirer of stock has an "investment-only intent." If that intent is not clear, the stockholder could be subject to FTC investigation. Among those actions that might prompt such an investigation are nominating a candidate for the board of directors; proposing corporate action requiring shareholder approval; soliciting proxies; and having a controlling shareholder, director, officer, or employee of the investor serve as a director of the company in which they have invested.

In addition, tax-exempt pension funds can lose their exempt status if it appears that they are taking an active role in management. The tax code stipulates that if an institutional investor actively provides direction to a firm in which it owns stock, it may be entering that business. If it is established that the investor has entered the business, any gains on sale of the stock become taxable, that is, the investor loses its tax exemption.

Thus, the ownership of corporate stock is moving more toward institutional investment *and* institutional investors have regulatory disincentives to become actively involved in management. At this point in the industrial life of America, laws and regulations that discourage the involvement of 40 percent of all corporate shareholders in support of long-term goals must be reexamined in light of current circumstances. It will be difficult, if not impossible, to compete with Japanese industry over the long-term when almost half of all Japanese shares are held by financial institutions (banks and insurance companies) that have Morgan-like relationships with those companies.

Lenders are also subject to restrictions under U.S. law. If a bank makes a long-term loan and exercises some influence over that company's activities, the bank could expose itself to potentially losing more than the amount of the loan to the firm. This possibility occurs when a firm is bankrupt and being liquidated. Other creditors may sue a bank that has influence over the business decisions of the bankrupt company and claim "equitable subordination" of the bank's claims. This means that the loans were effectively equity or stock investments and should not be paid until all true debt claims have been satisfied. If the other creditors can show that the bank used its influence to cause the company to make decisions that somehow benefitted the bank, they can then sue for damages over and above the amount of the bank loan, exposing the financial institution to unlimited liability. Obviously, the intent of such regulations is valid, that is, to protect the other creditors. However, in practice, they unnecessarily constrain bank lenders in the provision of financial and management services that could enhance a company's long-term viability.

Even if the constraints to more relationship banking were removed, the inability of banks to hold equity stakes in their client firms hurts the bank and the firm. When a bank has provided loans only, the bank is only concerned about the viability of the company to the extent that the loan is repaid. The most that the bank can expect is interest and principal repayment; there is relatively little upside potential. On the other hand, if the bank also has an equity stake in the company, it is in the best interest of the bank that the company perform up to its maximum potential.

In Japan, it has been shown that those companies that borrow on the market, that is, not from their *keiretsu* bank, often obtain a slightly lower interest rate. However, there is a significant loss of flexibility of financing in unexpected situations, such that the company must depend more on internal sources of funding (for example, retained earnings or employee bonus reductions). Those companies that borrow from their *keiretsu* bank can depend on financing in the event of an unexpected business opportunity or in the case of seasonal or cyclical cash shortages. Since U.S. banks have no equity stakes in their clients, they are far more likely to withdraw financing if economic trouble looms because there are few incentives to see the company through difficult periods.

This represents a significant loss of potential capital for long-term productive purposes. U.S. commercial banks hold almost $4.5 trillion in securities and loans that could be at least partially deployed to invest in the critical industries of the future. Moreover, if commercial banks were able to underwrite corporate securities, the vast network of banks could be used to mobilize even more capital for productive purposes.

The American Banking *Keiretsu*

The first step in developing such an organizational structure is to recognize that Glass-Steagall and other regulatory impediments to corporate cooperation are no longer warranted. In fact, there is some question as to whether they were ever warranted.

Virginia Senator Carter Glass, the primary framer of the Glass-Steagall Act, was himself a study in contradiction. Before being elected to office, Glass was a Lynchburg newspaper editor with little formal education. As a congressman, he helped write the Federal Reserve Act and advocated strong banker representation. He later served as Secretary of Treasury from 1918 to 1920 and maintained a close working relationship with the House of Morgan. He was elected to his senate seat in 1920 and later became a strong supporter of Franklin Roosevelt. Then in 1933, Senator Glass reversed his position and soundly criticized FDR's New Deal initiatives. While he maintained that he felt no animosity toward the House of Morgan, he allowed the provisions of the legislation that was to bear his name to severely hinder the strength, not only of the House of Morgan, but of the entire U.S. banking system.

The provisions of the act were politically motivated to punish the banking industry that was seen as being too powerful. At the same time, all too often the contributions made by bankers/industrialists like J.P. Morgan are overlooked. A stanch advocate of relationship banking, J.P. Morgan supported industrial development and never engaged in unsound banking practices. He took certain risks when necessary and he supported both the banking system and the U.S. monetary system. In all of these actions, he followed no political agenda.

If the United States is to renew its industrial infrastructure and increase its competitiveness, the initiatives must be led by those who also have no political agenda. First, those rules and regulations that discourage healthy collaboration must be repealed. Some are outdated; others are counterproductive. In the case of institutional investors, shareholders that represent 40 percent of outstanding common stock should not be prohibited from having input into management decisions.

In the case of commercial banks, small- and medium-size firms should not be prohibited from receiving technical assistance from their most readily available source of financing. Nor should commercial banks be prohibited from promoting the stock of client firms or taking equity positions. These activities can be insulated from the federally insured deposit-taking functions by forming subsidiaries of the bank holding company. In fact, in the absence of Congressional action, the Federal Reserve has already begun to exploit a loophole in Glass-Steagall for this purpose.

Beginning in 1987, the Federal Reserve interpreted the Glass-Steagall Act in such a way as to permit banks, upon special application, to engage indirectly in securities activities. Section 20 of the Glass-Steagall Act prohibits Federal Reserve member banks--state or national charter--from affiliating with any organization "engaged principally" in the issue, flotation, underwriting, public sale, or distribution of securities. (Other provisions of the act prohibit a bank from participating in these activities *directly*.) The Federal Reserve interpreted Section

20 as permitting a bank to affiliate with a firm engaged in securities transactions as long as securities transactions are not the principal business of the firm.

The Federal Reserve gave bank holding companies the right to establish nonbank subsidiaries that earn up to 10 percent of revenue from otherwise prohibited securities transactions. The maximum was later increased to 25 percent. These transactions include underwriting of and dealing in commercial paper, mortgage-backed securities, municipal revenue bonds, securitized assets, corporate bonds, and corporate equities. To ensure that the affiliation with banks is truly indirect, "firewalls" must be constructed and maintained. These firewalls limit transactions between the Section 20 subsidiary and the bank so as to limit the risk to the bank, restrict bank subsidies to the Section 20 subsidiary, and prevent conflicts of interest between the two.

There are less than 50 Section 20 subsidiaries, with approximately 10 being affiliated with foreign banks. One of the reasons that more banks have not taken advantage of this loophole is the 25 percent limit on securities revenue. In order for this 25 percent to be meaningful, the subsidiary must be large. Thus, only the money center banks and several large regional banks have taken advantage of this provision.

To facilitate more financial support of small- and medium-size industrial firms, the relevant provisions of Glass-Steagall should be repealed. Banks should be given incentives to invest in securities firms that specialize in the stock of these middle-market firms. This would be similar to the special permission that Congress gave banks in 1982 in order to stimulate U.S. exports. The Export Trading Company (ETC) Act defined ETCs as any businesses engaged in international trade with over 50 percent of revenues derived from the export of goods or services. The act gave bank holding companies the power to lend to ETCs or to acquire, partially or wholly, ETCs through equity investment. Within just two years, 24 bank holding companies had received approval from the Federal Reserve to establish ETC subsidiaries. If banks were given similar permission to invest in special-purpose securities firms, several banks could perhaps capitalize such a firm, pooling their capital and limiting their individual risk.

Once the banking system has been freed of the unnatural obstacles that have been placed between banks and industrial firms, the issue of industrial policy must be addressed. J.P. Morgan had a strong distaste for what he considered destructive competition. The German *Mittelstand* system was built on company specialization so as to compete not with each other, but with the rest of the world. The Japanese Ministry of International Trade and Industry saw to it that low-cost bank loans were available to the targeted industries through the chain of command that went from the Bank of Japan to the *keiretsu* banks to the *keiretsu* industrial firms.

It does not appear reasonable to assume that the U.S. private sector with no form of central guidance will make the necessary industrial investments that will ensure U.S. market share in the industries of the future. Nor does it seem reasonable to expect the government to lead the way in the United States as it has in Japan.

Consider Article 65--the Japanese equivalent of the Glass-Steagall Act. This law was instituted during the U.S. occupation after World War II. Within *two years* of the end of the U.S. occupation, the law was changed to allow banks to own up to 10 percent of an industrial firm. *Immediately* after the occupation ended, MITI was mobilized to target and foster critical industries. The Income Doubling Plan that sought to double Japanese GNP between 1960 and 1970 had realized its goal by 1967. In the United States, the Glass-Steagall restrictions on the ownership of industrial stock by banks remain after *60 years* and the country's political leaders are still debating the *merits* of the concept of an industrial policy.

U.S. industrial policy should be set by a nonpartisan commission of accomplished industrialists and bankers with vested power to tackle an aggressive agenda of economic development. Such an agenda would include identifying the investment needs of the United States, filling technology gaps, stopping the exportation of jobs, and rebuilding America's manufacturing infrastructure. In order to be effective, this group must be completely autonomous--as independent as the U.S. Federal Reserve and as far-sighted as the Japanese Ministry of International Trade and Industry. With a focus on small- and medium-size firms, such a blue-ribbon industrial commission can lead the way to economic revitalization.

Once it has been freed of the outdated and unnecessary restrictions of the past, the U.S. banking system can become a central part of the implementation of these industrial policies. In this way, the United States can benefit from the positive examples of other countries and create its own version of the American banking *keiretsu*.

Selected References

Chernow, Ron. *The House of Morgan: An American Banking Dynasty and the Rise of Modern Finance*, New York: Touchstone/Simon & Schuster, 1990.

Greider, William. *Secrets of the Temple: How the Federal Reserve Runs the Country*, New York: Touchstone/Simon & Schuster, 1987.

Jacobs, Michael T. *Short-Term America: The Causes and Cures of Our Business Myopia*, Boston: Harvard Business School Press, 1991.

Kelly, Kevin, Otis Port, James Treece, Gail DeGeorge, and Zachary Schiller. "Learning from Japan," *Business Week*, January 27, 1992, pp. 52-60.

Kupfer, Andrew. "How American Industry Stacks Up," *Fortune*, March 9, 1992, pp. 31-46.

Porter, Michael. "Capital Disadvantage: America's Failing Capital Investment System," *Harvard Business Review*, vol. 70, no. 5 (September-October 1991), pp. 65-82.

Index

acquisition 72, 153
Agricultural Bank of China 171
Allfinanz 124, 126
Allgemeine Zeitung 115
alliances 136
All-Japan Automobile Industry Union 136, 137
American Banking Association 209
Antimonopoly Act 140
antipollution 145
apprenticeships 114
arbitrage 96
Article 65 134
Asian dollar market 88
Asian NIC 184
authorization 99

bancherius 6
bank 6, 29, 202
bank commercial 186, 219
bank deposit 79
bank failure 48, 211
bank loan 86
bank note 39, 53, 58, 59, 132, 197, 198
Bank of China 35, 166, 173, 180
Bank of Communications 35
Bank of England 8, 34, 59, 70, 71, 91, 92, 96,
Bank of England, Governor of 78, 85
Bank of Japan 133, 143, 149, 156, 157, 158
Bank of Seoul 188
Bank of Sweden 8
Bank of Tokyo-Mitsubishi Bank 141
bank, joint-stock 21, 22, 56, 57
bank, merchant 44, 71–73, 93, 118, 119
bank, national 197, 199, 200, 202
bank, nationally chartered 205
bank, network 125
bank, regional 205
bank, universal 92, 105, 109, 116, 117
banker, merchant 74, 78, 94, 95
banking 51, 56, 64, 101
Banking Copartnerships Act of 1826 21

banking industry, consolidated 124
banking regulation 61
banking system 132
banking system, joint-stock 29
banking system, national 196, 198
banking system, private 29
banking, commercial 209
banking, corporate 177
banking, Japanese 35
banking, network 126
banking, private 51
banking, relationship 1, 46, 47, 84, 195, 215, 217
banking, universal 107, 119, 122, 124
bank-lending 77
banks, unit 57
Barclays 94
Barings 9, 10, 11, 14–22, 96, 97
BDI (Bundesverband der Deutschen Industrie) 121, 122
Bethmann Brothers and Rueppell & Harnier 14, , 23, 24
Big Bang 73, 91, 92, 95, 125
bills of exchange 6, 7, 10–12, 30, 71, 108
Board of Trade 136
bond issues 49
bond trading 14
bonds 39, 43, 44, 47, 64, 79, 137, 157
bonds, corporate 219
bonds, long-term 61
bonds, municipal revenue 219
British Department of Trade and Industry 91
British East India Trading Company 31, 40, 176
British Stock Exchange 90
broker 73
Buderus 23
buyout 118

California gold rush 18
call loan 60
Capital Adequacy Directive of the European Union 98
capital 95
capital market 212
Carnegie 48
cartel 40, 73, 133
cash reserves 60
Cathay Pacific 178
Central Bank Committee of Governors 80
certificates of deposit 86
ch'ien chuang 29, 31, 34, 35
chaebol 164, 184–188
Chamber of Assurance 8
Chambers of Commerce and Industry 120
Chartered Bank 175
Chartered Mercantile Bank of India, London and China 175
charters 132
China 15, 163

Chinese banking 31
Cho Heung Bank 186, 188
chonin 37
chung-p'iao 30, 34
Citibank 2, 43, 64
City Bank 58, 59, 60
City, the 69, 72, 74, 77, 78, 79, 85, 88, 93
Civil War 18, 165
Clapp 53
Clayton Antitrust 194
clearing bank 70, 73, 78, 90–94, 119
clearing system 70
coal 79, 106
coal mine 75
codetermination 113
cold-calling 92
collective ownership 170
Commercial Bank 188
commercial paper 219
Commerzbank 108, 124
commodity exchange 8
communist 163
Competition and Credit Central policy 89
competition 42, 153
Comprador 33, 34
Comptroller of the Currency 200, 201
concentrations of capital 40
conflict of interest 210
conglomerate 130
consent 113
consumer funds 124
contract, combination or conspiracy 194
contracts to exchange 88
conversion 84
convertibility 197
corporate and government bonds (domestic and foreign) 64
correspondent balance 59
credit 173
credit crunch 87
creditbank 106, 107
crises of confidence 196
cross-shareholding 159
currency 7, 28, 33, 81–85, 88, 91, 139, 173, 182
currency exchange 23, 138, 173
currency exchange market 83
currency exchange rate system, pegged 149
currency exchange services 175
currency exchange transactions 167
currency swaps 88
currency, hard 35
currency, liberalizing 139
currency, uniform 56, 198

Daewoo Group 187
Dai-Ichi Kangyo Bank 141
daimyo 36, 37, 39
decentralization 168

decentralized bank 204
dedicated capital 214
default 52
demand 21
democratization 135
deposit 58
deposit insurance 209
deposit interest rate 209
deposit rate 86, 87
deregulation 91, 125
destructive competition 48
Deutsche Bank 1, 28, 107, 108, 117, 118, 119, 124
discount rate 156, 206
diversification 92
division of labor 180
domestic borrowing 35
Douglas Amendment 134
Draper, William Undersecretary of the Army 135
Dresdner Bank 108, 109, 117, 124
due-on-demand checking 71
Duncan, Sherman and Company 45
duties 170

East India Company 10, 15, 32
economic development 106, 182
Economic Planning Board (EPB) 181
education 131
embargoes 166
EMS (European Monetary System) 80, 81
endaka 149, 150, 157
equitable subordination 216
equity, corporate 220
Eurobond (long-term instrument) 88
Eurocommercial paper 88
Eurodollar 79, 87
Eurodollar market 84, 87, 88
Euroequity (common and preferred stocks) 88
Euromarket 91
European Asian Bank 118
European Atomic Energy Community 80
European Central Bank (ECB) 81
European Coal and Steel Community 80
European Common Market 79
European Economic Community (EEC) Treaty 80
European Monetary Cooperation Fund 80
European Monetary Institute (EMI) 80
European Monetary Union 82, 83
European System of Central Banks (ESCB) 81
European Union 81, 82
exchange 197
exchange bank 8
exchange controls 91
exchange rate 82, 172
Exchange Rate Mechanism 82, 83

Exchequer 8
Executive Board (Vorstand) 111
expansion of trade 177
export-import bank 137, 167
export market 63
Export Trading Company (ETC) Act 220
exporting dollars 85

Fang Chieh-t'ang 30
federal charter 58
federal deposit 57
Federal Deposit Insurance Corporation 158, 209
federal depository institution 58
federal funds market 172
Federal Reserve 148, 172, 207, 208, 210, 219, 220, 221
Federal Reserve Act 205, 218
Federal Reserve Board 205
Federal Reserve System 194, 196, 204
Federal Trade Commission (FTC) 215
feudal 36, 37, 132
feudal lord 39
feudal system 164
feudalism 36
Finance Ministry 158
financial crisis 87
financial executives 214
financial institution 186
financial requirements, long-term 123
financial service 177
Financial Services Authority 98
financial system 195
financing, long-term 78, 125, 212
financing, short-term 77, 88
First Bank of the United States 56, 57, 197
First National Bank 203
fit and proper 92
Five Articles Oath 130, 131
fixed interest 70
fixed rates 69
flow of credit 194
foreclose 50
foreign direct investment, marginal 85
Foreign Direct Investment Program (FDIP) 85
foreign investment 146, 166
free banking era 199
Frick 53
FSA 100
FTC 216
Fuji Bank 141

Galey & Guffey 54, 55
German banking 28
German Deutsche Bank 46, 95
German universal banks 108
Germany 105

gilt-edged bonds 52
Glass-Steagall Act 2, 5, 84, 134, 194, 208–212, 218, 219, 221
gold 49, 201, 207
gold convertibility 149
gold prospecting 54
gold standard 49, 50
Gould, Jay 46
government 181, 189
government bond 39, 132
government finance 47
government loan 42
government securities, long-term 61
goyokin 40
grain exchange 8
Great Depression 195, 196, 208
gross domestic product (GDP) 82, 213
gross national product 110, 145, 221, 207
Grover, President 49
Guarantee Fund 20

Hanil Bank 187, 188
Hart-Scott-Rodino Act 215
Hausbank or House Bank 124
Hawley-Smoot Tariff Act 208
high-leverage potential 198
holding company 56, 159
Hong Kong 146, 163
Hongkong and Shanghai Banking Corporation 175, 179, 180
Hope and Company 10, 15, 16
hostile takeovers 115
house bank 105
House of Bardi 6
human capital 115
Hunt 53
Hutchison Whampoa 179
Hyundai Group 186

imported 208
income 123
Income Doubling Plan 139, 142
income tax 75
Industrial and Commercial Bank of China 171
Industrial development 40, 115
industrialization 133, 182
inflation 144, 201
inflation rate 81
informed 113
ING Group 97
initial offering 50
insolvency 196
institutional investors 215
insurance 209, 210
interbank market 172
interest 209
interest coupons 14, 23
Interest Equalization Tax (IET) 85
interest rate 47, 49, 82, 83, 86, 123, 148, 149, 172, 182, 207
interest rate ceiling 211

intermediary activity 34
international banking center 180
International Monetary Fund 75
international relations 131
international trade 166
investment 23
investment banker 72
investment banking 64, 209
investment management 177
investments, short-term (CDs) 88

J.P. Morgan and Company 43, 193, 215, 203
Japan 15, 35
Japan Development Bank 137
Japanese industries 41
Japanese model 189
Jardine Matheson 177
jobber 73, 74, 89
joint venture 185
joint-stock companies 40, 107
judgment bond 50

keiretsu 2, 4, 124, 125, 129, 140–144, 149,150, 152–154, 156, 159, 194, 195, 214, 217, 221
Kleinkredit 123
Knickerbocker Trust Company 202
Kohl, Helmut 122
Korea First Bank 186–188

Labor Party 75
labor union 134
Landgrave, the 14, 24, 25, 26
Landgrave, William 13, 23, 106
large-firm model 116
large-scale investments 181
lending 77
letter of credit 51, 212
leveraged buyout 153
liberalization 89, 90, 138, 182, 183, 185
liberalized conditions 169
liens 50
Ligonier Valley Railroad 52
Lincoln, Abraham 49
liquidity 27, 58, 212
Lloyds of London 72
loan 39, 40, 41, 69, 71, 166, 171, 189, 197, 207, 208, 209
loan, long-term 77, 216
loans, short-term 182
London and Scottish Committee of Bankers 70
London Futures and Options Exchange 72
London International Financial Futures Exchange 72
London Stock Exchange 100
Lucky-Goldstar Group 186

Maastricht Treaty 80, 83
MacArthur 134
Medici 7

medium of exchange 37
Meiji Restoration 137
Mellon 2, 15, 43, 50–53, 56, 62
merchant 37
merger 72, 92, 95, 153
minimum commission system 91
Ministry of Commerce and Industry 136
Ministry of International Trade and Industry (MITI) 136, 138, 139, 143, 145, 146, 149, 181
Mitsubishi 2, 4, 129, 141
Mittelstand 105, 121, 124, 125, 220
Mittelstand model 119
modernization 131, 168
monetary control 71
monetary convergence 82
monetary policy 80, 83
monetary standard 49
monetary unification 106
money 37, 39, 48, 59
money crunch 48
money market 173
money market mutual funds 211, 212
money supply 200
money trust 194
money trust and cartel 50
monobank system 166
monopoly 167, 186, 194
moral suasion 85
Morgan 15, 43, 44, 62, 84, 49, 50, 96, 216, 201, 203, 218, 220
mortgage 52
mortgage-backed securities 219
most favored nation 33

National Bank Act of 1863 199, 200
National City Bank 62, 63, 64, 203
national debt 198
National Income Doubling Plan 138
National Westminster 94
nationalized 74
negotiation 120
network 94
New York Stock Exchange 203, 204
niche market 120
non-resident holding 70
nontradeable debt 82
note, promissory 30, 34, 50, 79
notes 57, 58

Office of Fair Trading 91
oil 87, 144
oil venture 55
OPEC 87, 88
opium trade 32
Opium War 32, 41, 164, 177
Oppenheim 11
Organization for Economic Cooperation and Development 139
Oriental Banking Corporation 175
overdraft 71
overdraft loan 77
overseas investment 78

overseas operations 123
oversubscribed 76, 178

panic 202, 203, 204, 205, 207
Panic of 1873 51
partnerships 74, 90
Peabody 44
pension 39, 216
People's Bank of China 166, 171
People's Construction Bank of China 166
People's Republic of China 165
Perry, Commodore Matthew 131
Pittsburgh National Bank of Commerce 53
placing power 64
Plaza Accord 148, 149, 157
prefecture 39, 42
primus inter pares or first among equals 112
private capital 41
privatization 75, 76
privatized 69, 133
productive purposes, long-term 217
protected domestic market 182
providers of capital
Pujo Hearings 193
Pyne 61

quota, mandatory 169

ready money 60, 61
recession of 1920-1921 48, 156, 206
regulate 99, 172
regulated 98
regulation 86, 100, 139, 196, 217
Regulation Q (RegQ) of the Federal Reserve 86, 211
regulatory structure 93, 98
reserve requirement 87
reserves 49, 200, 201
restructuring 94, 156
rice riots 38
risk-based approach 98
risk calculated 56
risutora 156
Robin Leigh-Pemberton 78
Rockefeller 62
Rockefeller and Andrews 63
Rothschild 9, 11–14, 20, 22, 24–28, 49, 50, 96

S.B. Hale and Company 20
safety and soundness 4
sales contract 194
Samsung Group 185
samurai 37, 38, 39, 43
scarcity 168
Second Bank of the United States 59, 198, 199
securities 50, 59, 69, 72, 73, 76, 85, 132, 210
Securities and Exchange Act, (Japanese) 134

securitized asset 219
senior management responsibility 98
separation of commercial and investment banking 210
separation of power 210
Shanghai 30
shareholder 39, 52, 58
shareholder, corporate 216
shares 42, 46, 76, 117
Sherman Antitrust Act 194
shogunate 36
silk 132
silver coinage 49
Singapore 146
single capacity rule 89, 92
Single European Act 80
Sino-Japanese War 177
solvency 34
South Korea 146
Special Economic Zones or SEZs 170, 171, 189
specialization 110, 111, 120, 125
specialized 116, 172, 182
specie (gold and silver) 57, 59, 60, 199
Specie Circular of 1836 59
sprecher 112
standard 99
Standard Oil 62, 63
state banks 57
Stillman 61
stock 52, 179, 207, 215, 108, 112, 157, 158
stock broker 74, 89
stock brokerage 177
stock exchange 8, 72–74, 78, 79, 89, 91, 92, 100, 108
stock market 109, 157
stock market crash 208
stock speculation 207
stock, corporate 216
stockholding, intercorporate 194
strategic industries 41, 42
subscription method 108
subsidies 42, 132, 135, 138
Supervisory Board (Aufsichtsrat) 111, 112, 124
Swire Pacific 177, 178
syndicate 50
system of single capacity 91
system of true competitively priced commission 91

Taiping Rebellion 164
Taiwan 146
tariff 208
tax code 216
tax exemption 216
taxes 37
Thatcher, Margaret 69, 75, 88
Third World country 75
Tokyo Stock Exchange 154
Tory Party 75

trade 34, 36, 38, 180, 194
trade associations 121, 122
trade deficits 148, 149
trade embargo 175
trade finance 11, 44
trade surpluses 146
trade union system 111
trading 97
trading company 177
tranche 76
Transfer of Regulations or Law on the Factories 42
Treasury 48, 199
Treasury bills, short-term 211
Treaty of Nanking 33, 38
Treaty of Rome 80, 83
treaty ports 33
trust (or cartel) 40, 48
trust-busting 195
two-tiered board system 111
two-tiered financial system 84

U.S. dollar 84, 85
U.S. House Banking and Currency Committee 193
U.S. Treasury bills 86
U.S. Treasury Department 200
underwriter 72, 76
underwriting 35
unfair competitive practice 4
unfair pricing 194
unfair trading system 153
uniformity 200
union 137
Union Pacific Railroad 62
United East India Company 8
United Kingdom 69, 83
users of capital 214
usurpers 38, 39

viability, long-term 77, 143, 167, 205
volatility 61, 198
Voluntary Foreign Credit Restraint Program (VFCRP) 85
vote of no confidence 111
voting trust 47

Wall Street 49, 202, 203
window guidance 143
Wisselbank 8
works council 113
World War II 177

Yom Kippur War 144

zaibatsu 40, 41, 43, 133, 136, 140, 159